STRATEGIC TECHNOLOGY SERIES

UNDERSTANDING

ActiveX™
AND OLE

DAVID CHAPPELL

Understanding ActiveX and OLE

Published by **Microsoft Press**
A Division of Microsoft Corporation
One Microsoft Way
Redmond, Washington 98052-6399

Library of Congress Cataloging-in-Publication Data pending.

Printed and bound in the United States of America.

1 2 3 4 5 6 7 8 9   QMQM   1 0 9 8 7 6

Distributed to the book trade in Canada by Macmillan of Canada, a division of Canada Publishing Corporation.

A CIP catalogue record for this book is available from the British Library.

Microsoft Press books are available through booksellers and distributors worldwide. For further information about international editions, contact your local Microsoft Corporation office. Or contact Microsoft Press International directly at fax (206) 936-7329.

Acquisitions Editor: **David Clark**
Project Editors: **Stuart J. Stuple and Mary Renaud**
Technical Editor: **Stuart J. Stuple**
Manuscript Editor: **Mary Renaud**

Contents

Foreword

Throughout its history, OLE (and, more recently, ActiveX) has been understood as something to be, at one extreme, lamented, condemned, and crucified as utterly complex and completely impossible or, at the other extreme, praised, preached, and worshipped as if it were a direct manifestation of the Divine. OLE is, like all else, somewhere in the middle. But often those in the latter camp, once they've seen the fundamental simplicity of the Component Object Model (COM) on which OLE and ActiveX rest, seem to perpetuate the myth of complexity, perhaps in a subconscious, ego-driven effort to protect their expertise. "OLE," they say, "is hard enough for developers to grasp, let alone managers and other corporate executives."

You might find the same kind of attitude among, say, particle physicists who understand the physical universe (in at least the current opinion of science) to be made up of a handful of fundamental particles and a few equations that govern their behavior, with all else deriving from this small set of primitives. This understanding is generally reserved for a relatively small group of disciples (initiates into a discipline) who work around the central esoteric texts of the field. The masses, uninitiated into such secrets, see only the dizzying complexity of the details that follow from the core. Without seeing the basic connections, most find the foundations of physics incomprehensible and inaccessible.

For many, the implementations of COM also seem much like that branch of the physical sciences: incomprehensible and inaccessible. My own work on this subject (*Inside OLE,* 2nd ed., Microsoft

Press, 1995) is, I can say without reservation or regret, the essential "esoteric" text of the field for those who really wish to explore the depths. Embarrassingly enough, this work has its share of fanatical disciples (of the technology, not myself, fortunately). While the pages of *Inside OLE* guide you from the innermost details of the core and then expand the journey outward into increasingly complex details, the journey is not for everyone.

Here, however, in David Chappell's *Understanding ActiveX and OLE,* the author has assumed the role of making the foundation of OLE and ActiveX more accessible to those who need to understand implications and concepts rather than details. In his own style and with a fine sense of discrimination, Chappell has delivered a book that gives substance and coherence to the concepts while using only the essential details, enabling readers at all levels to easily wrap their minds around these rich technologies.

In reviewing the chapters of this book and following its progress, I have been repeatedly impressed with Chappell's ability to sow and nurture a fine harmony of ideas, details, figures, and analogies, much as a skilled organic gardener brings soil, insects, flowers, vegetables, and weeds together for a unified purpose. Where added details would choke a particular concept into confusion, Chappell has carefully weeded and thinned his garden. At the same time, he never hesitates to include beneficial elements that increase the harvest of your understanding.

Understanding ActiveX and OLE comes at an important point in the evolution of COM, OLE, and now all the technologies that fall under the ActiveX blanket—an evolution that will continue for the foreseeable future. At an early point in the history of computers themselves, only a few people really needed to know how to work with them in order to get their work done. Now, however, "computer literacy" is given such urgency that it has become part of grade-school curricula. In the same way, software developers who in any way operate in Microsoft's sphere of influence are quickly finding that an understanding of COM, OLE, and ActiveX is no longer a specialization but rather has become a necessity. As all the ActiveX technologies are based on COM and as the Internet feeding frenzy continues to grow, developers will only see this need amplified further. ActiveX or no, many of Microsoft's new technologies—such as transaction processing, object databases, and even core parts of Windows itself—are being built on top of the COM foundation. This includes not only those technologies of recent and near-term introduction but also those that won't see daylight until (if you'll pardon a shamelessly clichéd exploitation of an event that is now nearer than the '92 presidential campaign) the next millennium.

Thus, as increasing percentages of new systems and third-party components become COM-based, and as a component market takes shape, nearly all developers, managers, and executives alike are finding it necessary to understand how to work with components. Managers and executives especially need to understand the component software marketplace and what makes it succeed. This has become even more important with the release of Distributed COM in Windows NT version 4, which expands COM from the desktop to the enterprise. Managers and executives need to acquire basic knowledge about how the technology works in order to gauge how it affects their business and how it might affect their competitors in the expanding market. It is this level of knowledge that they will gain from *Understanding ActiveX and OLE*, without having to invest the effort required by their development staff.

This book expands the distance at which COM, OLE, and ActiveX can be examined and compared, offering you a chance to see the potential of these technologies where you might otherwise miss them altogether. For those who need to dive into the smallest details, *Inside OLE* awaits as a companion. But for many others, *Understanding ActiveX and OLE* will serve as a beacon, helping you adjust whatever course you might be on in order to avoid much larger and costlier adjustments down the road.

Kraig Brockschmidt

Preface

When writing a book on ActiveX and OLE, the first problem an author faces is deciding exactly what to include. These labels are applied to a large group of technologies, all of which rely on the Component Object Model (COM). But other technologies rely on COM, too, even though the term *ActiveX* or *OLE* might not appear in their name. In this book, I've focused on the most fundamental and most widely used COM-based technologies, regardless of whether they are officially labeled *ActiveX* or *OLE*.

The second problem is keeping the book under a thousand pages. Attempting to provide complete, exhaustive coverage of all today's COM-based technologies is guaranteed to result in a bookshelf-straining tome, one that only the most dedicated readers would ever finish. This book makes no attempt at completeness. Instead, I've tried to create a readable, understandable, largely architectural introduction to what COM is and how the major COM-based technologies created so far work. Toward this end, I've simplified topics and omitted details left and right. The intent is to present the bigger picture without getting lost in the fine points.

Who Can Use This Book

This book is aimed at anyone who's interested in knowing what ActiveX and OLE are, why they're important, and how these technologies work. This includes application developers who want to use ActiveX and OLE technologies in the software they develop, but it encompasses a broader audience as well. As you can quickly determine by flipping through the pages, this is not a programming book—it contains almost no code. Although I do assume that the reader is a software professional of some kind, I do not assume knowledge of C++ or Windows-based programming. ActiveX, OLE, and COM are important, and knowing what they are and how they work matters to a broader group than those who program for Microsoft Windows. Some familiarity with using Windows is taken for granted, however; this seemed safe to me, as it's hard to find anyone in this field who hasn't used Windows at least a little.

A Timestamp

The ActiveX and OLE technologies are a moving target. This book describes the fundamental COM-based technologies as of mid-1996. In particular, Chapter 10 on Distributed COM and Chapter 11 on the ActiveX Internet-related technologies were completed before those technologies actually shipped. Accordingly, some details described in these chapters might not exactly match what is finally delivered.

Where to Find More Detail

For some people, the depth of coverage offered in this book will be enough. (For others, it will surely be too much.) Developers who need a more intimate understanding of the topic will want to get a copy of the OLE "bible" for programmers, Kraig Brockschmidt's *Inside OLE*, 2d ed. (Microsoft Press, 1995). Another useful book, one that covers an important topic that's not fully addressed in *Inside OLE*, is *OLE Controls Inside Out*, by Adam Denning (Microsoft Press, 1995). (Watch for a new edition of this book, too, one that describes the recent changes in what are now known as ActiveX controls.) For the truly hard-core reader, nothing beats the two-volume *OLE 2 Programmer's Reference Library* (Microsoft Press, 1994) and the more recent *OLE Automation Programmer's Reference* (Microsoft Press, 1996). And, finally, for the mother lode of current, straight-from-the-source information, visit Microsoft's web site, *www.microsoft.com.* The fundamental specifications for COM, Distributed COM, and many ActiveX technologies can be found there, and new information is added often. Checking this site regularly is guaranteed to remind you of how much you don't know (yet).

Acknowledgments

The roots of this book are in the one-day seminar on COM and OLE that I have presented to hundreds of attendees in the past few years. The questions and concerns of those attendees have helped enormously in shaping the presentation of this material. To every one of you, thanks.

My largest debts to individuals are owed to Scott Newman, who suggested the idea of a book like this, and especially to Kraig Brockschmidt, who both contributed a foreword and provided detailed, painstaking reviews that vastly improved the text. Big thanks are also due to Nat Brown, Charlie Kindel, and Mark Ryland from Microsoft's OLE team, each of whom reviewed and provided useful comments on parts of this book. I'm also grateful for the help I received from others at Microsoft, including Jeff Alger, Rick Hill, David Kays, Srini Koppolu, Sam McKelvie, Alex Mitchell, Joe Quaglian, and Sara Williams. My outside reviewers—Pat Bonner, Bill Estrem (who read everything), Scott Lien, Lucy Suits, and Mark Thomas—were also very helpful. Every one provided useful, insightful suggestions that significantly improved the book. Despite all this assistance, however, the responsibility for any remaining errors lies solely with me.

At Microsoft Press, I'm grateful for the unfailingly professional and remarkably polite efforts of editors Mary Renaud and Stuart Stuple to make my writing readable, correct, and clear. Thanks also to David Clark, Microsoft Press acquisitions editor, for accepting my rather informal proposal for this book.

Finally, my wife, Karen, has been eternally patient and endlessly supportive through this and many other projects, something I too often forget to mention. Without her, it would be hard to do any of the things I do.

David Chappell
www.chappellassoc.com
July 1996

Chapter One

Introducing ActiveX and OLE

Writing good software is hard. Writing software that's large and complex, as most code is today, is even harder. As computers continue to infiltrate our lives, as we depend on them for everything from running our cars to writing letters to making toast, the effectiveness and reliability of software become more and more important. Good code is becoming the bedrock of our civilization.

In some ways, the history of software is the history of efforts to write better code. Applications and system software both have suffered from endless delays, mind-boggling complexity, and more bugs than anyone cares to admit. But creating software is tough—there's no way around it. Doing it well requires the ability to take a big-picture view coupled with a willingness (an eagerness, even) to deal with a myriad of small details. The intellectual effort required is substantial, and the tools are never perfect.

Writing good software is just plain hard

Microsoft's ActiveX and OLE are a step toward the creation of better software. "Better" here means software that's more reliable, certainly, and more effective as well. But it also means software that can do things that were impossible before, software that enables solutions to new problems. Although ActiveX and OLE are built on a quite simple idea, this idea turns out to have profound implications for improving how we create software.

ActiveX and OLE are about writing better software

From OLE to ActiveX

OLE 1 provided a
way to create
compound
documents

The first incarnation of OLE, Object Linking and Embedding 1,
was a mechanism for creating and working with compound
documents. To its user, a compound document appears to be a
single set of information, but in fact it contains elements created
by two or more different applications. With OLE 1, for example, a
user could combine a spreadsheet created using Microsoft Excel
with a text document created using Microsoft Word, as shown in
Figure 1-1. The idea was to give users a "document-centric" view
of computing, to let them think more about their information and
less about the applications they were using to work with that
information. As the name suggested, compound documents could
be created either by linking two separate documents together or
by completely embedding one document in another.

Figure 1-1   *A user's view of a compound document.*

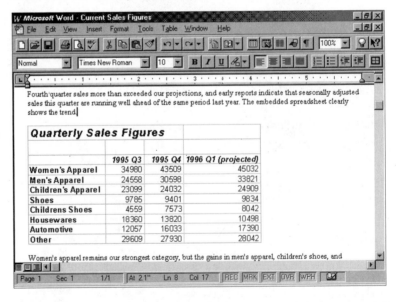

OLE 2 introduced
the Component
Object Model

Like most version 1 software releases, OLE 1 wasn't perfect. The
architects of the next release set out to improve on the original
design. They soon realized that the compound-document problem
was actually a special case of a more general problem: how

should various software components provide services to one another? To address this larger problem, OLE's architects created a set of technologies that were applicable to much more than compound documents. Foremost among these technologies was the Component Object Model (COM), which provided the foundation for OLE 2. This new version of OLE supported compound documents even better than the first release, but clearly a lot more was going on here than simply combining documents created by different applications. OLE 2 offered the potential for a new way of thinking about how software of all kinds should interact.

This potential was largely the result of COM. COM establishes a common paradigm for interaction among all sorts of software—libraries, applications, system software, and more. Accordingly, virtually any kind of software technology can be implemented using the approach COM defines, and doing so offers some very tangible benefits.

COM is a foundation for interaction among all kinds of software

Because of those benefits, COM soon became a part of technologies that had nothing to do with compound documents. Microsoft, however, still wanted to have a common name to refer to all COM-based technologies as a group. The company decided to reduce the name *Object Linking and Embedding* to just *OLE*—this three-letter combination was no longer treated as an acronym—and to drop the version number.

The name Object Linking and Embedding became simply OLE

Under this new regime, the term *OLE* was applied to anything built using the paradigm COM provides (although COM was also used in products that didn't have *OLE* in their name). OLE no longer meant only compound documents but was now a label assigned to any COM-based technology. In some ways, grouping under a single name all software written using COM makes no more sense than, say, grouping together all software written in C++. Both COM and a programming language such as C++ are general tools that can be used to create all kinds of software. Still, both for historical reasons and to mark the advent of this new and far-reaching technology, the term *OLE* was used to identify many (but not quite all) COM-based technologies.

The OLE label was applied to any technology that used COM

Today, most
COM-based
technologies
are assigned
the label
ActiveX

In early 1996, Microsoft dropped another term into the fray: *ActiveX*. In its first appearances, this new term was associated with technologies related to the Internet and applications that grew out of the Internet, such as the World Wide Web. Because most of Microsoft's efforts in this area were based on COM, ActiveX was directly connected to OLE. Soon, though, this new term began to usurp more and more of OLE's traditional territory, and today things have come full circle. Now the term *OLE* once again refers only to the technology used to create compound documents through Object Linking and Embedding. The diverse set of technologies built using COM, once all grouped under the OLE label, are now grouped under the ActiveX banner. In several cases, technologies that had *OLE* in their name have been rechristened as ActiveX technologies. New COM-based technologies that once might have been given the OLE label are now frequently tagged with ActiveX instead.

Is this the end of the naming saga for COM-based technologies? Given the history so far, the answer is probably no. What Microsoft's marketing mavens will think up next is anybody's guess. But despite these adventures in nomenclature, what's really important hasn't changed. What's really important is COM.

Understanding COM

Traditionally,
different kinds of
software provided
services in
different ways

All OLE technologies and all the ActiveX technologies described in this book are built on the foundation provided by COM. So just what is COM? To answer this question, think first about another: how should one chunk of software access the services provided by another chunk of software? Today, as shown in Figure 1-2, the answer depends on what those chunks of software are. An application might, for example, link to a library and then access the library's services by calling the functions in the library. Or one application might use the services provided by another, which runs in an entirely separate process. In this case, the two local processes typically communicate by using an interprocess communication mechanism, which usually requires defining a *protocol* between the two applications (a set of messages allowing one application to specify its requests and the other to respond appropriately). A third example is an application that might use services provided by an operating system. Here the application commonly makes system calls, each of which is handled by the operating system. Or, finally, an application might need the services of software that is running on a completely different machine, accessible via a network. Many different approaches can be used to access these services, such as exchanging messages with the remote application or issuing remote procedure calls.

Without COM, different mechanisms are used to access the services provided by libraries, local processes, the operating system, and remote processes.

Figure 1-2

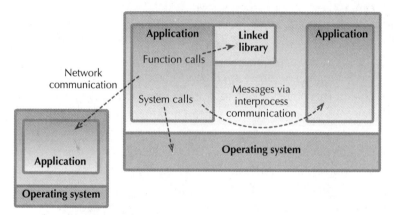

The fundamental need in all these relationships is the same: one chunk of software must access services provided by another. But the mechanism for getting at those services differs in each case—local function calls, messages passed via interprocess communication, system calls (which in fact look pretty much like function calls to the programmer), or some kind of network communication. Why is this? Wouldn't it be simpler to define one common way to access all kinds of software services, regardless of how they are provided?

Accessing services in different ways is needlessly complex

This is exactly what COM does. It defines a standard approach by which one chunk of software supplies its services to another, an approach that works in all the cases just described. By applying

COM defines a common way to access software services

this common service architecture across libraries, applications, system software, and networks, COM is transforming the way software is constructed.

How COM Works

COM objects provide services via methods that are grouped into interfaces

With COM, any chunk of software implements its services as one or more *COM objects*.[1] Every COM object supports one or more *interfaces*, each of which includes a number of *methods*. A method is typically a function or a procedure that performs a specific action and can be called by the software using the COM object (the *client* of that object). The methods that make up each interface are usually related to one another in some way. Clients can access the services provided by a COM object only by invoking the methods in the object's interfaces—they can't directly access any of the object's data.

For example, imagine a spell checker implemented as a COM object. This object might support an interface that includes methods such as LookUpWord, AddToDictionary, and RemoveFromDictionary. If the object's developer later wanted to add support for a thesaurus to this same COM object, the object would need to support another interface (perhaps with a single method such as ReturnSynonym). The methods in each interface collectively provide related services, either spell checking or access to a thesaurus.

The methods in each interface usually focus on supplying a particular service

Or imagine a COM object representing your bank account. It might support an interface that you access directly, one with methods such as Deposit, Withdrawal, and CheckBalance. This same object might support a second interface containing methods such as ChangeAccountNumber and CloseAccount, which can be invoked only by bank employees. Again, each interface contains methods that are related to one another.

---

1 Don't confuse COM objects with the objects in programming languages such as C++. Although they're similar in some ways, they're not the same. Later, this chapter describes how COM objects relate to other kinds of objects.

Figure 1-3 illustrates a COM object. Most COM objects support more than one interface, and the object in Figure 1-3 is no exception: it supports three interfaces, each represented by a small circle attached to the object. The object itself is always implemented inside a server, shown as the rectangle around the object. This server can be either a dynamic-link library (DLL), which is loaded as needed when an application is running, or a separate process of its own.

A COM object is implemented inside a server and usually supports multiple interfaces

A COM object's services are accessed via its interfaces.

Figure 1-3

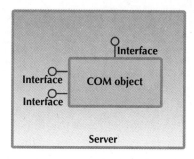

Figure 1-4 shows a close-up of a single interface supported by this COM object. This interface allows access to a spell checking service and contains the three methods previously listed. If another of the object's interfaces allowed access to the thesaurus service described earlier, a close-up of it would contain only the Return-Synonym method. (In fact, this diagram is a bit simplified—all interfaces actually include a few more standard methods, which aren't shown here.)

Each interface provides one or more methods.

Figure 1-4

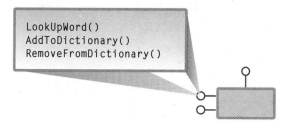

A client uses an
interface pointer
to invoke an
interface's
methods

To invoke the methods in a COM object's interface, a client must acquire a pointer to that interface. A COM object typically provides its services through several interfaces, and the client must have a separate pointer to each interface whose methods it plans to invoke. For example, a client of our sample COM object would need one interface pointer to invoke the methods in the object's spell checker interface and another pointer to invoke the method in the object's thesaurus interface. Figure 1-5 shows a client with pointers to two interfaces on a single COM object.

Figure 1-5   *A client with pointers to two of a COM object's interfaces.*

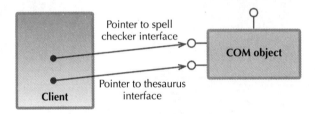

Every COM object is an instance of a specific *class*. One class, for example, might contain objects that provide spell checking and thesaurus services, while another might contain objects representing bank accounts. Typically, you must know an object's class to begin running an actual instance of that object, which you can do using the *COM library*. This library is present on every system that supports COM, and it has access to a directory of all available classes of COM objects on that system. A client can, for example, call a function in the COM library specifying the class of COM object it wants and the first supported interface to which it wants a pointer. (The COM library provides its services as ordinary function calls, not through methods in COM interfaces.) The COM library then causes a server that implements an object of that class to start running. The library also passes back to the initiating client a pointer to the requested interface on the newly instantiated COM object. The client can then ask the object directly for pointers to any other interfaces the object supports.

Once a client has a pointer to the desired interface on a running object, it can start using the object's services simply by invoking the methods in the interface. To a programmer, invoking a method looks like invoking a local procedure or function. In fact, however, the code that gets executed might be running in a library or in a separate process or as part of the operating system or even on another system entirely. With COM, clients don't need to be aware of these distinctions—everything is accessed in the same way. As shown in Figure 1-6, one common model is used to access services provided by all kinds of software.

With COM, an application accesses an object's services (no matter where that object resides) by invoking a method in an interface.

Figure 1-6

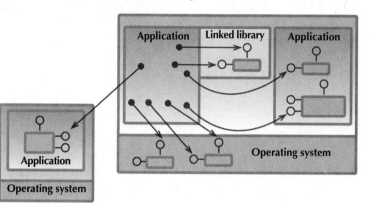

COM and Object Orientation

Objects are a central idea in COM. But how COM defines and uses objects sometimes differs from the way objects are used in other popular object technologies. To understand how COM relates to other object-oriented technologies, it's useful to describe what's commonly meant by the term *object-oriented* and then see how COM fits in.

Defining an object The term *object* has been blurred by marketeers trying to latch on to the latest fad, but in the minds of most, object-oriented technologies have a few key characteristics. Chief among these is a common notion of what constitutes an object. There is widespread agreement that an object consists of two elements: a defined set of data (also called *state* or *attributes*)

An object is a combination of data and methods

and a group of methods. These methods, commonly implemented as procedures or functions, allow a client of the object to ask the object to perform various tasks. Figure 1-7 shows a simple picture of an object.

Figure 1-7   *An object has both methods and data.*

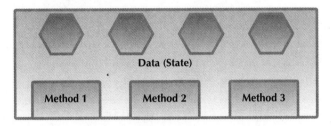

So far, so good—objects in COM are exactly like this. But in most object technologies, each object supports a single interface with a single set of methods. In contrast, COM objects can—and nearly always do—support more than one interface. An object in C++, for example, has only a single interface that includes all the object's methods. A COM object, with its multiple interfaces, might well be implemented using several C++ objects, one for each COM interface the object supports (although C++ isn't the only language that can be used to build COM objects).[2]

Unlike COM, most popular object technologies allow only a single interface per object

Another familiar idea in object technology is the notion of class. All objects representing bank accounts, for example, might be of the same class. Any particular bank account object, such as the one representing your account, is an *instance* of this class.

In COM, a class identifies a particular implementation of a set of interfaces

COM objects, too, have classes, as already described. In COM, a class identifies a specific implementation of a set of interfaces. Several different implementations of the same set of interfaces can exist, each of which is a different class. From the client's point of view, what matters are the interfaces. How those interfaces are implemented, which is what the class really indicates, isn't the

---

2   It's worth noting that, like COM objects, objects in the Java programming language can have multiple interfaces. In fact, as described in chapter 11, Java is a good fit for developing COM objects in several other ways, too.

client's concern. This ability to work identically with different kinds of objects, each supporting the same interfaces but implementing them differently, is called *polymorphism*. It's described a bit more in the next section.

Encapsulation, polymorphism, and inheritance If a technology models things as groups of methods and data and then organizes those groups into classes, is that sufficient to qualify it as object-oriented? Although there's plenty of debate, the answer from most quarters is no. In general, being object-oriented requires support for three more characteristics: encapsulation, polymorphism, and inheritance.

Encapsulation means that an object's data is not directly available to the object's clients. Instead, that data is encapsulated, hidden away from direct access. The only way to access the object's data is by using that object's methods. These methods collectively present a well-defined interface to the outside world, and it's only through this interface that a user of the object can read or modify its data. Encapsulation protects the object's data from inappropriate access and lets the object itself control how the data is accessed. By preventing inadvertent, incorrect changes from being made directly to an object's data, encapsulation can help enormously in the creation of better software.

Encapsulation prevents a client from directly accessing an object's data

C++ provides direct support for encapsulation (although it also offers ways around it). If a programmer inappropriately attempts to directly modify an object's data, the compiler can flag the attempt as an error. Although COM isn't a programming language, the same idea holds. A client can access a COM object's data only through the methods in that object's interfaces. A COM object's data is encapsulated.

COM objects support encapsulation

The second defining characteristic of object-oriented technologies is *polymorphism*. Simply put, polymorphism means that a client can treat different objects as if they were the same, and yet each object will behave appropriately. For example, think of an object representing your checking account. This object probably has a

Polymorphism lets a client treat different objects as if they were the same

Withdrawal method, which you implicitly call each time you write a check. You might also have an object representing your savings account, an object that also has a Withdrawal method. To a client, these two methods look just the same; and when either method is invoked, the same thing happens: the object's balance shrinks.

Different objects can implement the same method in different ways

In fact, however, the implementation of these two methods might be quite different. The implementation in the savings account object might simply check the requested debit amount against the account balance. If the debit amount is smaller than the balance, the request succeeds; if not, it fails. The Withdrawal method in the checking account object, on the other hand, might be a bit more complex. Checking accounts commonly offer an automatic loan up to a certain amount if a check would otherwise bounce. In implementing the Withdrawal method, the checking account object could check the requested debit amount against both the current account balance and the maximum loan currently available. In this case, the request succeeds and the check clears if the requested debit amount is less than the sum of the current balance and the available loan amount.

To a client, these two Withdrawal methods look alike; the differences in their implementation, important as they are, are hidden. This ability to treat different things as if they were the same, with each nevertheless behaving appropriately, is the essence of polymorphism. This example also demonstrates the great benefit of polymorphism: clients can remain blissfully unaware of differences that don't concern them, which simplifies the development of client software.

COM objects provide polymorphism

COM objects fully support this idea. It's entirely possible for two objects of different classes to present the same interfaces or perhaps only a single common method definition to their clients, even though each object implements the relevant methods differently.

The final defining characteristic of traditional object-oriented technologies is *inheritance*. The idea is simple: given an object, you can create a new object that automatically includes some or all of the features of the existing object. Just as a man might, with no effort on his part, inherit male-pattern baldness from his parents, an object can automatically inherit characteristics of another object.

Inheritance allows a new object to build on an existing object

There are various kinds of inheritance. One distinction that's worth making here is between *implementation inheritance* and *interface inheritance*. With implementation inheritance, an object inherits code from its parent. When a client of the child object calls one of the child's inherited methods, the code of the parent's method is actually executed. With interface inheritance, however, the child inherits only the definitions of the parent's methods. When a client of the child object calls one of these methods, the child itself must provide the code for handling the requests.

Implementation inheritance and interface inheritance are different

Implementation inheritance is a mechanism for code reuse, one that's widely used in languages such as C++ and Smalltalk. Interface inheritance, in contrast, is really about reusing a specification—the definition of the methods that an object supports. An important reason for using interface inheritance is that it makes it easier to provide polymorphism. Defining a new interface by inheriting from an existing interface guarantees that an object supporting the new interface can be treated like an object that supports the old one.

Interface inheritance reuses a specification rather than actual code

Programming languages such as C++ support both implementation inheritance and interface inheritance. COM objects, however, support only interface inheritance. COM's creators believed that, given COM's very general applicability, supporting implementation inheritance was an inappropriate (and even potentially dangerous) way for one COM object to reuse another. For example, because implementation inheritance often exposes the inheriting object to details of its parent's implementation, it can break the encapsulation of the parent. Supporting only interface inheritance, as COM does, allows reuse of a key part of another object—its interface—while avoiding this problem.

COM objects support only interface inheritance

But without implementation inheritance, how can one COM object reuse another's code? In COM, this is done with mechanisms called *containment* and *aggregation*. With containment, one object simply calls another object as needed to help carry out its functions. With aggregation, an object presents one or more of another object's interfaces as its own; what a client sees as a single object providing a group of interfaces is in fact two or more objects aggregated together. As you might imagine, aggregation takes a bit more work to implement than containment does, but both provide an effective way to build on existing COM objects.

COM objects can reuse code through containment or aggregation

Is COM really object-oriented? COM has a great deal in common with other object-oriented technologies. Its basic notion of an object as a collection of data and methods resembles that idea in languages such as C++, although COM allows a single object to have multiple interfaces. COM also provides encapsulation, polymorphism, and interface inheritance, but it reuses code through containment and aggregation rather than through implementation inheritance. Objects are fundamental to COM, but the way those objects are defined and exactly how they behave differ somewhat from other widely used object-oriented technologies.

COM is object-oriented, but it differs from other popular object-oriented technologies

So is COM really object-oriented? The answer depends on what this question means. If it's asking "Are COM objects exactly like objects in languages such as C++?", the answer is obviously no. This shouldn't be too surprising, since COM solves a problem that is quite different from the one addressed by an object-oriented programming language. But if the real question is instead "Does COM provide the key features and benefits of objects?", the answer is just as obviously yes, and it's this second question that really matters. The goal isn't to get lost in debates about whose definitions to use. The goal is to write better software.

COM and Component Software

Hardware has progressed faster than software

In the past 35 years, hardware designers have gone from building room-size computers to creating lightweight laptops based on tiny, powerful microprocessors. In the same 35 years, software developers have gone from writing large systems in assembler and COBOL to writing even larger systems in C and C++. While this is (arguably) progress, the software world isn't advancing at the same rate as the hardware world. Just what do hardware designers have that software developers don't?

The answer is components. If hardware engineers had to start from sand every time they built a new device, if their first step was always to extract the silicon to make a chip, they wouldn't progress very quickly, either. But, of course, this isn't what they do. Instead, a hardware designer typically builds a system out of prepackaged components, each of which performs a particular function, and each of which provides a defined set of services through well-specified interfaces. Hardware designers can greatly simplify their task by reusing the work of others.

Reuse is also a path to creating better software. Software developers today often start with something that's not too far from sand and then proceed to retrace the steps of a hundred programmers before them. The result is often very good, but it could be even better. Creating new applications from existing, tested components is likely to produce more reliable code. And, just as important, it can be much faster and significantly cheaper.

This idea of defining reusable parts, each presenting its services through well-specified interfaces, is exactly the approach that COM takes. COM objects provide an effective mechanism for software reuse by allowing the creation of discrete, reusable components. These components can act much like the various chips that hardware designers use, with each one supporting a specific function. Perhaps because of this analogy, this approach has become known as *component software*.

This is hardly a new idea. Developers have recognized the potential power of software reuse since the days before compilers. Some of the strictures on reuse are cultural—incentives in many organizations encourage reinvention rather than reuse, for example. But technology also constrains the potential for reuse.

Existing reuse mechanisms, important as they are, don't go far enough. To understand why this is so, it's helpful to examine the two reuse schemes that are most commonly seen today: libraries and objects.

Software reuse through libraries can help

As a mechanism for reuse, libraries have a lot to offer. This is especially true of dynamic-link libraries, which can be loaded on demand and are typically shared rather than statically linked into only one application. Libraries are familiar and easy to use. Since they can be distributed in binary form, there's no risk of revealing proprietary source code to prying eyes. And, with a little care, a program written in one language can call the routines from a library written in a different language. Libraries aren't without problems, however. One significant headache is the difficulty of adding functionality: how can you install a new version of a library without breaking applications that use the old version? And how can you easily and safely have more than one implementation of the same library on your system, which might be required in some circumstances? Libraries just aren't enough.

Software reuse with objects can also help

By encapsulating data and methods, objects can also provide a clean way to package reusable chunks of functionality. Much like traditional libraries, objects that solve specific problems can be created once and reused many times. But objects have even more to offer than libraries do. Through inheritance, one object can reuse another object's interface definition or its code or both. And polymorphism simplifies reuse by hiding irrelevant differences from an object's clients.

But no large market in re-usable objects exists today

Despite these advantages, object technology hasn't achieved its full potential for enabling software reuse. To see why, consider this: why can't an organization that wants to write a new application start the process by visiting the software store, checking a catalog, or searching the World Wide Web for the objects it will need? Why is there no large market in business-focused, reusable objects? Hardware developers benefit from this kind of market, so why can't creators of software have one, too? Why is there no object bazaar, rich with choices?

The answers are rooted in the object technologies we use today. Object-oriented languages such as C++ were designed to allow reuse within workgroups or, at most, a single organization. While you can certainly find some reusable C++ objects for sale, the kind of worldwide object bazaar envisioned here isn't feasible with existing technology. Standing in the way are three major problems.

Traditional object technologies present three obstacles to creating a component software market

The first and perhaps most important problem is that standards for linking binary objects together don't really exist. Although you can compile a C++ object and then use that compiled binary object from a library, this is guaranteed to work only when the same compiler is used for both the library and the application using the library. C++ doesn't have cross-compiler standards for the format of binary objects, so building and distributing binary object libraries is problematic, at best. As a result, currently available C++ object libraries almost always include source code. A related point: reusing code through implementation inheritance tends to bind parent and child objects together tightly. The creator of the child object should usually have access to the parent's source code, if only to know exactly what happens when an inherited method is called.

Problem 1: Distributing objects with their source code

Is it reasonable to expect that the creators of the software available in our hypothetical object bazaar will be willing to distribute their source code, thus revealing their proprietary secrets? The answer appears to be no, since no such bazaar exists. Although source-code–based reuse is entirely reasonable within a development group or even inside a single company, for a worldwide object bazaar binary distribution is essential.

The second problem is that, despite its dominance in object-oriented development, C++ is not the only language in the world. An object written in C++ can't be easily reused in, say, a Smalltalk program. And what about tools such as Powersoft's PowerBuilder or Microsoft's Visual Basic? While one can argue about whether these environments are really object-oriented, one cannot argue with their popularity. An object bazaar should offer objects that

Problem 2: Reusing objects across different languages

can be used and reused across various languages and development environments, but currently it's difficult to reuse an object written in one language in an application written in another language.

Problem 3: Relinking or recompiling an entire application when one object changes

The third problem is this: if you create an application out of objects written in a language such as C++ and then decide to change one of the objects, you must at best relink, and perhaps even recompile, the application. If several applications on one system use this changed object, you must relink or recompile all of them. Ideally, you'd have a way to drop in a new version of a single object and have all applications that use this object automatically use the new version. And, of course, this should happen without relinking or recompiling any of those applications.

COM solves all three problems

All of these problems are solved by COM. COM objects can be packaged into libraries or executable files and then distributed in a binary format (without the source code). Since COM defines a standard way to access these binary objects, COM objects can be written in one language and used in another. And since COM objects are instantiated as needed, when a new version is installed on a system, all clients will automatically get the new version the next time they use the object. COM offers the reuse benefits of both libraries and objects, along with other benefits that neither libraries nor objects alone can provide, chief among them a common approach to accessing all kinds of software services.

COM aims to create a large market in reusable components

COM brings the benefits of widespread reuse, prevalent for so long in hardware design, to the creation of software. In fact, sites full of COM-based components already exist on the World Wide Web, where you can browse or even download components, and magazines are chock-full of component advertisements. The object bazaar is becoming a reality, allowing software developers to create applications that are at least partially built from reusable parts. COM's general service architecture is useful for many tasks, but supporting the creation of component software was perhaps the single most important goal in the minds of its creators.

The Benefits of COM

Anything that simplifies the complex endeavor of creating large pieces of software is good. The conventions defined by COM do this in several ways.

COM offers a useful way to structure the services provided by a piece of software. Developers can design their implementation by first organizing it into COM objects and then defining the interfaces for each object. This is one of the traditional benefits of an object-based approach to design and development. And, as just described, COM goes further by allowing developers to create software components that can be safely distributed and reused in a variety of ways.

COM offers the benefits of object orientation

A second benefit of COM has already been mentioned: consistency. By providing a single approach for accessing all kinds of software services, COM simplifies the problems developers face. Whether the software in question is in a library, in another process, or part of the system software, you can always access it in the same way. A side effect of this consistency is that COM tends to blur the distinction between applications and system software. If you can access everything as a COM object, you'll perceive little significant difference between these two kinds of software, which have traditionally been quite distinct. Instead, you can develop applications that build on the software services available in your environment, whatever they happen to be and whoever happens to provide them.

COM provides consistency

In addition, COM is blind to the programming language being used. Because COM defines a binary interface that objects must support, you can write COM objects with any language that can support this interface. You can then use any language capable of making calls through this binary interface to invoke the methods in the interfaces of those objects. An object and its client neither know nor care what language the other is written in. While it's fair to say that some languages are better suited for use with COM than others, COM itself strives to be language independent.

COM is language independent

Another benefit of COM stems from its approach to one of the most persistent problems in developing and deploying software: *versioning*—that is, replacing an existing version of software with a new version that offers new features, while not breaking any existing clients. COM objects provide a simple answer, based on an object's ability to support more than one interface. As explained earlier, a COM object's client must acquire a pointer to each specific interface it needs to use. To add features in a new version of a COM object, then, you can simply offer the new features through a new interface on the object. Existing interfaces aren't changed (in fact, COM prohibits changes to existing interfaces), so clients using those interfaces are unaffected. And these existing clients never ask for pointers to the new interfaces. Only new clients know enough to ask for the interfaces that offer the new features, and so only new clients are affected by the new version.

COM also solves the other side of the versioning problem: what if a client expects an object to provide certain functionality, but the object hasn't yet been updated to offer it? The client requests a pointer to the interface through which this service would be available but gets nothing in return. Because COM supplies a clean way to learn that an object isn't all the client hoped it would be, developers can write clients to handle this situation gracefully instead of crashing. This simple, clean approach to versioning, which allows independent updates to both clients and the objects they use, is among COM's biggest contributions.

Microsoft itself is adopting COM in most of its products. The company is using COM to define extensions to Microsoft Windows and Microsoft Windows NT, applying it in various ways in many Microsoft applications, and using it to define standard interfaces for many kinds of services. COM's approach can be applied profitably to the development of all kinds of software.

COM's Availability
COM, which was developed by Microsoft, was originally made available on Windows and Windows NT. Microsoft now also provides support for COM on the Macintosh. Although Microsoft

does not support COM on other operating systems, this void has been filled by third parties. Several companies, large and small, provide implementations of COM and various COM-based technologies on a wide range of operating systems. Software developed using COM objects will be available on all kinds of systems, ranging from workstations that run Windows and Windows NT to IBM mainframes that run MVS. And, as you'll see later, Distributed COM (DCOM) allows COM objects on all kinds of systems to interact. COM's increasingly central role in software developed for Windows and Windows NT, coupled with the ubiquity of these systems, suggests that this new approach to creating software will work its way into all parts of the enterprise.

COM will be available on many operating systems

Defining Standard Interfaces with COM

COM provides the basic mechanisms needed for one chunk of software to provide services to another through well-defined interfaces implemented by COM objects. But who defines those interfaces? Unless a COM object and its client agree on what interfaces exist, what methods those interfaces contain, and what the methods actually do, it's not possible for them to accomplish anything useful.

In some cases, developers must define application-specific interfaces. For example, an investment bank creating its own custom software for carrying out trades might decide to design and build that software using COM. The software's developers can define appropriate custom interfaces as they see fit and then implement support for those interfaces in their own COM objects. There's no need to contact or seek approval from Microsoft.

Application developers can define interfaces as they see fit

But suppose that all investment banks have similar requirements for objects and their interfaces. Why not bring them together to define industry-standard interfaces for these objects? This would allow the creation of a market for standard components produced by competing companies. OLE Industry Solutions, a Microsoft-sponsored program to define these sorts of interfaces, has precisely this goal. Through this program, groups from financial

The OLE Industry Solutions program is designed to create industry-standard interfaces companies, healthcare organizations, providers of point-of-sale equipment, and others have defined standard interfaces for components useful in each area.

There are other kinds of services where new standard interfaces might become even more well known. For example, suppose that the owners of an operating system decided to make the services of its file system available via COM. They would need to define one or more COM objects, each with a specific class and supporting a defined set of interfaces. Then they would have to make those interface definitions available to the potential users of the COM objects—that is, to developers of applications that use the new file system.

Microsoft itself defines standard interfaces in many cases

The original problem addressed by OLE, creating compound documents, is another example of the need for standard interfaces. A compound document (as you saw in Figure 1-1 on page 2) contains elements from two (or possibly more) applications that share a single window on the user's screen, allowing the user to work with information from both applications. Clearly, both applications must cooperate to make this possible, providing services to each other that allow them to present a seamless interface to the user. They can do this by each supporting certain COM objects, each of which in turn supports specific interfaces. And since the goal is to allow all kinds of applications to cooperate in a standard way, someone must define and publicize the required COM objects and interfaces.

Every ActiveX and OLE technology defines a set of interfaces using COM

Defining (and sometimes implementing) standard interfaces to perform well-defined functions is what ActiveX and OLE are all about. In Structured Storage, for example, a COM-based technology provided with Windows and Windows NT, COM objects and interfaces define elements of a file system. The technology for creating compound documents, one of the most commonly supported COM-based technologies, is implemented by COM objects with standard interfaces that allow applications to share screen real estate and create compound documents.

ActiveX and OLE technologies are nothing more than software that provides services to clients through COM interfaces supported by COM objects. Various parts of ActiveX and OLE define standard interfaces for various purposes. Some of those interfaces are supported by system software, as in the file system example; others, like those for creating compound documents, must be supported by individual applications. In either case, the fundamental mechanism used to provide services to clients of the software is the same: COM.

Describing ActiveX and OLE Technologies

OLE, which once again refers only to technologies for creating compound documents, and the broad set of technologies assigned the ActiveX label are all built using COM. Many of these technologies have their roots in compound documents, but others address entirely different problems. This section provides a brief introduction to the most important COM-based technologies.

Automation

Spreadsheet applications, word processors, and other personal productivity software give people all sorts of useful capabilities. Why not let other software access those capabilities, too? For this to be possible, applications must expose their services to programs as well as to people. In other words, they must be programmable. Providing this programmability is the goal of *Automation* (originally known as *OLE Automation*).

Automation provides programmability

An application can become programmable by exposing its services through ordinary COM interfaces. This is seldom done, however. Instead, applications expose their services through *dispinterfaces.* A dispinterface is much like the interfaces described so far—it has methods, clients access those methods using an interface pointer, and so on—but it also differs in significant ways. In particular, dispinterface methods are much easier to invoke from clients written in simple languages such as Visual

Automation clients typically access an object's methods via a dispinterface

Basic. This is a crucial point because Visual Basic and tools like it are the first choice for most people who want to write programs that access an application's internal services.

To get a sense of how useful this idea can be, think of Microsoft Excel. This spreadsheet program offers a wide range of functions that are typically accessed directly by the person using Excel. It's also possible, of course, to create complete applications using Excel by writing them in Excel's built-in macro language.

Excel allows access to its services through dispinterfaces

Today, however, Microsoft Excel supports Automation—that is, Excel makes its internal services available through dispinterfaces supported by various COM objects, which provide methods such as Average, CheckSpelling, and many more. Applications built on Excel no longer are restricted to using Excel's built-in macro language but instead can be written in virtually anything. Excel itself is no longer only a tool for end users—it's now a toolbox for application builders, too.

Many other applications also support Automation

This same feature, programmatic access to internal services through Automation, is supported by a host of other applications. This ability to easily access the powerful features offered by an existing application is what makes Automation among the most widely used COM-based technologies. For a more detailed discussion of Automation, see Chapter 4.

Persistence

COM objects can make their data persistent

Objects have data and methods, and many objects need a way to store their data when they're not running. In the jargon of the cognoscenti, an object needs a way to make its data *persistent,* which typically means storing that data on disk. COM objects have many choices for how to accomplish this. One of the most commonly used is known as *Structured Storage.*

To understand Structured Storage, think first about how applications save their data in ordinary files. Traditional file systems allow applications to share a single disk drive without getting in one another's way. Each has its own files and maybe even its own directories to work with, independent of what other applications might be doing. Applications don't need to cooperate in storing their data, since each one can be assigned its own storage area.

With COM, however, the situation gets more complicated. Because COM allows all kinds of software to work together using a single model, independently developed COM objects might become part of what the user sees as a single application but might still need to store their data on disk separately. While each COM object could use its own file, to the application's users the objects are invisible—this is a single application—and having to keep track of multiple files is unlikely to make users very happy.

What's needed is a way for multiple COM objects to share a single file. This is exactly what Structured Storage provides. By essentially building a file system inside each file, Structured Storage allows the components comprising a single application to each have its own discrete chunk of storage space, its own "files." To the user, only a single file exists. To the application, however, each component has a private area for storing data, all of which are actually contained within a single disk file.

Structured Storage allows COM objects to share a single disk file

To make this work, Structured Storage defines two kinds of COM objects, each supporting appropriate interfaces. Called *storages* and *streams* (illustrated in Figure 1-8 on the following page), these objects are analogous to the directories and files, respectively, of common file systems. With Structured Storage, a single file can contain data stored by many COM objects, each storing its data in its own storage or stream. Just as a conventional file system allows different applications to share a single disk drive, Structured Storage provides a way for different applications to share a single file.

Structured Storage organizes a file into storages and streams

There's more to persistence than Structured Storage, however. A COM object can save its persistent data in other ways, such as in an ordinary file or even on the World Wide Web. Also, an object must supply a way for its clients to tell it when to load and save its persistent data. To allow this, an object can support one (or perhaps more) of several standard interfaces defined for this purpose. Chapter 5 presents a more complete description of persistence in COM objects.

Figure 1-8

With Structured Storage, a single file contains several storages and streams.

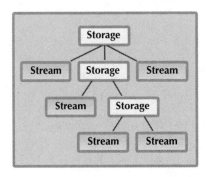

Monikers

A client can create and initialize a COM object

Imagine an instance of a COM object that represents your bank account. To access your account, a client needs to start this object and then have the object load its data (your account balance and other information). COM offers a way to do this—that is, it provides mechanisms that allow a client to instantiate and initialize a COM object.

To perform this task, the client needs to know quite a bit. It must know, for example, how to locate the correct data for your account and how to tell the appropriate COM object to load this data. While it's sometimes reasonable to expect the client to know all this, it would be nice if there were some way to hide this detail, to let the client simply say, "Create this object instance" (your bank account) and have everything happen automatically.

A moniker knows how to create and initialize another object

This is exactly what monikers do. A *moniker* is itself a COM object, but it has a very well-defined purpose: each moniker knows how to create and initialize one other object instance. If I had a moniker for your bank account object, for instance, I could ask that moniker to create, initialize, and connect me to your account. All the details of what's required to do this are hidden from me (the client). If I wanted to work with two bank accounts, using monikers to access them, I'd need two separate monikers, one for each account object. In general, monikers aren't required in the COM environment; they just make things easier for the client. Monikers are described in Chapter 6.

Uniform Data Transfer and Connectable Objects

Exchanging data is a fundamental software operation. Applications copy data back and forth, for example, when their user moves data via the clipboard. Various kinds of system software, such as device drivers, provide information from their devices to software using those devices. Given the plethora of reasons for different chunks of software to exchange data, it's not surprising that an overabundance of schemes have been invented to do it.

Uniform Data Transfer lets all kinds of software exchange data in a common way

In the COM world, *Uniform Data Transfer* is the standard way to exchange information. As with all ActiveX and OLE technologies, the applications involved must support particular COM interfaces. The methods in these interfaces define standard ways to describe the data being moved, to specify where that data resides, and to actually move it. They even define a simple mechanism that lets one application inform another when an interesting piece of data becomes available. Although it's hardly the most exciting thing that COM has to offer, Uniform Data Transfer plays an important part in much of the work that COM-based applications perform.

While it's useful in some situations, the simple scheme defined by Uniform Data Transfer for notifying a client when interesting data has appeared isn't entirely sufficient, however. A COM-based technology known as *Connectable Objects* has been created to address this deficiency. By providing a more general mechanism through which an object can talk back to its client, Connectable Objects makes it easy for clients to receive notifications of interesting events. Both Uniform Data Transfer and Connectable Objects are discussed in Chapter 7.

Compound Documents

Applications get more complicated every day. Word processors add graphical capabilities, spreadsheets add charting functions, and it can seem as if we'll eventually wind up using one big application for everything. But that isn't really the aim; rather, the goal is integration among different applications. A word processor doesn't need to add graphing functions, for instance, if you can use an existing graphing application from within the word processor. The intent is to have applications work together smoothly. A user should be able to see what appears to be a single document but have different applications cooperate to work on various pieces of that document.

OLE technology allows the creation of compound documents

The OLE technology (formerly known as *OLE Documents*) addresses this problem. By supporting appropriate COM objects, each with its own set of interfaces, separate applications can cooperate to present one compound document to the user, as shown in Figure 1-9. These interfaces are completely generic—neither application knows what the other one is. A user might, for example, work with a Word document that contains an Excel spreadsheet, as shown in the figure. When the user modifies the text, Word is in control. Double-clicking on the spreadsheet part of the document silently starts Excel, allowing the user to manipulate the spreadsheet's data using Excel. The word processor doesn't need to build in the functions of a spreadsheet; with OLE, an existing spreadsheet application can simply be plugged in as needed.

The standard interfaces defined by OLE enable this kind of interaction among all sorts of applications from any vendor, not just spreadsheets and word processors produced by Microsoft. You can include sound in graphs, create presentations with integrated video clips, and more. Many applications today, from a wide range of vendors, support OLE as a way to interact with other applications.

Documents can contain elements managed by separate applications.   *Figure 1-9*

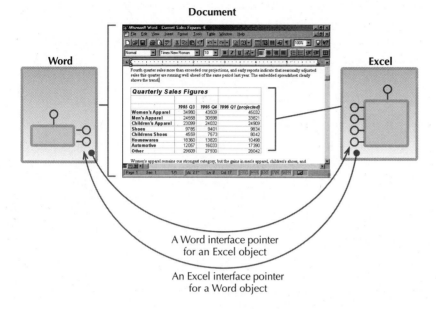

A Word interface pointer
for an Excel object

An Excel interface pointer
for a Word object

When you create a compound document with OLE, one application always acts as the *container*. As the name implies, a container defines the outermost document, the one that contains everything else. In Figure 1-9, Word is the container. Other applications, called *servers*, can place their documents within the container's document. In Figure 1-9, for example, Excel is acting as a server.

Applications act as containers and servers

Using OLE, a server's document can be *linked* to or *embedded* in the container's document. If the server's document is linked, it's stored in a separate file, and only a link to that file is stored in the container's document. (The link is actually a moniker.) If a server's document is embedded, that document is stored in the same file as the container's document. (The two applications share a single file using Structured Storage.)

Documents can be linked to or embedded in other documents

Creating compound documents was the problem that led to the creation of COM. Although COM is used much more widely today, the fingerprints of compound documents are visible on many

COM-based technologies. This challenging problem motivated the design of a large number of core technologies in this area. Chapter 8 describes the interfaces that OLE containers and servers must support and explains how those interfaces work to give a user the illusion of a single document.

ActiveX Controls

If you want to include a spreadsheet in a text document, why should you be forced to use all of Excel? If you need only basic spreadsheet functions, maybe you can get by with a simpler, faster, and probably cheaper spreadsheet component. Or suppose that you're using Visual Basic to build an application that needs to include some spreadsheet functionality. It'd be great to just plug in the basic functions you need without dragging along (or paying for) a complete spreadsheet application. In fact, you might like to build your entire application largely from existing components that you plug together.

ActiveX Controls defines standard interfaces for reusable components

This desire is what led to the idea of component software, an area where COM has much to contribute. You can build reusable components solely with COM itself, but it's also useful to define some standard interfaces and conventions for this purpose. Using these, you can build components that perform common tasks, such as providing a user interface and sending events to a client, in a common way. The *ActiveX Controls* specification defines these standards.

An ActiveX control is a stand-alone software component that does specific things in a standard way. Developers can plug one or more ActiveX controls into an application created in, say, Visual Basic to take advantage of existing software functionality. The result is software built largely from prefabricated parts—that is, component software.

ActiveX controls were originally called OLE controls or OCXs

ActiveX controls were originally known as OLE controls or OCXs. Microsoft changed the name to reflect several newly defined features that make these controls much more usable with the

Internet and the World Wide Web. For example, an ActiveX control can store its data on a page somewhere on the Web, or it can be downloaded from a web server and then executed on a client machine. And the container in which the control executes need not be a programming environment—it can instead be a web browser.

Hundreds of controls are available from dozens of companies, including spreadsheet controls, controls for mainframe data access, and many more. You can even select ActiveX controls by browsing sites on the World Wide Web and then download them for immediate use. By far the largest number of components today are built as ActiveX controls.

ActiveX controls are not separate applications. Instead, as shown in Figure 1-10, they're servers that plug into a control container. As always, the interactions between a control and its container are specified through various interfaces supported by COM objects. ActiveX controls actually make use of many other OLE and ActiveX technologies. Controls typically support the interfaces defined for embedding, for example, and they also commonly allow access to their methods via the dispinterfaces defined for Automation. ActiveX controls are described in Chapter 9.

ActiveX controls rely on many other COM-based technologies

The functions packaged in an ActiveX control can be used by any control container, such as Visual Basic or a web browser.

Figure 1-10

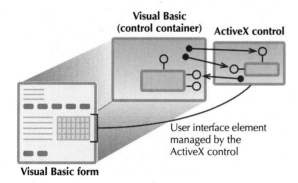

Visual Basic (control container)
ActiveX control
User interface element managed by the ActiveX control
Visual Basic form

Distributed COM

Although designed from the start to support distribution, the original implementation of COM ran on only a single system. COM objects could be implemented in DLLs or in separate processes running on the same machine as their client, but they couldn't reside on other machines in the network. *Distributed COM* (DCOM) changes this. With DCOM, COM objects can provide their services across machine boundaries, as shown in Figure 1-11.

Figure 1-11   ***Illustrating Distributed COM.***

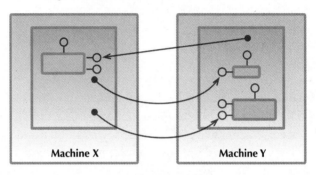

Machine X   Machine Y

To achieve this, DCOM relies on remote procedure call (RPC). With RPC, a client can make what appears to be a local call to a component, although that call actually executes in an object across the network. DCOM also includes support for security services (controlling which clients can use which COM objects) and a way to specify the machine on which an object should be created. The services supplied by DCOM can be used to build secure, distributed, COM-based applications, and they are described in more detail in Chapter 10.

COM-Based Service Interfaces

It's often useful to have a common interface to access different implementations of a service. For example, the Open Database Connectivity (ODBC) interface built into Windows and Windows NT defines a group of C function calls that can be used to access any relational database management system. With the arrival of

COM, these kinds of interfaces can be specified in a common, object-oriented way. Microsoft has defined several such interfaces, including those for databases, transactions, and directory services based on COM.

Databases A database management system (DBMS) provides a way to organize, store, and retrieve information. DBMSs are widely used tools that underlie many applications. Local access to a DBMS is usually through a library linked into a client process or perhaps through some kind of interprocess communication. Really, though, a DBMS is simply a collection of services provided by one chunk of software to another. Why not model and deliver those services as COM objects?

DBMS services can be accessed using COM objects

A typical DBMS includes a query processor, various data storage mechanisms, and more. If standard objects and interfaces were defined and widely supported, a client could access various DBMSs in the same way or even use only the best parts from different ones. For instance, an application might benefit from using a data storage scheme from one DBMS and the query processor from another. And there's no reason why those same interfaces couldn't be applied more generally and used to access data that's not in a DBMS. Why not have a common approach to accessing relational data and, say, data stored in spreadsheets?

COM-based database technology (originally called *OLE Database*, or OLE DB) addresses these issues. By defining standard COM objects and interfaces for data access, this technology establishes a common means for clients to access data stored in various fashions. In many ways a generalization of ODBC, OLE Database goes beyond this earlier standard interface by viewing everything as COM objects. A source of data can be modeled as a DataSource object, for example, and then have a Command object defined for it. This Command object might specify an SQL query or another kind of command that manipulates the data. Every Command object provides an interface containing an Execute method, which (not surprisingly) executes the command. The result

A COM-based database technology provides a way to access data stored in various ways

is yet another object, called a Rowset, that contains the result of the command's execution. This object, in turn, supports an interface with methods that allow examination of the data contained in that object.

All of these objects are defined using COM, and all present their services through methods in COM interfaces. The result is an abstracted view of data access, one that can be implemented in numerous ways and for a range of data access mechanisms.

A transaction's operations either all succeed or all fail

Transactions In accessing data, especially distributed data, the notion of a transaction can be useful. Suppose that you'd like to modify two databases, but either both changes must happen or neither should—partial success is not acceptable. For example, to transfer $100 from your savings account to your checking account, two actions must occur: $100 must be subtracted from your savings account, and that same amount must be added to your checking account. If only the first request succeeds, you won't be happy. If only the second succeeds, the bank won't be happy (although you might be). To arrive at a consistent result, either both operations must succeed or both must fail.

To carry out this kind of indivisible atomic operation, you must define a transaction that includes both modifications. This service can be built into the data access mechanism itself, but a separate transaction service that can be used with different data access mechanisms is often a better idea. Once again, the goal is for one piece of software, the transaction service, to provide services to another. Why not describe this interaction using COM?

COM-based transactions technology models a transaction service as COM objects

Just as COM-based database technology models data access mechanisms using COM objects, COM-based transactions model a transaction service as COM objects. The objects defined include resource managers (for example, a DBMS), transaction coordinators, and the transactions themselves. And since transactions are common in data access, the interfaces defined for transactions are designed to work well with those defined for databases.

Directory services Much like a telephone directory, a directory service in a distributed environment allows its user to look up information.[3] With a telephone directory, you can find someone's phone number if you know that person's name. With a directory service, the client supplies a name, and the directory service returns information about the named item. For instance, a client might supply the name of a particular machine and get back the information it needs to contact that machine, such as a network address. Or a client might provide the name of a user and receive that user's e-mail address.

A directory service maps a name to information about the named object

A directory service is extremely useful in a distributed environment. Because no single directory meets everyone's needs, numerous directory services exist, and many different technologies are used. The most well known services include the Windows NT directory service, the internationally standardized but not widely used X.500, and the Novell Directory Service (NDS) used primarily with Novell NetWare, but there are many more.

COM-based directory services (originally known as OLE Directory Services or OLE DS) do for directory services what OLE Database does for database systems: they provide a common interface that can be used to access all kinds of directory services. Just as COM-based databases make it easier to create clients that must handle all kinds of data, COM-based directory services make it easier to create clients that must work with all directory services.

COM can be used to define a common interface to diverse directory services

To define this standard interface, the technology must provide a general way to model the information stored in diverse directories. Fortunately, directory services typically organize their information in some type of hierarchy. For example, all the information a company maintains in its directory might appear below a single

---

3 Don't confuse a directory service with a directory in a file system. The use of the word *directory* is broadly similar, but the two are not the same thing.

node that represents the company itself. The next level in the tree might contain entries for divisions of the company, and so on. Alternatively, an organization's directory hierarchy might reflect physical rather than organizational boundaries. One branch might contain entries for all the company's machines, for instance, while another might include entries for all the printers.

Directory entries are modeled as container objects or leaf objects

The COM-based solution is to model each directory entry as a COM object. Mirroring the kinds of objects in a hierarchy, every directory entry is either a *container object* or a *leaf object*. Regardless of the particular directory service being used, a client sees all the directory's entries as container objects or leaf objects. Container objects, as their name suggests, can contain leaf objects or other container objects. For example, a container object might represent a directory entry that is the parent node for all entries about printers. Below this container object might appear many different printer entries, each describing a specific printer. Each kind of object provides appropriate interfaces that let clients access the data and methods that object provides. The goal is to make life simpler for developers who create clients that use multiple directory services.

COM and Internet Technologies

Most of Microsoft's Internet-related technologies use COM

The Internet and the style of data access provided by the World Wide Web have crashed like a tidal wave on the shores of computing. Although Microsoft wasn't the first to recognize the impact this wave would have, the company wasted no time in responding once that recognition hit. Not surprisingly, most of the new technologies Microsoft has created in this area are built using COM. As described earlier, the ActiveX brand name originated in COM's collision with the Internet, although it has now spread to include many other COM-based technologies.

COM's component-oriented approach is applied to Microsoft's Internet and web technologies in several ways. For example, Microsoft's web browser, Internet Explorer, relies heavily on an extension of OLE compound documents called ActiveX Documents. With this enhancement, a user can browse through many types of information in addition to the conventional Hypertext Markup Language (HTML) pages. The ActiveX Controls technology has been enhanced to allow a control's code and data to be intelligently downloaded as needed from a web server and executed inside a web browser. ActiveX Scripting provides a generic way for clients to execute scripts written in any scripting language, while the ActiveX Hyperlinks technology, based on monikers, allows the creation of Web-style hyperlinks not only between HTML pages but between all kinds of documents. All of these technologies are described in Chapter 11.

The Future of COM

From its humble beginnings as a way to create compound documents, COM has evolved into a fundamental underpinning for application and system software. COM has been so widely applied because the architecture it defines for providing software services offers an attractive solution to so many problems. Given this generality and its obvious benefits, the applications of COM described here are in all likelihood only the beginning. While the broad label applied to COM-based technologies has changed over time—from OLE to ActiveX—this matters little from a purely technical perspective. Whatever the name, the benefits of COM and applications of COM continue to spread throughout this part of the software world.

The use of COM will continue to grow

Chapter Two

The Component Object Model

ActiveX and OLE rest on the foundation of the Component Object Model. COM specifies the abstractions and rules needed to define objects and interfaces, and it also includes software that implements key functions. Understanding COM is a prerequisite to understanding anything else in ActiveX or OLE. Although COM is neither large nor especially complicated, it differs somewhat both from other architectures for providing software services and from traditional object-oriented approaches. Prepare yourself to think in new ways about what might be familiar concepts.[1]

Understanding ActiveX and OLE requires understanding COM

Describing COM Objects

As Chapter 1 explained, software built using COM provides its services through one or more COM objects. Each COM object is an instance of a particular class, and each supports a number of interfaces, generally two or more. Each interface includes one or more methods, functions that can be called by the object's client. One of the hypothetical objects discussed in Chapter 1, for example, supports both a spell checker and a thesaurus, providing access to their services through separate interfaces. The spell

A COM object's services are accessed through the methods contained in its interfaces

---

1 Distributed COM (DCOM) also plays an important role in ActiveX and is discussed in Chapter 10.

checker interface includes methods such as LookUpWord, Add-ToDictionary, and RemoveFromDictionary, while the thesaurus interface has only the single method ReturnSynonym. To invoke any of these methods, an object's client must hold an interface pointer to the interface that contains the method. Figure 2-1 summarizes this example.

Figure 2-1   *A COM object, its interfaces, and its client.*

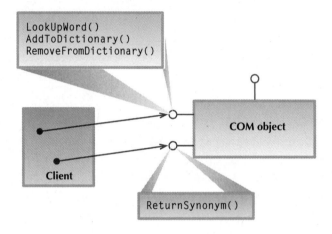

Interfaces

An interface is a contract between an object and its clients

Each interface an object supports is really a contract between the object and its clients. The object promises to support the interface's methods exactly as the interface defines them, and the clients promise to invoke the methods correctly. To make this contract work, the object and the clients must agree on the following: a way to explicitly identify each interface; a common way to describe, or define, the methods in an interface; and a concrete definition of how to implement an interface.

Every interface has two names, one used by people and one used by software

Identifying an interface Every interface in COM has two names. One name, which is meant for people to use, is a string of characters. The other name is more complex and is intended for use primarily by software. The human-readable, character-string name isn't guaranteed to be unique—it's possible (though not common) for two interfaces to have the same one. The name used by software, however, is unique, providing a way to identify precisely one interface.

By convention, the human-readable name of most COM interfaces begins with the letter *I* (for *interface*). Different technologies based on COM define interfaces with various names, but the names typically begin with *I*, and all attempt to be at least a little descriptive of the interface's function. For example, the spell checker interface described earlier might be called ISpellChecker, and the thesaurus interface might be IThesaurus.

Human-readable interface names begin with the letter *I*

Simple, friendly names like this are convenient to use when talking about an interface or choosing variable and type names for interface pointers. But when client software must specify exactly which of an object's interfaces it needs to use, these simple names aren't enough. For instance, if two groups of developers independently define two different interfaces, both groups might happen to pick the name ISpellChecker for their interface. If a client knows about only one of these interfaces and asks an object for a pointer to ISpellChecker, the object might implement the other interface, leaving the client with the wrong pointer. Or if an object needs to implement both interfaces, the object's clients are left in a quandary—when they ask for an interface pointer to ISpellChecker, which one do they get?

An interface's human-readable name isn't guaranteed to be unique

The solution is simple: the creator of every interface must assign it a unique name, called a *globally unique identifier* (GUID). An interface's GUID is called its *interface identifier* (IID). A GUID (pronounced either *goo-id* or *gwid*) is a 16-byte value that is typically created by running a software utility. Anybody on any machine can run this utility and be guaranteed (for all practical purposes) to produce a GUID that's different from all others.

Interface names used by software are globally unique

That's a neat trick. Is there some global clearinghouse that keeps track of all allocated names, some central name nanny that says, "No, you can't use that name"? How can I be sure that the GUID I create on my machine doesn't coincidentally happen to match the one you produce on your machine?

The problem boils down to ensuring that each GUID is unique in time and space. Uniqueness in time is easy: each GUID contains a timestamp indicating when it was created, thus guaranteeing that all GUIDs produced on a given machine will be different. To ensure uniqueness in space, every machine on which GUIDs can be created must have a unique machine identifier. For this identifier, the GUID-producing software uses a unique value already present on most machines: the address on the machine's network interface card. [2] (Ethernet, Token Ring, and some other networks use a 6-byte value called a MAC address to uniquely identify each system.) If a machine has no network card, a spurious machine identifier is synthesized from various random elements in that system. Even in this case, the odds are overwhelmingly in favor of each machine having a different identifier.

Although GUIDs aren't particularly easy for people to work with, they're perfect for assigning guaranteed unique names to interfaces, names used by software. People commonly use the simple, human-oriented names, rather than GUIDs, to refer to interfaces. Don't forget, though, that every interface really has two names—the human-readable one and the IID (which is, of course, a GUID)—and that compiled, running software nearly always uses the latter.

COM doesn't
mandate a
particular
language or
notation for
describing
interfaces

Describing an interface An object and its client must have a mutually agreed-upon way to describe an interface—that is, a way to define the methods an interface contains and the parameters of those methods. COM doesn't mandate how this must be done. A COM object might describe its interfaces using true

---

2 Because GUIDs typically include a network address, you might expect that the address could be extracted later from the GUID and somehow used to locate the machine that generated the GUID. This never happens, however. GUIDs include the network address of the machine on which they were created only because it's a convenient way to uniquely identify each machine. The address value is never pulled out of a GUID and used to locate a machine. (Since the system that's running the code where a GUID is being used isn't likely to be the same system on which that GUID was produced, trying to use the GUID's embedded address wouldn't be very useful anyway.)

C++ or some kind of pidgin C++ or anything else that the object's creator and the creators of its clients can agree on. The important point is that an object must correctly implement COM's binary interface standard (described in the following section).

It's convenient, though, to have a standard tool for defining interfaces. In COM, this tool is the Interface Definition Language (IDL). COM's IDL is largely an extension of the IDL already used in Microsoft's remote procedure call (RPC), which was itself borrowed from the IDL in the Open Software Foundation's Distributed Computing Environment (OSF DCE). Using IDL, a COM object's interfaces can be precisely and completely specified. For example, here is an IDL definition of our hypothetical spell checker interface, ISpellChecker:

COM's Interface Definition Language (IDL) is often used to define interfaces

```
[ object,
  uuid(E7CD0D00-1827-11CF-9946-444553540000) ]
interface ISpellChecker : IUnknown {
    import "unknwn.idl";
    HRESULT LookUpWord([in] OLECHAR word[31],
                    [out] boolean *found);
    HRESULT AddToDictionary([in] OLECHAR word[31]);
    HRESULT RemoveFromDictionary(
                    [in] OLECHAR word[31]);
}
```

As you might recognize, IDL looks a lot like C++. The interface specification begins with the word *object,* indicating that the extensions COM defines to the original DCE IDL will be used. Next is the inter-face's IID, a GUID. In DCE, from which the idea was borrowed, GUIDs are called *universal unique identifiers* (UUIDs). Because COM's IDL is based on DCE IDL, the term *UUID* is used in interface definitions. Don't be confused—UUID is just another name for GUID.

An interface definition includes its IID

Next comes the interface's name, ISpellChecker, followed by a colon and the name of another interface, IUnknown. This notation indicates that ISpellChecker inherits all the methods defined in IUnknown—that is, a client that holds a pointer to ISpellChecker

Every interface inherits from the IUnknown interface

can also invoke IUnknown's methods. IUnknown is a crucial interface in COM, as you'll learn later in this chapter, and every other interface inherits from it. [3]

Next in the interface definition is an *import* statement. Because this interface inherits from IUnknown, a software tool that might read the interface will also need to locate the IDL definitions for IUnknown. (Chapter 3 explains why a software tool would be interested in reading an interface.) The *import* statement tells the tool which file to locate to find these definitions.

A method
definition
specifies the
method's name,
its return value,
and (optionally)
a parameter list

Following the *import* statement are this interface's three methods—LookUpWord, AddToDictionary, and RemoveFromDictionary—and their parameters. All three return an HRESULT, a standard return value that indicates whether the call was a success. Parameters in IDL can be arbitrarily complex, using types such as structures and arrays, all of which are derived from their analogs in C++. Each parameter is labeled *[in]* or *[out]*. Values of *[in]* parameters are passed from the client to the object when the method is invoked, whereas the values of *[out]* parameters are passed back to the client. (Parameters whose values are passed in both directions can be labeled *[in, out]*.) These labels can help a reader better understand the interface, but their primary purpose is to allow the software tool that's processing this interface definition to decide exactly which data needs to be copied where.

---

3   As Chapter 1 explained, COM supports only interface inheritance, not implementation inheritance. Although a COM object is free to inherit from an existing interface in defining one of its own, this new object will inherit only the interface definition itself, not the existing interface's implementation. As it happens, interface inheritance is used sparingly in COM. Instead, an object typically supports each interface it needs separately (with the exception of IUnknown, from which every interface inherits).

Unlike C++, COM supports only single inheritance, allowing an interface to inherit from only one other interface at a time. Multiple inheritance, inheriting from more than one interface simultaneously, isn't supported. C++ programmers are free to use C++ multiple inheritance to implement COM objects (in fact, this technique is common), but it can't be used in defining interfaces with IDL.

This simple definition is all that's required to specify the contract between a COM object and its client. Although interfaces don't have to be defined this way, doing so can make a developer's life much easier. Besides, it's useful to have one standard scheme for defining the interfaces of COM objects.

You should note one more important point about interface definitions: once an interface has found its way into the world, once it has been implemented in released software, the rules of COM dictate that it cannot be changed. If its creator wants to add a new method or change a method's parameter list or modify anything else in the interface, that's too bad. Interfaces are immutable.

Interfaces are immutable—once made public, they can't be changed

To add new functionality or to modify existing functionality requires defining an entirely new interface. This new interface can inherit from the existing one, but it remains distinct, with a new and different IID. The creator of the software that supports this new interface might also continue supporting the old one (to keep current customers happy, since clients probably depend on this interface), but it's not required. The creator of the software is free to stop supporting the original interface (although this is usually a bad idea) but is absolutely prohibited from changing it. [4]

Adding new functionality requires defining a new interface

Implementing an interface To invoke a method, a client must understand the exact details of what's required to do it. An interface definition like the one just described is an important part of this. But COM specifies even more: it also defines a standard binary interface format that every COM object must support for every interface. Having a standard binary format means that a client can invoke an object's method regardless of the programming language either is written in. Figure 2-2 on the following page, which illustrates the ISpellChecker interface and its methods, shows what that binary format looks like.

COM defines a standard binary format for interfaces

---

4   Following this rule is the responsibility of software designers and developers. It's not enforced by COM software, and no COM police will hunt down offenders. But disobeying this rule is a sure path to chaos. As it turns out, this draconian restriction, coupled with the QueryInterface method in IUnknown, provides a very nice way to deploy new versions of COM objects (as described later in this chapter).

Figure 2-2

Figure 2-2   *What an interface looks like in an object.*

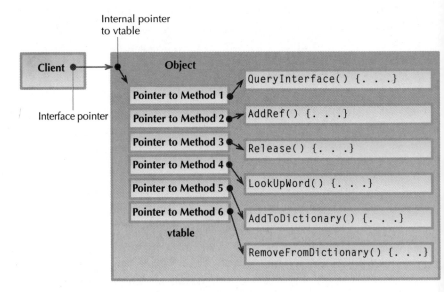

An interface's
vtable contains a
pointer to each of
its methods

As you can see in the figure, the client's interface pointer actually points to a pointer inside the object. [5] This pointer, in turn, points to a table that contains even more pointers. The table, called a *vtable*, contains a pointer to each method in this interface.

All vtables begin
with pointers to
IUnknown's
methods

Notice in Figure 2-2 that ISpellChecker's three methods appear in positions 4, 5, and 6 in the vtable. What are the first three methods? These three are the methods defined by IUnknown. Because ISpellChecker inherits from IUnknown, a client must be able to invoke IUnknown's methods via a pointer to the ISpellChecker interface. To make this possible, the vtable for the ISpellChecker interface must contain pointers to those three methods. In fact, since every interface inherits from IUnknown, the vtable for every COM interface begins with pointers to IUnknown's three methods.

An object must
implement this
binary format for
each interface

This binary structure exists for each interface an object supports. For example, if this object also supports the IThesaurus interface, that interface would have its own separate vtable with a pointer to

---

5   The truth can sometimes be a little more complicated than this. The full story is
     described in more detail in Chapter 3.

the IThesaurus interface's method (as well as a pointer to each of the three methods inherited from IUnknown).

The format of a COM interface is modeled after the data structure created by a C++ compiler for a class. This similarity means that it's quite straightforward to write COM objects using C++. Although COM objects can be written in any language capable of supporting these standard binary structures, it's fair to say that COM has some bias toward C++ implementation (which shouldn't be surprising, given the popularity of C++).

COM's binary interface format is like what a C++ compiler produces for a C++ class

When a client invokes a method in an interface, this structure of pointers is traversed (the pointer to the vtable leads to the pointer for the method, which in turn leads to the code that actually provides the service), and the correct method is executed. If the client is written in C++, this traversal is invisible, since this is what C++ does anyway. (If you are a C++ programmer, don't expect it all to be so simple, though—some parts of COM really do require you to do new and different things.) Calling the methods of a COM object from a C program is a little harder. In C, the writer of the client must be aware that a chain of pointers is being traversed and must write the call accordingly. In any case, the result is the same: a method in the object is executed.

A programmer writing clients might need to be aware of this binary format

What about making calls from an environment such as Microsoft Visual Basic? Here the tool itself can hide all the complexity of pointers behind higher-level language structures. And, today at least, Visual Basic clients commonly access COM objects using a special vtable interface called IDispatch, which makes things even easier. Chapter 4 explains how methods are invoked using IDispatch.

Tools such as Visual Basic can hide the details from a client programmer

IUnknown, the Fundamental Interface

Every COM object must support the IUnknown interface—it's the sine qua non of being a COM object. IUnknown contains only three methods: QueryInterface, AddRef, and Release. Since every interface inherits from IUnknown, IUnknown's methods can be

Every COM object must support IUnknown

invoked using any interface pointer to an object. IUnknown is a distinct interface, however, with its own IID, so it's possible for a client to acquire an interface pointer that points specifically to IUnknown. Diagrams of COM objects commonly show IUnknown on top of the object.

The QueryInter-face method lets a client ask for a pointer to another interface

Using IUnknown::QueryInterface A client commonly gets its first interface pointer to an object when it creates that object. (See "Creating COM Objects," on page 56.) Once it has that initial pointer, how does it get pointers to the object's other interfaces whose methods it needs to invoke? It's easy: the client simply asks the object for these pointers, using IUnknown::QueryInterface. [6]

To use QueryInterface, the client invokes this method on any interface pointer it currently holds for an object. The client passes in the IID of the interface it needs, as a parameter to the method. In the example shown in Figure 2-3, the client already has a pointer to interface A and needs a pointer to interface B. The client requests this pointer by invoking QueryInterface on its pointer to A, specifying as a parameter the IID of interface B (step 1). If the object supports B, it returns a pointer to that interface (step 2), and the client can invoke B's methods (step 3). If the object doesn't support B, it returns NULL.

Figure 2-3 *Using IUnknown::QueryInterface.*

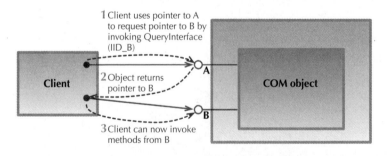

1 Client uses pointer to A to request pointer to B by invoking QueryInterface (IID_B)

Client

2 Object returns pointer to B

A

COM object

B

3 Client can now invoke methods from B

---

6 The notation IUnknown::QueryInterface refers to the QueryInterface method of the IUnknown interface. This notation is commonly used when referring to a method of a particular interface.

If pressed, COM's creators will sometimes say that QueryInterface is the most important element in COM. It might seem a little counterintuitive that such a simple mechanism could rate so high in the technological pecking order. But this simple scheme solves a very important and difficult problem: versioning.

QueryInterface helps to solve the problem of versioning

Imagine a world where applications are routinely built from COM objects. The objects that comprise these applications are provided by many different organizations, each of which updates its objects independently. Given that objects add new features at different times, how can this work? How can you install a new version of an object with new features and not break software that's using only the old features? And once a client is updated to know about the new features, how can it smoothly begin using them? The answer to all of these questions is QueryInterface. An example can best demonstrate how this works.

New versions of software with added features can present problems

Suppose there exists a set of text tools implemented as a COM object that supports the ISpellChecker interface. Once I install this object on my system, my word processor (and other clients too) can use it. To access the object's services, the word processor might use QueryInterface to ask for a pointer to ISpellChecker. Because the text tools object supports this interface, it returns that pointer, and the word processor invokes the methods in ISpell-Checker. Everything works smoothly.

Now assume that the company that sells this text tools object decides to add support for a thesaurus function that can be accessed via the IThesaurus interface. The next version of the object, then, supports both ISpellChecker and IThesaurus. When I install this new version on my system, everything works as it did before. My word processor asks for a pointer to ISpellChecker as always and happily uses its methods. (Remember that COM prohibits changing an interface.) The fact that the object now supports IThesaurus is totally unknown to my limited word processor, since it doesn't support a thesaurus option. Consequently, it never asks the object for that interface pointer.

Exposing new features requires adding a new interface

Now suppose that I install the next release of my word processor, which does support a thesaurus option. The next time I use the word processor, it starts the text tools object as usual and queries for a pointer to the ISpellChecker interface. This new version of the word processor, however, also knows enough to ask for a pointer to IThesaurus. Since I've already installed the version of the object that supports this interface, a pointer is returned, and my word processor can now use this new function. I was able to install a new version of the text tools object without breaking any of its current clients, and I was also able to have those clients smoothly begin using this new version's functions when they themselves were updated.

But what about people who've installed the new word processor but haven't yet forked out the cash for the new version of the text tools object? In this case, everything works just fine, except that the word processor won't provide those users with a thesaurus function. The word processor starts the text tools object and successfully uses QueryInterface to get a pointer to ISpellChecker. When it asks the object for a pointer to IThesaurus, however, it gets NULL in return. The word processor, written to allow for this possibility, then grays out the Thesaurus menu option seen by its user. Since no object with IThesaurus is available, the user can't access those functions. Once the user decides to invest in an updated text tools object, this option will come to life without any changes to the word processor.

There's one more interesting case. What happens when the creator of the text tools object wants to change or add features to the object's spell checking function? Doing this means changing or adding to the methods seen by the object's client. COM doesn't allow changes to interfaces, however, so the existing ISpell-Checker interface can't be touched. Instead, the object's creator must define a new interface, say, ISpellChecker2, that includes the necessary new or changed methods. The object will continue to support ISpellChecker as before, but it now will also support ISpellChecker2.

Adding support for ISpellChecker2 to the object is like adding support for any new interface. This new interface, like all COM interfaces, has a unique IID that a knowledgeable client can use to request a pointer to it via QueryInterface. And, just as with IThesaurus in the previous case, clients that are unaware of the upgrade never ask for a pointer to ISpellChecker2 and so aren't affected by the changes—they continue to use ISpellChecker as before.

QueryInterface and the mandated immutability of COM interfaces allow separate software components produced by different organizations to be updated independently, yet still work together smoothly. This is no small consideration, and it's the reason that COM's creators sometimes describe QueryInterface as the most significant element in COM.

QueryInterface might be the most important element in COM

Reference counting To use a COM object, a client must explicitly cause a new instance of the object to start executing (as described in "Creating COM Objects," page 56). This brings up an obvious question: when does the object stop executing? The obvious solution is to have the client that started the object also tell it when to stop. But this solution doesn't work, because the client that started the object might not be the only one who winds up using it. It's fairly common for a client to start an object, acquire pointers to interfaces on that object, and then pass one of those pointers to another client. This second client can use that pointer to invoke methods in the same object and can itself pass the pointer to yet other clients. If the first client could kill the object instance at will, any other client using this same object would be very unhappy—having an object go away when you're using its services is annoying at best.

Once a new instance of an object starts executing, it needs to know when to stop

Although many clients can use the same object, none of them can know when all the others have finished. Therefore, it's not safe for a client to kill an instance of an object directly. Only the object itself can know when it's safe to stop running, and it can know only if all its clients tell it when they've finished. Objects keep

The object itself keeps track of how many clients are using it

track of all this with a mechanism called *reference counting,* which is supported by two of the methods in the IUnknown interface.

Reference counting is done with the IUnknown methods AddRef and Release

Every running object maintains a reference count. Whenever the object passes out a pointer to one of its interfaces, it adds 1 to this reference count. (In fact, an object can even maintain a separate reference count for each interface.) If one client passes an interface pointer to another client, causing the object to acquire another user without its knowledge, the client who receives the pointer must invoke the AddRef method using that pointer. (For simplicity, this is usually expressed as *calling AddRef on the pointer.*) This causes the object to increment its reference count. Regardless of how a client got an interface pointer, it must always call Release on that pointer when it has finished using it. Executing this method in the object causes the object to decrement its reference count. An object usually destroys itself when its reference count drops to 0.

Reference counting controls an object's lifetime

Reference counting can be problematic. If all clients don't follow the rules, an instance of an object can hang around indefinitely or, perhaps worse, die too soon. Still, reference counting appears to be the only workable solution for controlling object lifetimes in the diverse and dynamic environment that COM allows.

Classes

Every COM object is an instance of a class, and each class can be assigned a class identifier (CLSID)

Every COM object is an instance of a class, and each class can be assigned a GUID called a *class identifier* (CLSID). A client can pass this CLSID to the COM library to create an instance of the class, as described in "Creating COM Objects," page 56. Not every class must have a CLSID, however—objects of some classes aren't created using the COM library, and so these classes aren't required to have CLSIDs. It's entirely possible for one, two, or many objects of the same class to be active at the same time. A bank, for example, might represent each account as a COM object. If tellers, automatic teller machines, and other clients were working with many accounts at once, a COM object would be running for each one, each an instance of the same class.

The relationship between an object's class and the interfaces supported by that object is a little tenuous. The obvious assumptions are that an object of a specific class supports a certain set of interfaces and that adding a new interface to the object changes its class. This is not necessarily true, however—adding interfaces to an object without changing its class is not prohibited by COM. Instead, the primary use of a CLSID is to identify a specific piece of code for the COM library to load and execute for objects of that class. [7] In COM, an object's class identifies a particular *implementation* of a group of interfaces, not simply the group itself. Suppose, for example, that two different vendors decide to implement the text tools object described earlier and that both of the objects they create support ISpellChecker and IThesaurus. Although both objects support the same set of interfaces, the two objects are of different classes and are assigned different CLSIDs because their implementation differs.

A class identifies the implementation of a group of interfaces

Servers for COM Objects

Every COM object is implemented inside a server. The server contains the code that actually implements the methods for the object's interfaces and keeps track of the object's data while it's active. A single server can and often does support more than one object of a particular class and can even support more than one class. Figure 2-4 on the following page illustrates the three primary kinds of servers:

A COM object is implemented in a server (in-process, local, or remote)

- In-process servers, in which objects are implemented in a dynamic-link library and thus execute in the same process as the client.
- Local servers, in which objects are implemented in a separate process running on the same machine as the client.
- Remote servers, in which objects are implemented in a DLL or in a separate process that runs on a different machine than the client does. Distributed COM (DCOM) supports this option.

---

7   It's still useful to know in advance what interfaces an object supports. Component categories, described in Chapter 9, were created to allow this.

Figure 2-4   *Three kinds of servers.*

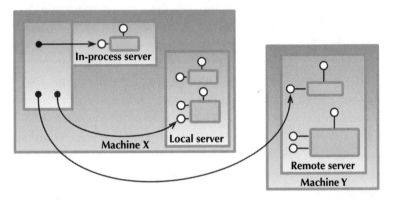

A client need not
be aware of the
kind of server in
which an object
is implemented

To a client, an object implemented in any of these kinds of servers
looks the same; the client still accesses the object's methods via
interface pointers. If necessary, a client can distinguish among the
various kinds of servers, but it isn't required. Starting an object,
acquiring pointers to the object's interfaces, invoking the methods
in those interfaces, and releasing the pointers all look the same to
a client, whether the object is implemented in an in-process
server, a local server, or a remote server.

COM and Multithreading

A multithreaded
process contains
several apparently
simultaneous
threads of
execution

In a traditional, simple process, only one action happens at a time.
Put another way, the process has only a single thread of execution.
In certain cases, however, it can be useful to allow a single process
to carry out several tasks simultaneously (or at least appear to
carry them out simultaneously). To allow this, a process can have
more than one thread of execution—that is, it can become *multithreaded.* A multithreaded process can lead to better performance
when, for instance, a machine has several processors and the
process can assign a thread to each one. Multithreading can also
be helpful in a distributed environment, where a process on one
machine makes a request of a second machine. Rather than waiting
idly for the second machine to fulfill its request, the calling process
can use a separate thread to do useful work while the request is
being handled.

Adding threads to a programming environment also adds complexity. The programmer must now be aware of possible conflicts in the process, for example, when two threads each want to update the same variable. Correctly handling issues like these requires extra work to ensure that the code is thread-safe. The libraries used by a multithreaded program must also be thread-safe, or bizarre and hard-to-find errors can occur. [8]

For some of COM's original target platforms, Microsoft Windows 3.x and the Macintosh, threads were not an issue. Because neither operating system supported threads, the concerns that come with ensuring thread-safety didn't arise. Both Microsoft Windows NT and Microsoft Windows 95 support the creation of multithreaded processes, however, as do other platforms that support COM, so effectively using COM in these environments requires dealing with the issue.

The original approach to allowing the creation of multithreaded COM objects is called the *apartment model*. The idea is that although a process can be multithreaded, individual COM objects cannot be. Each thread acts like an apartment, and each COM object lives inside only one apartment (that is, one thread). Only this thread is able to call an object's methods—calls from other threads are queued and then handled sequentially by this object's owning thread.

COM first supported multithreading using the apartment model

Apartment-model threading is certainly useful, but it's not perfect. Allowing a process to have multiple threads is a great benefit, but allowing each COM object to be simultaneously accessible by multiple threads would be even better. Support for this, an option known as *free threading* or just multithreading, appeared with the release of Windows NT 4.0 in 1996. With free threading, several threads can be active at once inside a single COM object.

COM now also supports free threading

---

8 One reason these errors are hard to find is that they can be hard to replicate. Since the details of which thread runs when can vary from one execution of the process to another, the exact circumstances required for an error to occur might crop up only occasionally. Sometimes the only sure way to replicate an error is to do a demonstration for upper management.

Free threading
requires more
from the
programmer

The programmer who writes the code for that object must be careful to make it thread-safe, but if this is done, COM no longer restricts each object to having only one thread at a time calling its methods.

Creating COM Objects

This discussion so far has assumed that, somehow, a client has acquired a pointer to an initial interface on a currently running object. Exactly how that pointer was procured has been left unsaid. It turns out that a client might acquire its first interface pointer to an object in any of several ways. For example, it might have been passed a pointer by another client, or it might have gotten the pointer from a moniker. (Monikers are described in Chapter 6). For every object, though, some client has created that object and has obtained the first interface pointer to it. Ultimately, this process relies on functions implemented by the COM library.

The COM Library

The COM library
provides basic
services that
objects and their
clients need

Every system that supports COM must include an implementation of the COM library. This library implements a group of functions that supply basic services to objects and their clients. Most important, the COM library provides a way for clients to start an object's server. The COM library's services are accessed through ordinary function calls, not by using methods in interfaces on COM objects. The names of COM library functions usually begin with the prefix *Co*—for example, CoCreateInstance.

The COM library
uses the system
registry to locate
the right server for
a particular class

Finding servers When a client requests the creation of an object, it passes to the COM library that object's class identifier, which the library must use to locate the correct server for this class of object. To accomplish this, some kind of system registry must exist, a table that maps CLSIDs to the actual server code. The classes of all objects that the COM library will be asked to create on this machine must be registered in this database.

COM has been implemented on many different systems, and the exact format of this system registry varies. Microsoft Windows and

Windows NT use a standard system table simply called the Registry. Other implementations of COM are free to use other variations, although the mapping must include the following:

- The CLSID, which acts as a key for the entry.
- An indication of what kinds of servers are available (in-process, local, or remote).
- For in-process and local servers (those that run on the same machine as the client), the pathname for the file containing the server's DLL or executable, respectively. For remote servers (those accessible on another machine via DCOM), an indication of where to find the server's executable.

An application typically adds its entries to this table when the application is installed. That application is then ready to have its objects created and used by clients.

Classes and instances Before describing how the COM library creates an object, it's worth taking a minute to think about what this means. To create an object is to cause an instance of that object's class to begin running. For at least the first instance of a class, this implies starting a server for the class. In fact, the COM library's primary job is to start this server, not necessarily to start the object itself.

Since the COM library knows only the object's CLSID, it can start only a generic instance of the object. A CLSID is enough to find the code for an object's methods, but what about the object's data? How can you specify not just any object of a certain class but instead a specific object of that class, complete with that object's data—that is, an initialized object?

An object created using only the COM library is an uninitialized instance of a class

The answer is that you can't, at least not if you are using COM alone. As described in "Initializing COM Objects," page 63, COM requires a client to ask the object to initialize itself, a distinct operation performed after the object is running. Thus, using COM by itself requires a two-step process to load and initialize an object. (It is possible to capture both class and data

If needed, a client can explicitly initialize a new object instance in just one reference, however. This technology, called monikers, is discussed in Chapter 6. A moniker can hide all the details from a client, providing a single reference to both methods and data for a particular object instance.)

Creating a Single Object

A client can call CoCreate- Instance to create a new instance of an object

The easiest way to create a single uninitialized instance of an object is shown in Figure 2-5. First a client calls the COM library function CoCreateInstance. This request specifies, among other things, the CLSID of the object to be created and the IID of an interface that object supports. The COM library then uses the CLSID to find the entry for this object's class in the system registry. (More precisely, the COM library delegates this task to what is called the Service Control Manager, or SCM. The SCM's role is especially interesting in DCOM, as explained in Chapter 10.) This entry specifies the location of the server capable of instantiating this class of object. Once this server is found, the SCM starts it.

Figure 2-5   ***Creating an object with CoCreateInstance.***

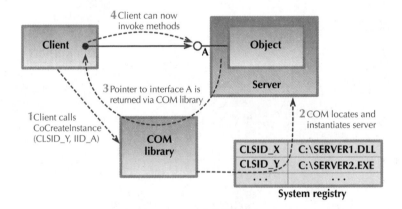

The client specifies a CLSID, an IID, and the kind of server it wants the COM library to start

Along with a CLSID and the IID of the first interface to which the client wants a pointer, the parameters of CoCreateInstance also allow the client to specify what kind of server COM should start—for example, in-process or local. A client is free to say, "I don't care—just start one" or to specify any combination of allowable server types.

The server that's started creates an instance of the requested object class and then returns the requested interface pointer to the COM library. The COM library, in turn, passes this pointer back to the client, who can then begin invoking that interface's methods. Since this process creates only an uninitialized object, the requested interface is often one that lets the client ask the object to initialize itself, although this isn't required.

The discussion so far has assumed that the object being instantiated is implemented in an in-process server or a local server—that is, that it will run on the same machine as the client. What happens with remote servers? How are remote objects instantiated?

DCOM provides support for remote objects. The process is much the same as for local objects: the client makes the same request to the COM library, the SCM checks the system registry, and so on. If a remote server is specified, COM will contact the remote system to do the work of instantiation. Like all machine-to-machine communication in DCOM, this request is made via a remote procedure call. The remote system then checks its registry, locates the server executable, and instantiates the object. Just as in the local case, an interface pointer is returned, and the client can now invoke the newly created object's methods. To a client, starting an object always looks the same, regardless of whether the object is in an in-process server, a local server, or a remote server; the client need be aware of the distinction only if it chooses to be. (Chapter 10 describes in more detail how DCOM creates remote objects.)

Whatever kind of server is started, COM establishes rules for security that determine which clients are allowed to start which servers. COM also defines relevant interfaces and COM library calls for security, although exactly how they are implemented depends on the operating system. And, for remote servers, DCOM defines how distributed security services should be accessed, as described in Chapter 10.

Creating Multiple Objects of the Same Class: Class Factories

A class factory can create multiple objects of the same class

If a client needs only a single instance of a particular object, the simplest solution is to create that instance with CoCreateInstance. It's possible, though, that a client might need multiple instances of objects in the same class. To create them efficiently, the client can access a *class factory,* a kind of object that can create other objects. Each class factory knows how to create objects of one specific class (although the name *class factory* is something of a misnomer because class factories actually create object instances, not classes). Class factories are COM objects in their own right—they are accessed via their interfaces, they support IUnknown, and so on. They are special, however, in that they're also able to create other COM objects.

CoCreateInstance uses a class factory that it hides from the client

The truth is that the objects seen so far were created by a class factory. Even when a client simply calls CoCreateInstance, the implementation of this function in the COM library relies on a class factory to create the object. CoCreateInstance hides those details from the client, but, in fact, it uses the methods in the IClassFactory interface, described next.

Every class factory supports the IClassFactory interface

The IClassFactory interface To qualify as a class factory, an object must support the IClassFactory interface. IClassFactory is remarkably simple, containing only two methods:

- **CreateInstance** creates a new instance of the class of object that the factory can instantiate. The client does not specify a CLSID as a parameter for this method, since the class of the object being created is implicit in the factory object itself. The client does, however, specify an IID, indicating the interface to which it needs a pointer. (A class factory written in C++ might implement this method by creating a new object using the C++ *new* operator.)

- **LockServer** lets a client keep a server in memory. A factory object is like any other object in that it maintains a reference count to keep track of how many clients are currently using it. But for various (fairly complex) reasons, this reference count isn't enough to keep the factory's server in memory. To ensure that this server stays running, IClassFactory::LockServer can be used.

In some ways, the IClassFactory interface is too simple. Today an interface called IClassFactory2 adds to these basic methods. (Remember that interfaces in COM can't be changed once they're disseminated—even COM's creators must follow this rule.) Because IClassFactory2 inherits from IClassFactory, it includes the CreateInstance and LockServer methods, but it also supports a few other methods that are concerned with licensing. Using these methods, it's possible to allow only licensed clients to create new objects—that is, clients who have a legal, presumably paid-for copy of the software on their system. Because this is especially useful with ActiveX Controls, Chapter 9 describes the additional methods in this interface.

The IClassFactory2 interface adds methods that support licensing

Using a class factory To access a class factory, a client invokes the COM library function CoGetClassObject. In this call, the client specifies the CLSID of the class of objects the factory will create, not a CLSID specific to the factory itself. The client also specifies an IID for the interface the client needs to use to access the factory. Normally, of course, this IID is the one for IClassFactory. And, as with CoCreateInstance, a client can also specify the kind of server that should be created for the factory and its objects. If an in-process server is requested for the factory, for example, the objects this factory creates will also execute within that in-process server.

A client calls CoGetClassObject to get a pointer to a class factory

A client can use IClassFactory:: CreateInstance to create a new instance of an object

Figure 2-6 illustrates the process of using a class factory. In the figure, the client has already called CoGetClassObject, and the COM library has started the class factory and returned a pointer to the factory's IClassFactory interface. Once the client holds this interface pointer, it invokes that interface's CreateInstance method (step 1). The parameters the client specifies on this call include the IID of the interface to which it needs a pointer. The class factory responds by creating the requested object (step 2) and returning this interface pointer to the client (step 3). The client can then use this pointer to invoke the interface's methods (step 4).

Figure 2-6   *Creating an object with a class factory.*

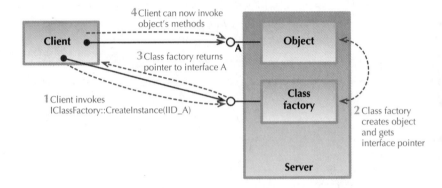

Emulation

Earlier this chapter discussed IUnknown's QueryInterface method and its ability to handle versioning smoothly. Adding a new interface to an existing object causes no problems for current clients of that object because they won't ask for a pointer to this interface. New clients ask for the pointer, get the new interface's services, and everybody's happy.

But there's a potential problem here. Suppose that I replace an existing class with another class, one that supports all the interfaces of the first class and more. In other words, this new class is polymorphic with the first one—a client can use it just as if it were the old class. But suppose that this new class has a different CLSID. Existing clients are written to create objects of the old class using the old CLSID. If I remove that old CLSID entirely, the existing clients will break. Something must be done to allow those clients to remain unchanged while still using the new class.

That something is called *emulation*. The idea is straightforward: let a client call CoCreateInstance with the CLSID of the old object, but actually create an instance of the new object. To allow this, the COM library provides a function called CoTreatAsClass, which takes two parameters: the old CLSID and the new CLSID. Once this call is made, attempts to create an object using the old CLSID will result in instantiating an object with the new CLSID. (The call is typically implemented by setting up an emulation relationship between the two CLSIDs in the system registry.) Because objects of the new class also support all the old interfaces, the existing clients continue to work as before.

Emulation lets one class play the role of another

This mechanism is also useful for creating generic components, such as the spell checker object described earlier. For example, a word processing application wants to know only a single CLSID identifying a spell checker object that supports a well-known ISpellChecker interface. In COM, however, because a CLSID identifies a particular implementation of an interface, two vendors' spell checker objects will have different CLSIDs even though both support the same interface. To make this work, a well-known CLSID must be defined that simply means "spell checker." The word processor will always use this CLSID when it creates a spell checker object. To determine which spell checker gets started on a given system, the CoTreatAsClass function is used to establish a mapping from this generic spell checker CLSID to the CLSID of the selected spell checker object.

Emulation also allows the creation of generic components

Initializing COM Objects
As described so far, a client requests creation of an object by specifying the object's CLSID and one of its IIDs. In response, a class factory creates a generic instance of this class. Essentially, this process makes the new object's methods available. But objects have more than methods—they also have data. When a client accesses a bank account, for example, it usually wants to

access a specific account. Completely instantiating an object, then, generally requires loading the object's data (such as the account balance) as well as its methods.

A client can ask a new object instance to initialize itself

In COM, a client usually asks a newly created object to initialize itself. For this to be possible, the object's data must be stored in a persistent way—that is, the object must be able to save its data when it's not actually running. One obvious place for an object to store its persistent data is in a file on disk.

The first interface pointer a client asks for is often to the interface used to request initialization

The first interface pointer a client requests when a new object is created is usually the one for an interface containing the object's initialization function. As Chapter 5 explains, standard interfaces, such as IPersistFile, IPersistStorage, and IPersistStream, are defined for this purpose. Each of these interfaces contains methods that allow a client to ask an object to load its persistent data (that is, to initialize itself). Although these are by no means the only interfaces that can be used for initialization, any one of these is a common choice.

Reusing COM Objects

One of COM's primary goals is to promote widespread and effective reuse of existing code. By allowing the creation of reusable components with well-defined interfaces, COM provides an infrastructure that makes this possible.

One COM object can't reuse another's code through inheritance

Many, perhaps most, object-related technologies rely on implementation inheritance (in which a new object inherits the actual implementation of methods in an existing object) as their fundamental mechanism for reusing existing code. COM's creators, however, believe that this kind of inheritance is impractical for an object system in a very heterogeneous environment. [9]

---

9 COM's lack of support for implementation inheritance in no way interferes with use of this feature in programming languages that support it, such as C++. Implementations of COM objects are free to use implementation inheritance as always. (In fact, Microsoft encourages it.) What's not supported is inheriting an implementation from another COM object. This is not a contradiction—C++ is a language for implementing objects, whereas COM is an enabling technology for component software and more.

Despite the isolation provided by interfaces, changes in base objects could have unexpected effects on objects that inherit implementation from them. In a world where base objects and objects that inherit from them are created, released, and updated independently, this can be problematic. Instead, COM provides reuse through two other mechanisms: *containment* and *aggregation*.

COM provides reuse through either containment or aggregation

Containment and aggregation are simple concepts. Both provide a means for reuse, and so both rely on a relationship between objects. In the terminology used in COM, an outer object is one that reuses the services of an inner object. The outer object might simply act as a client of the inner object, or the relationship might be a little more involved.

In both mechanisms, an "outer" object reuses an "inner" object

Containment

With containment (also called *delegation*), the outer object acts as a client of the inner object. As shown in Figure 2-7, the outer object invokes the inner object's methods to carry out its own functions, but it doesn't make those methods visible to its client. Instead, when a client invokes a method in one of the outer object's interfaces, the execution of that method might include a call to a method in an interface on the inner object. In other words, the outer object's interface contains methods that call the inner object's methods.

With containment, the outer object is simply a client of the inner object

Reusing an object through containment.

Figure 2-7

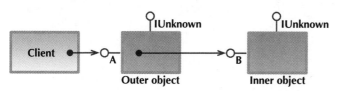

Implementing containment is as simple as implementing a client that uses any COM object. The inner object doesn't need to be written in a special way, and, in fact, it can't distinguish between containment and direct use by a client. (To the inner object, the outer object *is* just a client.) Because of its simplicity, containment is a very common mechanism for reuse in COM.

Containment is simple and frequently used

Aggregation

Although it's simple, containment isn't always the most efficient solution

If containment is so straightforward, why not always employ this technique to reuse an existing COM object? Even though you can always reuse existing objects via containment—nothing else is really required—there are nevertheless occasions where containment just isn't the best approach.

Consider the case, for example, in which an object needs to present a specific interface to its client, and another object that supports the interface already exists. The first object could implement an interface with the correct methods, each of which could be written to do nothing more than invoke the corresponding method in the existing object. This would certainly work, and the client might even be happy (as happy as a piece of software can be, anyway). But it's not very efficient. And if this same process is repeated through several objects, with each one delegating the call to another, invoking a method can become very inefficient, as several objects must be traversed to reach the actual implementation of the method.

With aggregation, the outer object presents the inner object's interfaces as its own

Aggregation avoids this problem. As shown in Figure 2-8, aggregation lets an outer object present as its own an interface that's actually implemented by an inner object. When a client asks the outer object for a pointer to this interface, the outer object returns a pointer to the interface on the inner, aggregated object. (The inner object's methods are added to—aggregated with—those of the outer object.) The client is none the wiser—this interface is provided by the only object it knows about, the outer object. Aggregation makes the process more efficient, but, like containment, it's completely invisible to the client.

Figure 2-8   *Reusing an object by aggregation.*

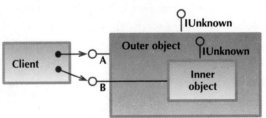

Aggregation is not invisible to the objects involved, however. Unlike containment, implementing aggregation requires support from the inner object. This object must be specifically written to support aggregation; otherwise, it can be reused only through containment. What's so different about aggregation that requires support from the inner object? The problems derive from the operations that all objects must support, those defined in IUnknown. Getting reference counts right and making sure that QueryInterface works correctly are the two big issues in implementing aggregation.

Because aggregation requires special support from the inner object, not all objects can be aggregated

To see why these problems exist, look again at Figure 2-8. The outer object provides interface A and, of course, supports IUnknown. The inner object, the one being aggregated, supports interface B and IUnknown. Because the outer object is aggregating rather than simply containing the inner object, interface B is directly available to the outer object's client.

Special support is needed to ensure that IUnknown's methods work as expected

Suppose that the client holds a pointer to interface B, as in the figure. As far as the client knows, this interface is provided by the same object that provides interface A. If the client calls IUnknown::QueryInterface on its pointer to interface B, it should be able to retrieve a pointer to interface A. But how can the inner object know that its outer object supports interface A? And if a client calls IUnknown::AddRef on interface B, how can the outer object learn about this? After all, to the client only one object exists, so each of these requests should succeed.

Both problems can be solved in a straightforward way. All the inner object needs to do is delegate all calls made on its IUnknown methods to the IUnknown methods in its outer object (the one aggregating it). To make this work, the inner object must somehow acquire a pointer to the outer object's IUnknown interface. This pointer, known somewhat metaphysically as the *controlling unknown*, is passed as a parameter on either CoCreateInstance or IClassFactory::CreateInstance when the aggregated object is created. If the controlling unknown parameter is NULL on these calls (the most common case), the object being created

The outer object passes the inner object a pointer to its IUnknown interface

knows that it's not being aggregated, and it will handle all calls on IUnknown's methods itself. If this parameter is not NULL, however, the new object will function only as the aggregated inner object of a particular outer object, the one that passes in its controlling unknown. Calls to the inner object's IUnknown methods are then delegated to the IUnknown methods in the outer object, that is, to the controlling unknown.

Even more complications are involved here to make everything turn out correctly. Suffice it to say that implementing aggregation is a bit of work. Still, with a little effort, it's not hard either to understand or to implement. And the effort is often worth it, as aggregation can greatly improve performance for certain kinds of object reuse.

The Importance of COM

While COM itself is simple, it enables the creation of powerful, effective software

COM allows all kinds of software to provide services through one common paradigm: COM objects. The relatively simple set of conventions that all COM objects follow—implementing interfaces in a certain way, always supporting IUnknown, and a few more—provides the underpinnings for an enormous diversity of applications. The ActiveX and OLE technologies, all built on COM, add all sorts of useful functionality to the basics described in this chapter. But even if the entirety of these higher-level services didn't exist, COM alone would nonetheless qualify as a great leap forward.

Chapter Three

Marshaling and Type Information

To invoke methods in a COM object, a client must hold one or more pointers to that object's interfaces. As explained in Chapter 2, the object and its methods can be implemented either in the same process as the client or in a separate process. Regardless of where the object is implemented, however, the client invokes the methods in the same way.

What kind of magic makes it possible to sustain this illusion? As with so many other questions, the answer is, "It depends." In some cases, there's no magic at all—the client simply invokes the method directly. In other cases, a process called *marshaling* is required. Additionally, to acquire the information necessary to perform marshaling, and sometimes for other reasons as well, it can be useful to obtain *type information* about the object. This chapter discusses both of these topics.

What an Interface Pointer Really Points To

When a client holds a pointer to an object's interface, what does this pointer really point to? If the object is implemented in an in-process server, the pointer can point directly to the binary interface structure shown in Chapter 2. (See Figure 2-2 on page 46.) If the object is implemented in a local or remote server, however, this isn't possible—an ordinary pointer can't point to something in

What a client's interface pointer points to depends on the kind of server in which the object is implemented

a different process or on a different machine. So what's actually going on? The answer depends on how the object is implemented. Just as COM has three primary kinds of servers—in-process, local, and remote—there are three possible answers to the question.

The first possibility, a COM object implemented in an in-process server, is shown in Figure 3-1. It couldn't be simpler: the client's interface pointer points directly to the object's interface. Calls made to a COM object implemented in an in-process server are as efficient as calls to a C++ function in the same process.

For an object in an in-process server, the client's pointer points directly to the object's interface

Figure 3-1   *Accessing a COM object in an in-process server.*

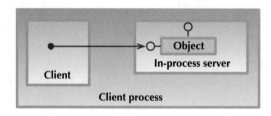

For a COM object implemented in a local server (a separate process running on the same machine), it's a little more complicated, as shown in Figure 3-2. Because the client's interface pointer can't point directly to the interface in the object, it points instead to the interface of a *proxy* within the client's process. A proxy is simply another COM object, but it's one that typically presents the same interfaces the client expects from the object in the local server that the client is trying to communicate with.

For an object in a local server, the client's pointer points to a proxy object

Figure 3-2   *Accessing a COM object in a local server.*

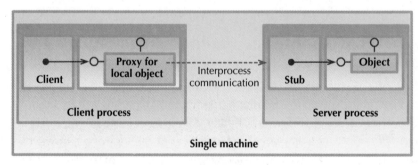

When a client invokes a method using this interface pointer, what actually executes is code in the proxy. The proxy takes the parameters passed by the client and packages them for transfer. It then sends a request via some kind of interprocess communication (the details depend on the operating system on which COM is implemented) and transfers the necessary parameters to the process that implements the real object.

When this request arrives in the local server process, it is handed to a *stub*. The stub unpackages the call's parameters and invokes the method in the object. The method executes, and any results are returned through the same path in reverse. To the client, this method invocation looks the same as that for an in-process server. This sameness, providing the client with a common view of in-process and out-of-process objects, is sometimes referred to as *local/remote transparency*.

The client might notice one difference, of course: a method call to an object in a separate local server process will be significantly slower than a call to an object in an in-process server. This is a consequence of the enormous difference in overhead necessary to make the two kinds of calls work. It could be worse, however— the object could be implemented in a remote server.

The architecture for supporting remote servers, a feature added by Distributed COM (DCOM), is much like that used with local servers, as Figure 3-3 shows on the following page. The client uses a proxy, and the server relies on a stub to make the actual call to the object. But here the two processes are running on different machines, and a relatively lightweight interprocess communication scheme is no longer adequate. Instead, invoking a method across machine boundaries requires a full-blown remote procedure call (RPC). Given that this kind of overhead is unavoidable for machine-to-machine communication, the RPC used by COM (described in more detail in Chapter 10) is quite efficient. Once again, however, to a client, a call made to an object in a remote server looks just the same as a call to an object implemented in an in-process or a local server.

Figure 3-3   *Accessing a COM object in a remote server.*

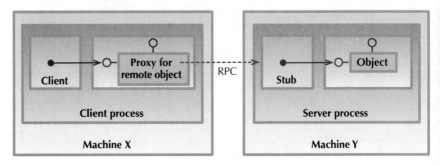

Marshaling and Unmarshaling

Invoking methods cross-process or cross-machine raises a deeper problem: exactly how are the request and its parameters packaged for transfer to the out-of-process object, and how are any results packaged for the return trip? For simple in-process objects, this isn't an issue; because the client's call winds up invoking a method in the same process, the parameters and results can be passed like those for any ordinary function call. When going between processes or machines, however, things aren't so simple.

Parameters passed between processes or machines must be packaged for the trip and then unpackaged when they arrive

In the cross-process case, the call's parameters and return values must be assembled into some standard format that both processes understand. The cross-machine case is more difficult still, because different machines commonly use different formats for representing the same information. In particular, machines differ in how they represent characters, integers, and floating-point numbers. In both the cross-process and cross-machine cases, a standard format for transmitting parameters and results is required, and code to perform the appropriate translations must exist in the client and the server.

This packaging and unpackaging are called marshaling and unmarshaling

Packaging a call's parameters into a standard format for transmission is called *marshaling*. The reverse operation, unpackaging from the standard format into a format appropriate for the receiving process, is called *unmarshaling*. Code that knows how to perform these operations is generically referred to as *marshaling code* or, for short, a *marshaler*. The primary purpose of proxies and stubs is to perform marshaling and unmarshaling as needed.

Each interface has its own set of methods, each with its own parameters. As a result, marshaling code is usually structured on a per-interface basis. The marshaler for a particular interface knows how to correctly package and unpackage the parameters for the methods in that interface. The marshaling code required for a client calling an interface's methods is generally different from that for an object that implements those methods and responds to the request. The code on the client side must be able to package each method's parameters and unpackage each method's results. The marshaler on the object side must be capable of doing just the reverse: unpackaging each method's parameters and packaging each method's results.

Proxies and stubs perform marshaling and unmarshaling

Creating Proxies and Stubs

Every interface that can accept calls from clients in other processes or on other machines needs to use marshaling and unmarshaling. But where does that code come from? Recall from Chapter 2 that interfaces can be defined using COM's Interface Definition Language. Although it's not required, using IDL provides a convenient and standard way to describe an interface's methods and their parameters. Apart from convenience, however, using IDL to define an interface also makes it easy to produce a proxy and a stub for that interface.

Masochists are free to sit down with an IDL definition and write a proxy and a stub by hand. The emotionally healthy among us can rely on a tool instead. This tool is called the MIDL (Microsoft IDL) compiler. Given an interface definition written in IDL, this compiler can read the definition and automatically generate the necessary marshaling code for this interface, contained in a proxy and a stub. Along with these essential pieces, the compiler produces other files that define such useful elements as function

A tool called the MIDL compiler can be used to create a proxy and a stub for any interface defined in IDL

prototypes for the interface's methods as well as a file that contains a named constant definition for the interface's IID. You can use the output of the standard MIDL compiler in code written in either C or C++.

Custom Marshaling

Proxies and stubs produced with the MIDL compiler use *standard marshaling*—that is, they do all their marshaling and unmarshaling in the same way. But for cases in which this standard approach isn't enough, COM also allows *custom marshaling*. To support it, a developer must provide an implementation of a COM-defined interface called IMarshal.

Why do custom marshaling? The most obvious reason is to improve performance. Defining one's own marshaling routines that take advantage of known restrictions in an object's implementation can lead to faster code. For example, the IStorage and IStream interfaces described in Chapter 5 rely on custom marshaling in their implementation to improve performance. And, with DCOM, in which objects and their clients can be separated by a network, custom marshaling allows the developer to define a private data representation for transfer across the network or even to create an interaction with the remote object that, while functionally identical to the local interface, actually behaves in an optimized way.

Building Marshalers Dynamically: Late Binding

Using marshaling code provided by proxies and stubs is the right approach in many situations. But it can be completely unworkable for certain kinds of problems. Because proxies and stubs are typically created during the development of a client and/or the objects it uses, they are a static way to produce marshalers. Although both proxies and stubs are implemented as DLLs and so can be loaded as needed, the assumption is that the client knows what interfaces it will use when it is written and compiled. Imagine a situation, though, where this isn't possible. Suppose that a client is already running and then learns about a new interface on an object. If no proxy for that interface exists, how can the client invoke the interface's methods?

The answer is that the client might be able to do something called *late binding*. The idea here is that a running client can dynamically construct calls on a newly discovered interface. Doing this lets the client decide at run time rather than compile time what interfaces it wants to use. Late binding can allow great flexibility and is useful for some types of clients.

An alternative, creating marshaling code dynamically, allows late binding

Imagine, for example, that a running client needs to load and use a new software component. If the client can dynamically learn about the new component's methods, it could also have the ability to dynamically construct new calls on those methods or even to allow the component to make new calls on it. (This is exactly what happens with many ActiveX controls.) The client needn't know at compile time all the details about all the methods it will use.

Late binding lets a client invoke methods in interfaces discovered while it's running

The ability to do late binding relies on being able to do dynamic marshaling. This in turn implies that a client must have a way to dynamically learn about the interfaces an object supports—that is, to discover this information while the client is running. The following section describes how a client can do this.

Type Information

A COM object's interfaces are typically defined using IDL. Formally describing an object's interfaces and their methods is useful for several reasons. For one, it's important to specify exactly what those methods look like so that developers will know precisely how to write code that implements or calls the methods. In this case, people directly use descriptive information about an object during the implementation of that object and the clients that use it.

IDL definitions precisely document an object's interfaces

A second reason to precisely define objects and their interfaces was discussed earlier in the chapter: IDL definitions can be used to generate marshaling code in the form of proxies and stubs. Using tools to accomplish this is a far better solution than forcing someone to read the interface and then manually create marshalers for it.

But if tools can use descriptions of an object's interfaces to generate marshalers, why not use the same information to build marshalers dynamically? This third possible use of object interface definitions requires a way for a running client to dynamically acquire this information, to access what's known as an object's *type information*.

Type information includes a description of everything a client needs to know to use an object's services. For each interface an object supports, for example, the object's type information includes a list of the interface's methods and properties, along with a description of the parameters for those methods. The type information for a simple object might include only a couple of interfaces, whereas the type information for a more complex object would define several. And although it's conceivable that other languages could be used, all type information today should be defined using IDL.[1]

To provide type information to an object's clients, the object's developer can create and make available a *type library*, which contains a standardized description of the object's interfaces. Type libraries are not required for all COM objects, but they can be very useful. The library can be distributed in various ways—in an ordinary file, for example, or as a stream in a file using Structured Storage. To create a type library, the developer typically uses IDL to describe the object's interfaces and then feeds that description

---

1   The original release of OLE also employed a second language, called the Object Description Language (ODL). ODL has since been superseded by an enhanced version of IDL, which incorporates ODL's functionality and even much of its syntax.

Proxies and stubs for an object's interfaces can be produced with IDL definitions

Type information created from IDL definitions can be used to generate marshaling code dynamically

A running client can access an object's type information, which describes its interfaces

An object can store its type information in a type library generated by the MIDL compiler

into the MIDL compiler described earlier.[2] Figure 3-4 shows a diagram of this process. Depending on the information provided in the IDL file, the MIDL compiler can produce marshaling code (proxies and stubs) for one or more interfaces, and/or a type library, and more. Once the library exists, clients can access it through standard interfaces.

The MIDL compiler can generate type libraries as well as proxies and stubs.

Figure 3-4

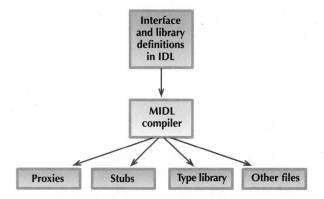

Obviously, this can all get a little involved. The place to start in understanding type libraries and type information in general is with the language used to describe everything, IDL.

Describing IDL

The easiest way to understand IDL is to look at an example. The object described here is the hypothetical text tools object from Chapter 2. As you might recall, this object supports an interface for a spell checker and an interface for a thesaurus. The IDL example on the following page defines these two interfaces as well as a type library that includes both.

This IDL example contains two interface definitions and the information needed to produce a type library

---

2 When type information was described with ODL, a tool called MkTypLib was used with ODL to create type libraries. With the demise of ODL, an enhanced MIDL compiler made MkTypLib obsolete.

```
[ object,
  uuid(E7CD0D00-1827-11CF-9946-444553540000) ]
interface ISpellChecker : IUnknown {
    import "unknwn.idl";
    HRESULT LookUpWord([in] OLECHAR word[31],
                       [out] boolean *found);
    HRESULT AddToDictionary([in] OLECHAR word[31]);
    HRESULT RemoveFromDictionary([in] OLECHAR word[31]);
}

[ object,
  uuid(5FBDD020-1863-11CF-9946-444553540000)]
interface IThesaurus : IUnknown {
    HRESULT ReturnSynonym([in] OLECHAR word[31],
                          [out] OLECHAR synonym[31]);
}

[uuid(B253E460-1826-11CF-9946-444553540000),
  version(1.0)]
library TextToolsLib {
  importlib ("stdole32.tlb");

    [uuid(B2ECFAA0-1827-11CF-9946-444553540000)]
    coclass CoTextTools {
        interface ISpellChecker;
        interface IThesaurus;
    }
}
```

This example has three distinct parts. The first two are the definitions of ISpellChecker and IThesaurus, the object's interfaces.
From these two interface definitions, the MIDL compiler will
produce proxies and stubs complete with marshaling code. The
third part creates a type library called TextToolsLib. From the
information here, the MIDL compiler will produce a type library.
If this third part were omitted, leaving only the interface definitions, the result would still be a completely legal IDL file, although
the MIDL compiler would generate only proxies and stubs, not a
type library, when the file was compiled.

You've already seen the definition of ISpellChecker—it's the same
interface described in the preceding chapter (and it contains the

same slightly unreal simplifications, such as using fixed-length character strings for words). The definition of IThesaurus is very similar, and even simpler. IThesaurus has only one method, ReturnSynonym, so that's all this interface needs to describe (and the *import* statement in ISpellChecker doesn't need to be repeated here). Using the two interface definitions in this IDL file, the MIDL compiler can generate two proxies and two stubs, a pair for each interface.

The third section of this type information is new: the IDL definitions that the MIDL compiler needs to create a type library. This type library begins with a UUID (that is, a GUID) and a version number. (This version number is for the type library, not for any interfaces described in that library. COM interfaces don't have versions.) Following this is the keyword *library* and the library's name, which in this case is TextToolsLib. Next is an *importlib* statement, which tells the MIDL compiler to include a standard set of IDL definitions found in the file STDOLE32.TLB.

A type library has a GUID

The library definition itself contains only one element: a component object class, or coclass, that lists all the interfaces (in this case, two) that this object supports. Like the interfaces, the coclass is assigned a GUID, which must be the same GUID used as the CLSID for this object. There's no need to repeat the interface definitions themselves in the coclass—simply listing their names is sufficient.

A component object class, or coclass, lists all the interfaces the object supports

From this definition, the MIDL compiler will produce a type library that includes descriptions of the coclass and each of this object's interfaces. Given an object's CLSID, a client can then use the registry to find its type library. Once it's found the library, the client can examine the object's coclass to get a list of its interfaces and can then learn the details of the interfaces' methods, parameters, and properties by examining the relevant parts of the type library. Understanding how all this works requires taking a look at how type libraries are accessed and used.

The type library contains descriptions of the coclass and each interface

Accessing a Type Library

The ITypeLib and ITypeInfo interfaces allow access to a type library and its elements

Although type libraries are just ordinary files, they are typically accessed using standard software that lets the library and its contents be viewed as COM objects that are accessible via standard interfaces. As shown in Figure 3-5, the library as a whole can be accessed through the ITypeLib interface, while individual objects in the library, such as the definitions of interfaces and the coclass, can be accessed through the ITypeInfo interface. The library shown in Figure 3-5 illustrates what the MIDL compiler would create from the IDL definition presented earlier (for the text tools object).

Figure 3-5   *A type library and its client.*

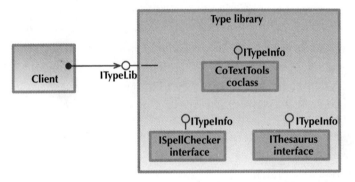

Each object in a type library describes part of the type information

Each object in the type library contains a description of one aspect of the object whose IDL definition was used to create the library. For example, the object in Figure 3-5's type library that describes the ISpellChecker interface contains all the information about this interface that was expressed in the IDL definition on page 78—the name of every method in the interface, the types of all their parameters, and more. Virtually anything that a human can learn from reading an IDL file can be determined by a program that uses the ITypeLib and ITypeInfo interfaces of the objects in the type library created from that IDL file.

The type library as a whole is accessed via ITypeLib

To access the contents of a type library, a client must first get a pointer to the library's ITypeLib interface. This process is usually fairly simple, since an application that provides a type library commonly registers the library's location in the registry when it is installed. To access a library, the client can call the LoadReg-TypeLib function (part of the standard library provided) and pass in as a parameter the CLSID of the object the type library describes. LoadRegTypeLib looks up the type library's location in the registry, loads the library's contents into the client's memory, and then returns to the client a pointer to the library's ITypeLib interface. Alternatively, a client that already knows the type library's filename can call LoadTypeLib instead.

The methods in ITypeLib allow a client to acquire pointers to individual sets of type information in the library—that is, to the library's objects. A type library built from the IDL file shown on page 78, for example, would allow access to ITypeInfo pointers for objects describing the ISpellChecker interface, the IThesaurus interface, and the CoTextTools coclass that includes both. The client can identify which object it's interested in either by giving the text name of the element the object describes (ISpellChecker, for instance) or by specifying its GUID.

Using methods in ITypeLib, a client can get pointers to the ITypeInfo interfaces of the library's objects

The ITypeLib interface is nontrivial. Some of its more interesting methods are listed here:

- **GetTypeInfoOfGuid** returns a pointer to the ITypeInfo interface of an object in the type library that is identified by a GUID. For example, a client might invoke this method, passing in the GUID that serves as the IID of the IThesaurus interface. In return, that client would receive a pointer to the ITypeInfo interface for the object in the type library that contains a description of IThesaurus. Using the methods in ITypeInfo, the client can learn about the methods in IThesaurus and their parameters.
- **FindName** returns a pointer to one or more ITypeInfo interfaces of objects in the type library that contain a particular text name.

- **IsName** determines whether an object with a specified name exists in the type library. ITypeLib::FindName can take a while to execute, so it can be prudent to call IsName first to ensure that the named element exists.
- **GetTypeInfoCount** returns the number of directly accessible objects in the type library.

Using methods in ITypeInfo, a client can learn about specific elements in the type library

When a client has a pointer to an ITypeInfo interface, it can ask specific questions about whatever the object describes. Like ITypeLib, ITypeInfo is not an especially simple interface. Among its methods are the following:

- **GetFuncDesc** returns information about a method in an interface, including the number and types of the method's parameters.
- **GetTypeAttr** returns information about the typeinfo object itself, including what the object contains (a description of an interface or a coclass, for example), its GUID, and more.
- **GetVarDesc** returns information about a variable or constant.

Using Type Information

Once a client knows the CLSID of an object, it can use LoadRegTypeLib to acquire a pointer to the ITypeLib interface of the object's type library. Using ITypeLib methods like GetTypeInfoOfGuid and FindName, the client can then get pointers to the ITypeInfo interfaces of the objects in the type library that describe the relevant interfaces, coclasses, and so on. Finally, the client can use ITypeInfo methods like GetFuncDesc and GetTypeAttr to learn what it needs to know to use those interfaces.

Today type libraries are most commonly used with IDispatch

But who would ever do this? How are type libraries actually used? Today by far the most common use of the information in a type library is by clients of objects that support an interface called IDispatch. Through IDispatch, a client can access methods in what is known as a *dispinterface*. Type information was first invented for use with dispinterfaces, and dispinterface clients typically make heavy use of it. (Chapter 4 describes dispinterfaces and IDispatch.)

None of the interfaces we've discussed earlier in this chapter are dispinterfaces, however, and there's no law that says the information in a type library can't be useful with any kind of interface. Just as the idea of type information has been generalized to include more than dispinterfaces, so too can its applicability be broadened. A foundation is in place—all that's needed is for creative software developers to implement their good ideas on top of it.

Chapter Four

Automation

Desktop applications—word processors, spreadsheets, and so on—are intended to improve the personal productivity of their users. The popularity of these programs is incontrovertible evidence that they succeed in this goal. Toward this end, applications today usually provide a graphical interface, an online help facility, and other features to aid the people who use them.

But why should people be the only users? A spreadsheet program, for instance, is chock-full of code that performs all sorts of useful actions, from calculating various formulas and sorting data to checking a document's spelling. Why not make these services available to other software as well as to people? In a word, why not make applications *programmable*, allowing them to be driven not only by people but also by other pieces of software? By allowing another program to do anything a human user can do, common personal productivity applications like spreadsheets and word processors can become much more useful.

Making an application programmable allows other software, as well as people, to use its services

Of course, plenty of desktop applications have long provided programmability through their macro languages. Spreadsheet applications, for instance, commonly let their users create macros that use the application's internal services. But macro languages have historically suffered from several significant problems. First, they're notoriously cryptic; it's not easy to become proficient in these languages. Second, no standard exists. Each application has its own distinct language, which makes it challenging at best to

An application's macro language does this, but only in a limited way

write a macro that spans several applications. Finally, for a given application, there's only one choice of macro language. Developers skilled in Microsoft Visual Basic, C++, or another language have traditionally been unable to use their favorite tools to write applications on top of Microsoft Excel, Lotus 1-2-3, or other programs.

What's needed is a standard way to make any application programmable

A better approach to providing application programmability would be to create a generic way for all kinds of applications to expose their internal services to other software. With this approach, built-in macro languages would wither and die. Developers would be able to employ any programming tools they like to use an application's services. Instead of being tools for end users only, desktop applications could become toolboxes for programmers, too.

Providing this general programmability using COM is called Automation

Programmability requires that one piece of software make its services available to another. This kind of interaction is precisely what COM is all about. Applications can allow access to their services through the interfaces exposed by their COM objects. Any piece of software that's capable of invoking methods in a COM object can then use these services. Freed from the tyranny of idiosyncratic macro languages, developers can use their favorite programming tools to build applications on top of the functions already provided by existing software. A program can be created to do automatically anything that a user can do manually. Providing this kind of general programmability with COM is called *Automation*.[1]

A User's View of Automation

Automation is widely supported today

Many applications, from both Microsoft and other software vendors, currently make their services available to clients through Automation. By doing this, they allow the creation of clients that in a very real sense are able to drive these applications from the outside. Microsoft Excel, for instance, supports Automation via COM objects whose methods mirror the tasks that can be carried

---

1   The name was originally *OLE Automation*. Now that Microsoft is again using the OLE label to refer only to compound documents, the term has been dropped from the name.

out through Excel's user interface, such as performing a calculation on a range of cells in a spreadsheet or checking the spelling of text. Using Visual Basic or another tool that can act as an Automation client, a developer can write code that does whatever a human user of the application can do—but that does it from a piece of software instead.

Imagine, for example, that the manager of a division needs to prepare a monthly status report. This requires extracting the current raw data from a database and manipulating that data in a spreadsheet. The manager then must create a chart from the result, embed the chart in a written report, and e-mail the final report to the staff. All of these steps need to be performed every month.

One way to prepare the report would be to do all these operations manually, copying data between applications as needed. But this would be painfully cumbersome. Why not devise a way to do it automatically? If every application involved supports Automation, writing a program to create the report would not be terribly difficult. (With a little programming knowledge, the manager might even be able to write the program without relying on anyone else.) Since applications that support Automation commonly allow programs to access many or all of the features that a user sees, the program could simply make the same requests as the user, as shown in Figure 4-1 on the following page. Then, rather than physically going through all of those steps each month, the manager could just run the program, and everything would happen automatically.

With Automation, you can write programs that automate repetitive tasks

Programmability using Automation can also be applied in more straightforward situations. Suppose, for example, that you want to create a simple interactive spell checker that lets you enter a word and then tells you whether that word is spelled correctly. If you've already installed an application (say, a word processor or a spreadsheet program) that includes its own spell checker and exposes its spell checker function via Automation, it's easy to write a program that meets your need. (This chapter will present a Visual Basic example that does this using Excel.)

Automation can also be used to access specific functions provided by an application

Figure 4-1   *Automating the creation of a monthly report.*

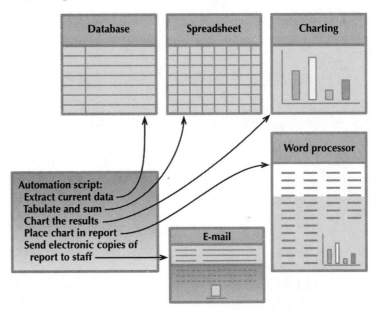

Programs that drive other applications are sometimes called scripts

It's common (although not mandatory) to use a relatively simple, graphically oriented tool such as Visual Basic to create programs that drive applications. These programs are sometimes referred to as *scripts*, and the set of visually oriented tools that are commonly used are generically known as *scripting languages*. Visual Basic is one example, but you'll encounter plenty of others as well.

Providing Programmability

The goal of programmability is to let an application expose its internal services to other software, making it possible for a script to do anything a human user can do. COM provides a way to do exactly this. To become programmable, then, an application can simply expose its internal functions as methods in COM interfaces. Programmability and COM sound like a perfect match.

And they can be. A developer could make an application programmable by defining ordinary COM objects and interfaces with methods that reflect the functions that need to be exposed. In practice, though, this is rarely done. Although COM *is* used to provide programmability, the mechanisms involved are usually a little more complex.

The problem is that the kind of COM interfaces you've seen so far aren't a great match for the capabilities of tools like Visual Basic. As Chapter 2 described, every COM interface is implemented using a vtable, a table of pointers to functions. To invoke a method in one of these vtable interfaces, a client must traverse the chain of pointers that includes the table. Furthermore, the call's parameters must be marshaled whenever the object that supports the interface is implemented in another process.

Unfortunately, until recently all this was beyond the reach of Visual Basic, one of the most common tools for writing scripts using programmable applications—and, more important, the major tool that Microsoft promotes for this purpose. Essentially, Microsoft's Visual Basic group faced this problem: although COM could be used to allow programmability, COM by itself offered no way to let a relatively simple language like Visual Basic make use of this programmability. Dispensing with COM wasn't an option, but what other choices existed?

Methods in vtable interfaces are hard to invoke from Visual Basic

IDispatch and Dispinterfaces

To solve the problem, the Visual Basic group defined a standard COM interface called IDispatch. Any application that exposes its internal functions to other software—that is, any application that is programmable—can do so using only this interface. Through IDispatch, the application can make any number of methods available.

IDispatch was originally defined to allow applications to be programmable from Visual Basic

IDispatch is an ordinary COM interface. Like any other, it is implemented using a vtable that contains pointers to its methods. Unlike others, however, it includes a method called Invoke that can be used to invoke other methods. By using Invoke, a client can actually invoke any of a group of methods, passing whatever parameters that method requires. In order to make this work, the

Through the single method IDispatch::Invoke, a client can invoke any number of methods

developer of an object that implements IDispatch must specify exactly what methods are available to be invoked. The developer does this by defining a *dispatch interface,* commonly called a *dispinterface.*

A dispinterface is a group of methods that can be invoked using IDispatch::Invoke

Just like an ordinary vtable interface, a dispinterface is a collection of methods. Dispinterfaces aren't implemented using vtables, however. Instead, an object lets its client invoke any method in a dispinterface by using IDispatch::Invoke. Each method in the dispinterface is assigned an integer called a *dispatch identifier* (DISPID). To invoke a method in a dispinterface, a client calls IDispatch::Invoke, passing in the DISPID of the appropriate dispinterface method, as shown in Figure 4-2. The object's implementation of the IDispatch::Invoke method is conceptually a big Case statement: based on the DISPID it receives, the object chooses the right method and executes it. Through a single method in the vtable interface—IDispatch::Invoke—a client can invoke any method in the dispinterface.

Using IDispatch, a Visual Basic program can easily invoke the methods in a dispinterface

But just how does this improve the situation? Why would the Visual Basic developers go to all this trouble? The answer is that this approach allows Visual Basic to provide a mechanism to invoke an object's methods using COM. The Visual Basic interpreter (or any other program taking advantage of IDispatch) simply needs to contain code that knows how to navigate through only one vtable

Figure 4-2   *Invoking a method in a dispinterface using IDispatch::Invoke.*

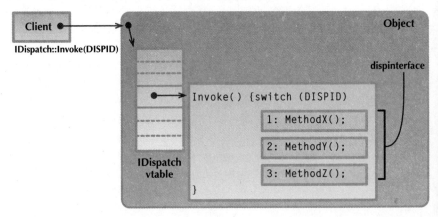

interface, IDispatch. Any object that implements IDispatch then provides something analogous to a vtable for the dispinterface, the (conceptual) Case statement that maps a DISPID to the correct method to execute. Finally, the method's parameters can be marshaled in a different way, as described in "Dispinterfaces and Marshaling," page 94. To a Visual Basic programmer, everything looks simple. But the result is the ability to invoke all kinds of methods in all kinds of objects—in other words, programmability.

Visual Basic is not the only tool that you can use to drive an application via IDispatch. Anything that's capable of correctly calling IDispatch::Invoke and the other methods in this interface will work. You can, for example, write Automation clients in C++. It's worth keeping in mind, though, that it was the Microsoft Visual Basic group who defined IDispatch and that the requirements (and limitations) of this relatively simple language have driven its design.

Programs in other languages such as C++ can also invoke methods using IDispatch

Because of Visual Basic's popularity, applications that need to be programmable commonly do so via IDispatch. Microsoft Word, Microsoft Excel, and many, many more applications now support IDispatch. An application might become programmable solely through one or more custom vtable interfaces, but this option is rarely chosen. The lure of allowing scripting with tools such as Visual Basic has been too strong.

Most applications today are made programmable by using IDispatch and one or more dispinterfaces

Clients and Servers

To allow its services to be accessed via Automation, an application must expose one or more COM objects. Originally these objects were called *automation objects,* and an application that made them available was called an *automation server.* Today these terms have changed. Automation objects are now referred to simply as objects or, in some cases, as ActiveX objects. An automation server is now described as an ActiveX component acting in the role of a server.

ActiveX components acting as servers were originally known as automation servers

Both of these changes make good sense. Automation objects have always been regular COM objects—they support IUnknown, they can be created using CoCreateInstance, and so on—and giving them a special name was a little confusing. In addition, although automation objects were originally required to support IDispatch, this is no longer strictly true. Most of these objects do support IDispatch for the reasons explained earlier, but it's also possible to provide programmability through ordinary vtable interfaces. Similarly, any server that supports externally accessible objects is potentially programmable, so no special name is required in this case either.

Clients capable of driving other applications through IDispatch were formerly called *automation controllers*. Despite the fancy name, however, controllers are ordinary COM clients, and they are now described as ActiveX components acting as clients. Because the term *Automation* once specifically referred to invoking methods through IDispatch, an automation client (known then as a controller) was once required to have this capability. Today, however, Automation refers to programmability in general, whether or not IDispatch is used. As a result, while clients of programmable applications are typically capable of invoking methods through IDispatch, this interface isn't absolutely necessary.

Figure 4-3 illustrates how an application can offer programmability through objects that support IDispatch. Note that an object can support more than one instance of IDispatch (and can allow access to more than one dispinterface within it). Note too that an object can support other interfaces, such as the fictitious IServices interface shown in the figure, alongside IDispatch. The client accesses these objects using various interface pointers, just as it would access any other COM object. Microsoft Excel, for instance, supports objects that are assigned names such as Application and Chart. (These objects also have CLSIDs, which are used to actually instantiate the objects.) The methods each object provides are made available in dispinterfaces accessed through IDispatch. Excel's Application object, for example, offers methods such as Calculate and Check-Spelling. Virtually any task that a human user of Excel can perform can also be performed by an ActiveX component acting as a client.

Applications typically provide programmability by implementing objects that support IDispatch.

Figure 4-3

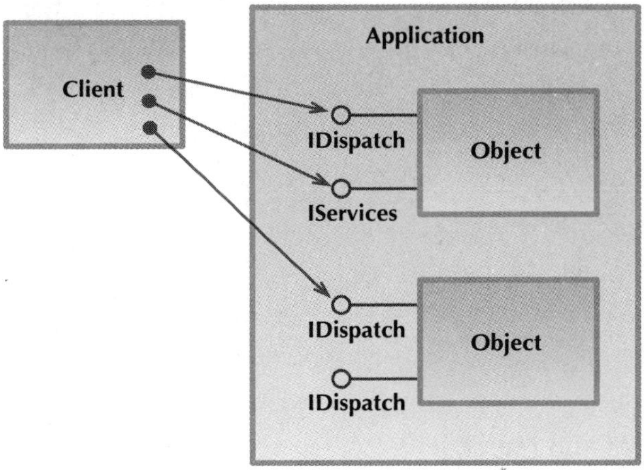

Describing Dispinterfaces

Like all interfaces, a dispinterface is just a group of methods. Because they were created to work with Microsoft Visual Basic, though, methods in a dispinterface are somewhat different from methods in a vtable interface. First, the parameters allowed with dispinterface methods can't be as complex as those in methods defined by vtable interfaces. The reason is simple: Visual Basic doesn't support certain data types, including, for instance, structures. To make them callable from Visual Basic, then, dispinterface methods are prohibited from using these data types.[2]

The parameter types allowed in dispinterface methods are simpler than those allowed in vtable interface methods

A second difference, again derived from the needs of Visual Basic, is that dispinterface methods can be explicitly designated as methods that get or set the values of specific *properties*. A method that gets a property is read-only—it simply returns a value. A method that sets a property does the reverse, setting the property to a new value supplied by the caller. Visual Basic development uses properties extensively, so providing a straightforward expression of this idea in dispinterfaces makes sense.

Dispinterface methods can be defined to explicitly get and set properties

---

2   When a future version of Visual Basic adds support for a wider range of types, these restrictions will probably be lifted.

Like vtable interfaces, a dispinterface can be described using COM's IDL. In the original release of OLE Automation (as it was then known), this wasn't true; a notation called Object Description Language was used instead. By the second half of 1996, however, ODL was primarily of historical interest, since its relevant features and even much of its syntax had been incorporated into IDL.

Like vtable interfaces, dispinterfaces can be defined in IDL

Because of their special requirements, dispinterfaces use IDL attributes that aren't relevant for describing vtable interfaces. For example, a dispinterface can specifically indicate that certain methods are used only to get and set a property. An example of an IDL-defined dispinterface appears later in this chapter.

Dispinterfaces and Marshaling

As Chapter 3 described, each vtable interface can use a proxy in the client and a stub in the server to marshal and unmarshal the parameters in that interface's methods. Marshaling converts parameters to a form that allows them to be transferred between processes or machines; unmarshaling converts them back to the destination format. Accessing methods using a vtable interface, then, implies that one of these three situations exists: the object supporting the interface is implemented in an in-process server (and thus no marshaling is required); a proxy and a stub for the interface are available; or the client uses the information in a type library to do dynamic marshaling (which is not a widely used approach with vtables today).

A vtable interface can rely on a proxy and a stub for marshaling

Using a dispinterface for marshaling, on the other hand, requires only a single proxy and stub, since only a single vtable interface—IDispatch—is in use. This proxy and stub know how to marshal and unmarshal the parameters for the methods in IDispatch. But since all kinds of methods with all kinds of parameters can be invoked through IDispatch::Invoke, how can any single stub know how to do all this marshaling? The answer is simple: it can't. There must be some code somewhere that converts a dispinterface method's parameters to a standard form and converts

A dispinterface doesn't require its own proxy and stub

them back when they reach their destination—but that code isn't in IDispatch's stub and proxy.

Instead, a client that calls a method in a dispinterface essentially does some of the marshaling itself. Before it calls IDispatch::Invoke, the client packages the dispinterface method's parameters into a *variant*. A variant defines a standard form for each parameter along with an identifier for each parameter type (short integer, long integer, character string, and so on). Once the client has constructed a variant containing a method's parameters, it passes the variant along with the DISPID on the call to IDispatch::Invoke. The object that implements the dispinterface unpackages the variant and uses the parameters it contains in executing the specified method. Any results returned by the method are wrapped in a variant by the object and then returned to and unwrapped by the client.

The parameters for a dispinterface method are packaged into a variant

Since proxies and stubs are not required to package and unpackage parameters, dispinterfaces allow late binding. If a type library is available, a client can access it to learn what interfaces and methods an object supports and then dynamically construct requests on those objects (creating a variant and passing it to IDispatch-::Invoke). If no type library is available, a client can ask the object itself for its type information in order to create a variant and determine the correct DISPID for IDispatch::Invoke, as described in "The IDispatch Interface," page 97. Dispinterface clients written in C++ must do all this themselves (although standard helper functions are provided to make it easier). The Visual Basic interpreter, however, hides all this from the developer. To a Visual Basic programmer, all the work of packaging and unpackaging parameters using variants is invisible.

Dispinterfaces allow late binding, even if no type library is available

A Visual Basic Example

To execute a method in a dispinterface, a client must instantiate the appropriate object, acquire the correct DISPID, package the correct parameters into a variant, and invoke the dispinterface method using the Invoke method in IDispatch. Doing this in a language like C++ is certainly possible, but it can be a bit of work. Doing it in Visual Basic is much simpler.

Invoking dispinterface methods from Visual Basic is easy

The following code shows how to take advantage of Automation by instantiating and using an Excel object from Visual Basic for Applications (VBA), the Visual Basic dialect that's included with Microsoft Excel:

```
Sub SpellCheck()
  Dim Obj As Object
  Set Obj = CreateObject("Excel.Application")
  Word = InputBox("Enter word")
  If Obj.CheckSpelling(Word) Then
    MsgBox ("Valid word")
  Else
    MsgBox ("Word not found")
  End If
End Sub
```

Visual Basic hides
all the details

As you can see, the object must be declared and then created with VBA's *CreateObject* call. This call invokes CoCreateInstance with the object's CLSID (thus loading Excel) and requests a pointer to the object's IDispatch interface. The object's methods can then be invoked using the syntax *object.method(parameters)*. This builds the appropriate request on the object, complete with the parameter list packaged as a variant, and calls the object using IDispatch-::Invoke. The object locates the method in the dispinterface, unpacks the variant, executes the method, and returns its result.

This example prompts the user for a word and then invokes Excel's spell checker through the Application object's CheckSpelling method. If the word is in the spell checker's dictionary, you'll see the output *Valid word*. If it is not, VBA outputs *Word not found*. All the complexity of interfaces, DISPIDs, and so on is hidden beneath the calm surface of VBA.

A ProgID is a
human-readable
synonym for a
CLSID

This description leaves several unanswered questions. How, for instance, does VBA translate the object's name (Excel.Application, in this case) into the correct CLSID? The answer is that the system registry (discussed in Chapter 2) contains a mapping from this name to the correct CLSID, a mapping supplied by Excel when it was installed. Excel.Application is an example of a *programmatic identifier*, known as a *ProgID*. ProgIDs provide convenient, human-readable synonyms for CLSIDs. ProgIDs don't have quite as strong a guarantee of uniqueness as CLSIDs do, but common ProgID naming conventions make duplicate names very unlikely in practice.

Here's another important question: how did the person who wrote this VBA code know that Excel supported an Application object? And how did this programmer know the object had a dispinterface method called CheckSpelling that took a single word as a parameter? The most likely source of this information is the Excel online Help, which contains a complete list of all the objects in Excel that can be used for Automation, their methods and properties, and everything necessary to invoke their services. In general, applications that provide services through Automation document those services quite thoroughly.

An application's documentation tells programmers which methods the application exposes

Finally, how does VBA translate the method name CheckSpelling into the correct DISPID to invoke this method? Most often, the client relies on information in the object's type library. But it's also possible to use another of IDispatch's methods, called GetIDsOf-Names. This method, along with the other methods in IDispatch, is described next.

Automation clients commonly rely on a type library to learn details about an object's methods

The IDispatch Interface

The IDispatch interface is very simple. It contains only these four methods:

- The **Invoke** method is used to invoke all methods in all dispinterfaces.
- The **GetIDsOfNames** method allows a client to pass in the name of a method in a dispinterface and get its associated DISPID in return. This can be used by Visual Basic, for example, to translate the method name given by the programmer (such as CheckSpelling in the preceding example) into the correct DISPID needed to invoke that method. (The current version of Visual Basic, however, prefers to use a type library instead.)

- If a type library exists for the object, a call to the **GetType-Info** method returns a pointer to the ITypeInfo interface of a typeinfo object (discussed in Chapter 3) that describes this dispinterface. Using the methods in ITypeInfo, a client can learn everything it needs to know to package parameters and invoke the dispinterface's methods.
- The **GetTypeInfoCount** method returns an indication of whether an object provides type information at run time—that is, whether a call to the GetTypeInfo method will return useful information.

Supporting Multiple Dispinterfaces in a Single Object

Like other vtable interfaces, IDispatch has an interface identifier (IID)

When a client wants to invoke the methods or access the properties in a dispinterface, it must first get a pointer to the object's IDispatch interface. IDispatch, like every interface, has a unique GUID that acts as its IID. If an object supports only a single dispinterface, a client can content itself with a pointer to IDispatch. Whenever it invokes a method using IDispatch::Invoke, that method will be one of those defined in the object's single dispinterface.

An object can allow access to more than one dispinterface via IDispatch

But what happens when an object needs to support more than one dispinterface? DISPIDs aren't required to be unique across multiple dispinterfaces, so invoking the method with DISPID 3 might mean different things in different dispinterfaces. A client requesting a pointer to IDispatch gets back a pointer that allows access to the methods and properties in one of those dispinterfaces, but which one?

A client can invoke methods in the default dispinterface or explicitly request a pointer to another dispinterface

If an object supports multiple dispinterfaces, one of them must be designated as the default. (An IDL attribute is defined to do this.) When a client asks for a pointer to IDispatch and starts invoking methods in a dispinterface with IDispatch::Invoke, the methods of the default dispinterface are invoked. To access methods in other dispinterfaces, the client can use QueryInterface to explicitly request pointers to them. Even dispinterfaces have distinct IIDs, different from the one assigned to IDispatch. Calls to those disp-interfaces' methods are made through IDispatch, as always, but the client sees each dispinterface as a distinct interface accessed through a specific interface pointer.

Dual Interfaces

Making an object's methods available via one or more dispinter-faces is the right approach in many cases. For clients created with tools like Visual Basic, for example, dispinterfaces make it easy to access those methods. But dispinterfaces also have drawbacks. For one, invoking a method through a dispinterface is slower than invoking the same method in a vtable interface. A dispinterface method call must first invoke a vtable interface method (IDispatch::Invoke) and then do a little more work to figure out which method in the dispinterface to execute. And the process of packaging the parameters into variants and then unpackaging them to pass to the dispinterface's method is also fairly time-consuming. Another drawback of dispinterfaces is that it's actually more work for a developer writing in C++ to create the necessary code to invoke a dispinterface method than to call the equivalent method in a vtable interface.

Methods in disp-interfaces are easier for Visual Basic clients to invoke, but C++ clients prefer vtables

Wouldn't it be nice to provide both options in the same interface, to access the same methods as either dispinterface methods or vtable methods? This is exactly what a *dual interface* offers. If an object implements a dual interface, the methods in that interface can be invoked through either IDispatch or direct vtable calls. A client can choose the option that's best for it.

A dual interface provides the benefits of both dispinterfaces and vtable interfaces

Every dual interface begins as an implementation of IDispatch. (More correctly, every dual interface inherits from IDispatch.) As shown in Figure 4-4 on the following page, IDispatch's vtable (like all vtables) begins with the three methods contained in IUnknown. Next come the four methods in IDispatch. One of these, IDis-patch::Invoke, contains a (conceptual) Case statement that lets it determine which dispinterface method to call based on the DISPID it receives from the client.

Figure 4-4

Figure 4-4 *A dual interface exposes its methods through both a vtable and IDispatch.*

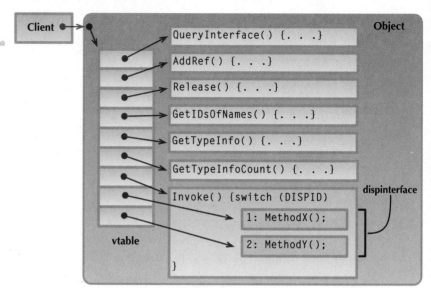

A dual interface is essentially an IDispatch vtable extended to include direct pointers to a dispinterface's methods

In an ordinary implementation of IDispatch, nothing more is required. In a dual interface, however, IDispatch's vtable is extended to include direct pointers to the methods in the dispinterface. These methods can now be invoked in two different ways: through IDispatch::Invoke or directly through the vtable. A client written in Visual Basic could use the simpler (for it) but slower mechanism offered by IDispatch::Invoke. A C++ client is free to call the same methods directly through the vtable, an option that both executes faster and is simpler for the programmer. Each kind of client can access the interface's methods using the approach that's best for it.

The following code shows an example of an IDL definition for a dual interface. This interface is the familiar spell checker interface used as an example in previous chapters. Earlier this interface was defined as a vtable interface; here it's defined as a dual interface.

```
[   object,
    uuid(E7CD0D00-1301-11CF-9946-444553540000),
    dual ]
```

```
interface ISpellChecker : IDispatch {
  import "unknwn.idl";
  import "oaidl.idl";

  [propget] HRESULT BritishSpellings(
                    [out, retval] boolean *sp);
  [propput] HRESULT BritishSpellings([in] boolean sp);

  HRESULT LookUpWord([in] BSTR word,
                    [out] boolean *found);
  HRESULT AddToDictionary([in] BSTR word);
  HRESULT RemoveFromDictionary([in] BSTR word);
}

[uuid(B623E460-1837-11CF-9946-444553540000),
  version(1.0)]
library SpellCheckerLib {
  importlib ("stdole32.tlb");

  [uuid(B23EFAA0-1849-11CF-9946-444553540000)]
  coclass CoSpellChecker {
    interface ISpellChecker;
  }
}
```

Defining ISpellChecker as a dual interface is much like defining
it as a vtable interface. As before, the interface definition begins
with the word *object* and a GUID. The keyword *dual* also appears,
however, indicating to the MIDL compiler that this interface should
be handled differently than an ordinary vtable interface.

The interface definition itself also contains some new elements.
First, ISpellChecker, like all dual interfaces, inherits from IDispatch
rather than from IUnknown. (IDispatch itself inherits from IUnknown, so ISpellChecker's vtable still begins with IUnknown's
methods, as shown in Figure 4-4.) In addition, this version of
ISpellChecker defines a property, BritishSpellings, that controls
whether the spell checker should use American or British spellings
when looking up words. The interface's first two methods, both
named BritishSpellings, are used to get and set the value of this
property. The *[propget]* and *[propput]* attributes that appear before
these methods indicate the purpose of each.

All dual inter-
faces inherit
from IDispatch

The rest of ISpellChecker's definition should look familiar. The interface's three methods are defined, each with appropriate parameters. One point worth reemphasizing is that the parameters of methods in a dual interface must adhere to the restrictions placed on dispinterface parameters. This means that parameter types such as structures, which are too complex for Visual Basic, can't be used. It also means that arrays of OLECHARs, the type used to pass words in Chapter 3's example, can't be used here. To be automation-compatible, this interface instead uses a Visual Basic–derived type called BSTR (for *Basic string*).

DISPIDs can be assigned automatically

As described earlier, dispinterfaces rely on DISPIDs, the integers assigned to each method and property. Given the IDL definition shown here, those DISPIDs will be assigned automatically to the interface's property and methods. There's also an IDL attribute that lets the creator of an interface definition explicitly assign DISPIDs to properties and methods.

This ISpellChecker example ends with the information required to create a type library for this object. Once again, this resembles Chapter 3's example, with a coclass containing an interface list. This simple object supports only ISpellChecker, so that list has only one element.

It's common to define new interfaces as duals

If you need a new dispinterface, it makes good sense to define it as a dual interface, and this is strongly recommended. A dual can do everything a plain dispinterface can do, and it's also easier to use from C++ clients. When defining a new vtable interface, however, it's not so obvious that making it a dual is the right choice. The limitations on parameter types imposed by dual interfaces might outweigh the advantages. Still, it's very common today to define a new interface as a dual. It's easy to do, and the result is an interface whose methods can be invoked naturally from all kinds of clients.

Remote Automation

Visual Basic 4 introduced something new and important: the ability to use dispinterfaces and dual interfaces to access objects on other machines. Called Remote Automation, this feature was in many ways a precursor of Distributed COM (DCOM). Like DCOM, Remote Automation uses Microsoft's OSF DCE–compliant remote procedure calls (RPC) to communicate between client and server. But while DCOM allows cross-machine access for any COM interface, Remote Automation supports it only for dispinterfaces and dual interfaces.

Like so much else in this area, Remote Automation was developed by Microsoft's Visual Basic group. Because it was released before DCOM, Remote Automation is a bit different from its more full-featured cousin. DCOM will eventually supersede Remote Automation, although applications built using Remote Automation will work over DCOM, too.

To understand how Remote Automation works, first recall from the last chapter how proxies and stubs are used to allow a client in one process to invoke methods in an object that's implemented in another process. If the two processes are on the same system, the client's proxy communicates with the server's stub through some kind of interprocess communication.

On a single machine, calls made with IDispatch or dual interfaces also work this way. An object acting as a client relies on a proxy for the IDispatch interface when it wants to invoke a method implemented by an object in another process. The request is conveyed to that object via interprocess communication, and the receiving object relies on a stub to invoke the correct method in IDispatch.

Making this work between processes on different machines requires little more than replacing the interprocess communication with RPC. A proxy and a stub are still used, of course, but now they handle remote requests rather than purely local ones. To both client and server, everything looks just as it does in the local case—all the changes are hidden in the proxy and the stub.

> Remote Automation allows methods in dispinterfaces and dual interfaces to be called across a network

> Remote Automation is not the same as DCOM

> Remote Automation uses RPC between proxy and stub

Remote Automation relies on one more component to make all
this work: the *automation manager*. As shown in Figure 4-5, the
automation manager is a separate process that sits between the
object acting as a client and the remote object. Running on the
same machine as the remote object, it receives requests from the
client and passes them on to the object. Results are sent back
through the reverse path: remote object to automation manager to
the object acting as a client. Remote Automation is invisible to both
objects—to them, everything looks just as it does in the local case.

Figure 4-5   ***Illustrating Remote Automation.***

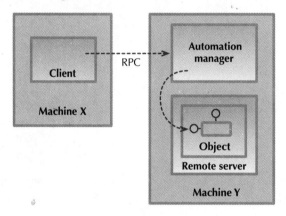

Automation Today

The word *Automation* originally referred exclusively to IDispatch
and dispinterfaces. Even type libraries were viewed as part of
Automation, since they were used almost entirely in concert with
dispinterfaces. A separate language, ODL, was defined as part of
the original Automation technology for creating those dispinterface-
oriented type libraries, and a separate tool called MkTypLib produced those type libraries.

Things are different today. Now the word *Automation* is used more
broadly to mean programmability, whether it is achieved via
IDispatch and a dispinterface, through a dual interface, or even
by using a vtable interface. Type information is useful with all
kinds of interfaces, not just dispinterfaces; and ODL is no more,

as its essential features have been merged with IDL. MkTypLib has also become obsolete, and its facilities for generating type libraries have instead been built into the MIDL compiler. Change can be confusing, but it's also unavoidable. As the technology has evolved, so too has the notion of Automation.

Chapter Five

Persistence

Most applications need to store their data in some way. A typical approach is to save data in a file and then read it back when it's needed. For example, a word processor might save a document in a file on disk when the user closes the program and then read the file back in when the user opens the document again.

In the world of objects, an object that stores its data on a relatively permanent medium such as a disk is said to have made its data *persistent*. Making its data persistent allows an object to stop running and then later pick up where it left off simply by loading that persistent data the next time it's instantiated. An object representing your bank account, for example, might allow changes to be made to the account balance while the object is running. When the changes are completed, the object might shut itself down—but not before making the changes to your balance persistent, perhaps by saving them on disk. The next time the object is started, it can load this persistent data and thus know the correct balance in your account.

An object's persistent data is information about the object's state that's saved between instantiations of the object

A mechanism that lets objects store and retrieve their persistent data is sometimes called a *persistence service*. A file system is a simple example of a persistence service, but there are many other possibilities, too.

A persistence service lets an object save and load its persistent data

Although some objects are able to autonomously decide when it's time to make their data persistent, many objects aren't this smart. In these cases, the object's client needs a way to tell the object

An object's client typically controls when the object's persistent data is loaded and saved

when to load and when to save its data. A client of your bank account object, for instance, would find it useful to have a means of telling the object to save any changes the client has made—that is, to make the changes persistent. The problem of persistence, then, really has two parts: providing a way for objects to store and retrieve their persistent data, and allowing the clients of those objects to control when (and perhaps where) that data is stored and retrieved.

Structured Storage is a COM-based persistence service

For COM objects, these two distinct aspects of persistence are addressed by defining two distinct sets of standard interfaces. One set focuses on providing a specific way for COM objects to store their persistent data. These interfaces are part of a particular kind of persistence service known as *Structured Storage*. Structured Storage is not the only persistence service available to a COM object, but it's an option that's applicable to many situations.

The IPersist* interfaces let a client control an object's persistence

The second set of standard interfaces focuses on allowing a client to control an object's persistence. An object can support one or more of these interfaces, which are collectively called the *IPersist* interfaces.* Which ones an object supports depends entirely on how that object saves its persistent data. Using the methods in one of these interfaces, a client can tell an object to load its data, save its data, and more. This chapter begins with an explanation of Structured Storage and then describes several of the IPersist* interfaces.

Structured Storage

A COM object can store its persistent data in many ways

A COM object can store its persistent data in any number of ways. In some cases, an ordinary flat file might be just the thing. In others, it might be useful for several objects to share a single file, each storing its persistent data in a discrete part of that file. In still other cases, a COM object might even need to store its persistent data on some other machine. Imagine, for example, an object whose persistent state is stored on a World Wide Web page somewhere on the Internet. COM objects using the standard interfaces defined in this chapter and the next can support all these possibilities and more.

Structured Storage is relevant to the case in which several objects need to store their persistent data in a single file. To understand why Structured Storage was created, imagine an application built from several independently developed components, each implemented as one or more COM objects. Each component might have its own persistent data that it needs to store when it's not running. How can the various components that comprise this application, each perhaps created by a different vendor, accomplish this?

One solution would be to have each component use a separate file for its data. Users of the application wouldn't like this, however; as far as they're concerned, they work with a single collection of data—the fact that it's built from several independent COM objects isn't visible to them. Having to deal with multiple files (for example, when copying data to a different location) for what is apparently one application would be annoying, to say the least. Another solution might be to assign each component its own location within the same file, a place that it can always use for its data. Once again, though, this becomes challenging when the components involved are written by different organizations at different times and for different purposes. How are these different organizations to agree on a common scheme to share a single file?

Structured Storage allows multiple COM objects to store persistent data in a single file

Other uses of COM also give rise to this problem. In OLE, for example, two or more independent applications cooperate via standard COM interfaces to create a compound document. If a document created by one application is embedded in another, the contents of both documents must be stored in the same file. In general, then, the problem is this: how can independently developed COM objects, whether yoked together into what a user sees as one application or separated into different applications, store their persistent data in a single file?

Applications creating compound documents also need to share a file

Structured
Storage is an
important
persistence
service in the
COM world

The answer is Structured Storage, which permits a single disk file to be shared by many different chunks of software, whether those chunks are independent COM objects comprising a single application or completely different applications. Although it's by no means the only choice, Structured Storage is a commonly used persistence service in the COM world.

Storages and Streams

The problem of allowing different objects to share a single disk file is analogous to the problem of allowing different applications to share a single disk. The latter problem is solved by providing a file system, which is commonly structured as a tree built from directories and files within those directories. Each application has its own file or maybe its own directory with some number of files below it, and the application is free to use this file or directory as it sees fit.

In Structured
Storage, a single
disk file becomes
a compound file
made up of stor-
ages and streams

To let many COM objects share one file, why not build an analogous structure inside the file? As shown in Figure 5-1, this is exactly what Structured Storage does. With Structured Storage, a single file is made up of *storages*, which function like directories, and *streams*, which act like files. In the Microsoft Windows implementation, files built this way are called *compound files*, or sometimes (although the term is now out of date) *docfiles*.

Figure 5-1   **A disk file containing storages and streams.**

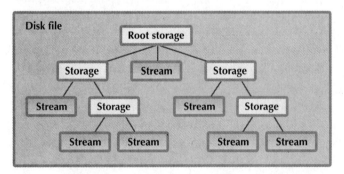

As Figure 5-1 shows, each compound file contains a root storage, below which other streams and storages can exist. Below these storages, in turn, live still other streams and storages, and so on. It's very much like a conventional hierarchical file system, except that the entire edifice exists within one file. Objects using Structured Storage treat their streams and storages just as conventional applications treat directories and files.

Structured Storage essentially creates a hierarchical file system inside each compound file

Each chunk of software that shares a compound file can be assigned its own stream in which to store data or perhaps even its own storage, allowing it to expand the hierarchy by creating any additional storages and streams it needs below that storage. Since each component has a distinct area in which to store its persistent data, all the components can use the file without getting in one another's way—and, just as important, they need no prior agreement in order to do so. Just as a file system allows many applications to share a disk drive in a standard way, Structured Storage allows many components to share a file.

Each component using a compound file is assigned its own storage and/or stream

Breaking up an application's data into the individual pieces stored by its component objects provides another benefit, too: applications no longer need to load and save their data in toto but can instead work incrementally. Long waits while an application loads or saves a complete file can be replaced with much shorter waits while the application loads only those pieces of data it needs.

Nothing is free, however, and perfect solutions don't exist. Building a structure such as the one shown in Figure 5-1 within a single disk file requires adding room for the overhead of managing the structure. Although Structured Storage offers a number of benefits, it does so at the cost of extra disk space—it tends to make the files involved bigger.

While storages don't do much besides keep track of the streams below them, each stream actually stores data. As its name implies, a stream is just a container for a stream of bytes—there's no implied organization of the bytes in the stream, no division into records or substreams or anything else. If an application needs to

Streams are just streams of bytes, with no system-defined internal structure

organize the information it puts into a stream, the application itself must define and enforce that organization. Streams themselves offer no help.

Each storage or stream is accessed via an IStorage or IStream interface

Storages and streams are themselves viewed as COM objects, each accessed via an appropriate interface. Storages support an interface called IStorage, whereas streams support one called IStream. Other COM objects interact with storages and streams in the usual way, by acquiring interface pointers and invoking methods. Figure 5-2 illustrates how an object, itself providing interfaces to its clients, relates to a storage and two streams. Note that the storage and the streams being accessed by the object might or might not be part of the same disk file—either situation is possible.

Figure 5-2 *A COM object using a storage and two streams.*

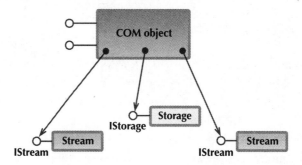

Naming storages and streams A file system defines rules for naming files and directories. In addition, it usually permits different users to name elements in different parts of the system. For example, on a multiuser system, each user is typically assigned a home directory and allowed to create and name files and directories within it. If this were not the case, if instead any user could name anything anywhere in the file system, chaos would result.

The owner of a storage can freely assign names to the streams and storages it contains

Structured Storage faces the same problem. Given that several independent chunks of software can potentially use the same compound file, how should that file's storages and streams be named? And, for any particular file, who should assign those names? The solution here resembles the solution to the same problem in a multiuser file system: just as each user is assigned a home directory, each object sharing a compound file can be assigned its own storage or stream, with one object "owning" the root storage. The owner of a storage gets to create and name any storages and streams below that storage.

What should those names look like? For the root storage, the solution is easy: the root storage is given the same name as the file itself. The names of all other storages and streams are dealt with by software, however, not by human beings, so those names need not be easily usable by people. As a result, storage and stream names can be pretty much anything.

The name of the root storage is the same as the filename

A few rules do exist, however. For example, an object that owns a storage cannot assign any names that start with ASCII control characters (hexadecimal 00 through hexadecimal 31) to the streams and subordinate storages below that storage. Names that begin with ASCII control characters are reserved for use by other objects that might need to use this storage. Although the purpose of this might not be immediately obvious, reserving certain names in a storage for software other than the object that owns the storage allows some very useful elements to be created.

Names starting with certain characters are reserved for use by other software

For example, the first time a user saves a file in Microsoft Word, Microsoft Excel, or many other programs (including many non-Microsoft applications), the program prompts the user for summary information about that file, including the name of the file's creator, the file's subject, and keywords indicating the file's content. This information is stored in a stream immediately below the file's root storage, a stream whose name consists of the ASCII character hex 05 (a control character indicating a reserved name), followed by the character string *SummaryInformation*. The format of the information stored in this stream is also well known. (It's a standard form called a *property set*.) Given all this, it's easy to write code that reads this information from a compound file created by any other application. Tools such as the Microsoft Windows 95 Explorer allow this data to be examined, letting a

Compound files commonly contain a stream with summary information user learn basic information about any kind of file without starting the application that created the file.

Transactions

According to the Structured Storage specification, both storages and streams are designed to be opened in either *direct mode* or *transacted mode*. When a client opens a storage or stream object, the client indicates the mode in which the object should be opened. In direct mode, all changes made to the data in the storage or stream occur immediately. If a storage or stream is opened in transacted mode, however, changes don't take effect until they are explicitly committed by the storage's owner. And until this commitment happens, all pending changes can be rolled back, allowing the storage or stream to revert to its previous state.

In other words, Structured Storage supports the notion of *transactions*. A transaction is a group of changes to data with the property that either all of the changes must happen or none of them do. An intermediate state, in which some changes are applied and some aren't, isn't possible. Storages must support transacted mode. However, a valid implementation of Structured Storage might elect not to support transacted mode for streams. (In fact, none of the current implementations on Windows 95, Windows NT, or the Macintosh support transactioning for streams.)

Why bother to support this kind of transacted access to information? The first application of this feature, and the initial reason for its existence, came from OLE compound documents. To see why transactions are useful, think again about our usual example: a Word document with an Excel spreadsheet embedded in it. When one document is embedded in another, the data for both is stored in a single compound file. The data for the "parent" document is stored in a stream just below the file's root storage, while the data for the embedded document is stored below a subordinate storage. In our hypothetical example, the Word document's data is stored in a stream below the root storage (managed by Word), while the data for the Excel spreadsheet is safely ensconced inside a stream

Storages and (potentially) streams can be opened in direct mode or transacted mode

A transaction allows a group of changes to be either committed or rolled back as a unit

below its own subordinate storage (one managed by Excel). (See Chapter 8 for a more detailed description of how this is done.)

OLE compound documents use transactions on storages

Imagine that a user who is working with this compound document decides to make a few changes to the embedded spreadsheet. The user double-clicks on the spreadsheet (starting Excel), makes the corrections, returns to the Word part of the document, and closes the document. The program then prompts the user to save the changes. If the user does so, all modifications made to the embedded Excel spreadsheet must be saved. If the user chooses not to save the changes, all modifications made to the spreadsheet must be discarded. Implicitly, then, at this point both the old and the new versions of the embedded spreadsheet must exist. Since embedded objects can potentially be very large, holding both versions in memory might not be feasible. Instead, the changes can be written directly below the spreadsheet's storage. If the user saves the modifications, the changes to this storage are committed; otherwise, the changes to the storage are rolled back. Although this could certainly be accomplished in other ways—by making Excel create a temporary storage, for example—building transaction support into compound files makes life simpler for application developers.

The IStorage Interface

As mentioned earlier, storage objects support the IStorage interface. The methods in this interface are analogous to the operations that can be performed on a typical directory in a file system. IStorage is a big interface, containing numerous methods. Some of its most interesting methods include the following:

The methods in IStorage are analogous to operations performed on a file system directory

- **CreateStream** creates a stream below the storage object.
- **OpenStream** opens a stream below the storage object.
- **CreateStorage** creates a new storage below the storage object.
- **OpenStorage** opens a storage below the storage object.

- **DestroyElement** destroys a stream or a storage below the storage object. If the storage object containing the stream or subordinate storage was opened in transacted mode, this destruction can be reversed.

- **RenameElement** renames a stream or a storage below the storage object. This change can be reversed if transacted mode is being used.

- **CopyTo** copies the contents of one storage object into another.

- **MoveElement** moves the contents of one storage object into another—that is, it copies the contents and then deletes the original.

- **EnumElements** returns a list of the elements contained in the storage object.

- **SetElementTimes** sets the creation, access, and modification times of a storage or a stream below the storage object. (Some implementations of Structured Storage might not support all three of these times.)

- **SetClass** persistently stores a CLSID in its own stream immediately below the storage object. This allows persistent storage of a complete object—its data is stored in one or more streams, and its methods are identified by this CLSID.

- **Stat** returns various information about the storage object, including the CLSID stored by a call to SetClass.

- For a storage object opened in transacted mode, the **Commit** method commits all changes made since the object was opened or since the last Commit request was made. For a storage object opened in direct mode, this method merely flushes its buffers to disk.

- For a storage object opened in transacted mode, the **Revert** method discards all changes made since the object was opened or since the last Commit request was made.

The IStream Interface

The IStream interface is a little simpler than IStorage. Given how simple a stream is (it's just a stream of bytes), this shouldn't come as a surprise. Just as the methods in IStorage are analogous to operations performed on a directory, the methods in IStream are analogous to file operations. Here are some of the more interesting methods found in IStream:

The methods in IStream are analogous to operations performed on an ordinary file

- The **Read** method reads a specified number of bytes from the stream object.
- The **Write** method writes a specified number of bytes to the stream object.
- The **Seek** method moves the seek pointer in a stream object to a specified place.
- The **CopyTo** method copies a range of bytes from one stream object to another.
- The **LockRegion** and **UnlockRegion** methods lock and unlock, respectively, a range of bytes within a stream object. (This option isn't currently supported on Windows or the Macintosh.)
- For stream objects opened in direct mode, the **Commit** method flushes any memory buffers to disk. For stream objects opened in transacted mode, this method makes permanent the changes made in a stream. (The Structured Storage specification explicitly allows the option of not supporting transacted mode for streams, and the current Windows 95, Windows NT, and Macintosh implementations don't support this method.)
- For stream objects opened in transacted mode, the **Revert** method causes all changes made since the stream was opened or since the last Commit request to be rolled back to their original state. (This method isn't supported in the Windows 95, Windows NT, or Macintosh implementations of IStream.)

Library functions
are used to create
and open com-
pound files

Structured Storage Library Functions

Every implementation of Structured Storage includes a library
with several useful functions, such as these:

- The **StgCreateDocFile** function creates a new compound
  file and returns a pointer to the IStorage interface of the
  new file's root storage.

- The **StgOpenStorage** function opens an existing compound file.

- The **StgIsStorageFile** function allows a client to determine
  whether a particular file is a compound file or an ordinary disk file.

Controlling an Object's Persistence

A client can
initialize an
object it creates
by asking the
object to load its
persistent data

The discussion so far has described how a COM object can use
storages and streams to load and store its persistent data. In reality, though, an object won't often make the decision to store or
load data by itself. Instead, the object's client will control exactly
when this happens. Recall, for instance, that an object created by
a client using only the COM library is uninitialized. That client
must have a way to ask the object to initialize itself by loading its
persistent data.

For a more concrete illustration, think of the compound document example described earlier: an Excel spreadsheet embedded in a Word document. The user starts Word, which then loads
the Word part of the document and a kind of snapshot of the
most recent state of the embedded spreadsheet to display to the
user—Excel itself is not immediately started. Only when the user
double-clicks on the embedded spreadsheet is it necessary to start
Excel. When the user does this, Word looks in the storage that
contains this embedded object (Word doesn't know that it's an
Excel object—the interfaces defined by OLE allow completely
generic interaction) and extracts the CLSID stored there. Word
then asks the COM library to start an instance of the object with

this CLSID using the CoCreateInstance function.[1] The COM library starts Excel, passing back as always a pointer to the initial interface Word requests. Using the methods in this interface, Word then asks Excel to initialize itself—that is, to load its persistent data from the storage embedded in the Word file. Excel does this, and the object (to the user, an embedded spreadsheet) is now ready for use.

But what is the interface that a client like Word first requests, the one it uses to ask the object to initialize itself? In general, an object and its client are free to use any interface, including custom interfaces designed for specific purposes. More likely, though, an object will support one of the standard IPersist* interfaces that have been defined for this purpose. The creator of an object decides which of these interfaces to support based on how the object stores its persistent data. Among the choices are the following:

- The **IPersistStream** interface lets a client ask an object to load its persistent data from and save it to a stream. An object with simple persistent data that could naturally be stored in a single stream would probably support this interface.

- The **IPersistStreamInit** interface is just like IPersistStream (in fact, it inherits all the methods from IPersistStream) except that it adds an extra method. Using this additional method, a client can let an object know that it's being initialized for the first time, something that isn't possible with IPersistStream.

- The **IPersistStorage** interface lets a client ask an object to load and save its persistent data using a storage. An object whose persistent data is contained in several streams below a single storage, for example, might support this interface. (IPersistStorage is what Word requests in the Word/Excel scenario just described.)

A client usually asks an object to load its persistent data via one of the IPersist* interfaces

---

1 Actually, Word calls the helper function OleLoad to perform all these tasks on its behalf.

- The **IPersistFile** interface lets a client ask an object to load and save its persistent data using an ordinary flat file.
- The **IPersistPropertyBag** interface allows a client to get and set an object's persistent data as a set of properties, each of which is a character string. An object whose persistent data is stored as HTML text on a web page might support this interface.
- The **IPersistMoniker** interface lets a client ask an object to load and save its persistent data using a moniker. An object whose persistent data is stored elsewhere—on a web page, for instance—might support this interface. (IPersistMoniker and monikers in general are described in Chapter 6.)
- The **IPersistMemory** interface resembles IPersistStream-Init, but the client can ask an object to load and save its persistent data using a specific piece of memory rather than some truly persistent storage medium.

An object can support one or more of the IPersist* interfaces

An object typically supports one or more of these interfaces, depending on how it stores its persistent data. When a client starts the object, the first interface pointer the client requests is commonly for one of the IPersist* interfaces. The client then calls a method in that interface to initialize the object.

How does a client know which IPersist* interface to request for a particular object? In some cases, the client might already be aware of how an object stores its persistent data and thus might know which interface to ask for. If this isn't the case, the client can use QueryInterface to run through the list of all the IPersist* interfaces the client knows about until it finds one the object supports.

An object typically doesn't know where to find its persistent data—it must be told by its client

Regardless of the IPersist* interface an object is using, the client determines exactly which storage, stream, or file the object should load from. With IPersistStream and IPersistStreamInit, for instance, the client passes in a pointer to an IStream interface when it asks the object to load its persistent data. With

IPersistStorage, the client passes in a pointer to an IStorage interface; and with IPersistFile, the client specifies a filename. In general, a newly created object instance doesn't know where its own persistent data is—its client must tell it.

In many, perhaps most, cases, this arrangement is entirely reasonable. In our compound document example, for instance, the client (Word) was able to tell the object (Excel) exactly where to get its data, which was embedded in a compound file the client was already using. In some cases, however, knowing how to locate an object's data and initialize the object is too much to expect from a client. In such situations, the entire process of instantiating and initializing an object can be performed by a moniker (described in the next chapter).

The IPersistStream and IPersistStreamInit Interfaces
As shown in Figure 5-3, both the IPersistStream and IPersistStreamInit interfaces are supported by objects that can store their persistent data in a single stream. Today, IPersistStreamInit is gradually replacing IPersistStream, since it offers all the features of its older relative plus one more: the ability to let an object know when it's first being initialized.

An object supports IPersistStream or IPersistStreamInit if its persistent data can be stored in one stream

Illustrating the IPersistStream and IPersistStreamInit interfaces.

Figure 5-3

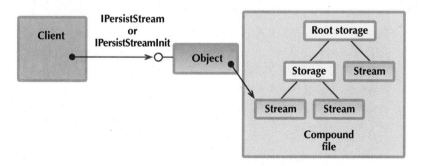

As befits this simple view of persistent storage, IPersistStream and IPersistStreamInit have only a few methods, which are listed on the following page.

- **Load** instructs the object to load its persistent data from a stream whose location is provided by its client.

- **Save** instructs the object to save its persistent data in a client-specified stream.

- **IsDirty** allows the object's client to determine whether the object's data has been modified and thus should be saved before the object is released.

- **GetSizeMax** returns the maximum size stream that would be required if the client called IPersist-Stream::Save immediately.

- **InitNew** (contained in IPersistStreamInit only) allows a client to let an object know that it's being initialized immediately after its first creation. This turns out to be very useful for certain kinds of COM objects, such as the ActiveX controls described in Chapter 9.

The IPersistStorage Interface

An object supports IPersistStorage if its persistent data is stored in one or more streams below a storage

An object that uses streams to store its persistent data but can't fit all the data into just one stream might decide that it needs its own storage. The object can then create and use as many streams as it needs beneath this storage. For example, when an Excel spreadsheet is embedded in a Word document, the embedded spreadsheet needs to store several elements—the actual spreadsheet data, Excel's CLSID, and other information. (For a more detailed description of what's stored, see Chapter 8's discussion of embedding in compound documents.) Cramming all this into one stream doesn't work. Instead, Excel gets its own storage and then uses streams as needed below this storage. As shown in Figure 5-4, a client can pass Excel (or any object) a pointer to this storage and take other actions to control the object's persistence via IPersistStorage.

Once a client has passed an object a pointer to a storage, the object can create new storages and streams below that storage. But the client might still need to work with this storage even after handing the pointer to the object. To allow this, IPersistStorage includes methods that let the client control when the object is allowed to modify the storage, thus avoiding chaos and providing a way to coordinate the shared use of the storage between client and object.

Illustrating the IPersistStorage interface.

Figure 5-4

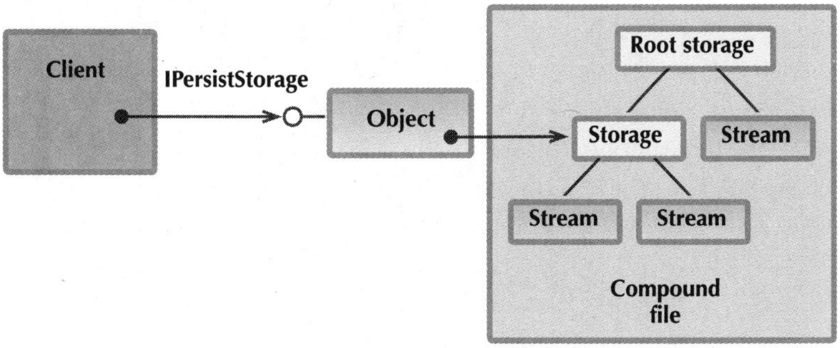

Here are the methods defined in the IPersistStorage interface:

- **InitNew** allows the object's client to pass it a pointer to the storage object it should use. This method is called on the first initialization of the object.
- **Load** instructs the object to load its persistent data.
- **Save** instructs the object to save its persistent data. After a request to save its data, the object is not allowed to write to its storage until it receives a call to SaveCompleted. (This, for example, allows the client to invoke IStorage::Commit directly on the storage object to make any changes permanent.)
- **SaveCompleted** indicates that the object can again write to its storage (that it's back to what's called *scribble mode*).
- **HandsOffStorage** causes the object to release any pointers to streams or subordinate storages that it has opened below its storage. This allows the object's client to safely copy or otherwise work with the storage. The client calls SaveCompleted when it finishes with the file, once again returning the object to scribble mode.

- **IsDirty** allows the object's client to determine whether the object's data has been modified and thus should be saved before the object is released.

The IPersistFile Interface

An object supports IPersistFile if its persistent data is stored in an ordinary flat file

There's no rule that says a COM object must use a compound file to store its persistent data. Storages and streams are quite useful for storing some kinds of data (such as embedded documents), but they're not right for everything. Imagine the case, for example, where an object needs nothing more than an ordinary flat file to store its persistent data. In this situation, that object could get away with supporting only the simple interface IPersistFile, as shown in Figure 5-5.

Figure 5-5 *Illustrating the IPersistFile interface.*

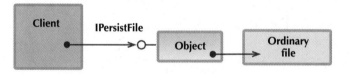

The IPersistFile interface contains these methods:

- **Load** instructs the object to load its persistent data from a client-specified file.
- **Save** instructs the object to save its persistent data to either a client-specified disk file or the file from which the data was loaded.
- **SaveCompleted** is necessary if a call to Save has left the object in a state that prohibits writing to the file. The client must then call SaveCompleted to instruct the object to return to its normal state.
- **IsDirty** allows the object's client to determine whether the object's data needs to be saved before the object is released.
- **GetCurFile** returns the name of the file in which the object is storing its persistent data.

The IPersistPropertyBag Interface

If an object supports any of the IPersist* interfaces described so far, its client passes it a reference to a stream, a storage, or a file, and the object itself saves its own persistent data. In some cases, however, an object's client wants to save that data itself. For such situations, the client needs a way to extract an object's persistent information.

A client of a COM object might want to store that object's data

Imagine, for example, a COM object that's being used by a Microsoft Visual Basic program. Such objects commonly organize their persistent data into a number of named properties, a concept that fits well into Visual Basic's worldview. (For more on this idea, see the discussion of ActiveX Controls in Chapter 9.) If the object is implemented in an in-process server and loaded when needed, it needs a place to store these properties persistently when it's not running. (Otherwise, the user of the Visual Basic program would have to reset them all every time the program was started.) The obvious place to store them is in the same file that contains the code for this Visual Basic program. But Visual Basic stores its code in a flat file—it doesn't use a compound file. So the obvious solution, giving each COM object used by this program its own stream or storage, won't work. Furthermore, since Visual Basic stores its programs as plain text, ideally each COM object used with this program should do the same. What's needed is a way for Visual Basic to extract an object's properties (its persistent data) one at a time. Once this is done, those properties can be stored however the client chooses—for example, as text strings kept in the program file Visual Basic ordinarily maintains.

As another example, imagine a COM object that stores its persistent data in a page on the World Wide Web. Web pages are typically described as text using HTML. Again, it would be nice to be able to keep the object's persistent data as character strings stored within that HTML document. It's the same problem—providing a way for an object to load and store its persistent data one property at a time, but giving the object's client complete control over how and where each property is actually stored.

If an object
supports IPersist-
PropertyBag, it
can store its
persistent data in
a client-supplied
property bag

The IPersistPropertyBag interface was defined to solve this prob- lem. As implied by this interface's ungainly name, an object can save its properties in a *property bag,* which is simply an unor- dered collection of properties supplied by the object's client. IPersistPropertyBag has only three methods:

- **InitNew** allows a client to let an object know that it's being initialized immediately after its first creation.
- **Load** allows a client to tell an object to load its persistent data from a client-supplied property bag.
- **Save** allows a client to tell an object to save its persistent data to a client-supplied property bag.

The client of an
object supporting
IPersistPropertyBag
must implement
the IPropertyBag
and IErrorLog
interfaces

IPersistPropertyBag works with two other interfaces: IPropertyBag and IErrorLog. As shown in Figure 5-6, the object with persistent properties implements IPersistPropertyBag, but the other two interfaces are implemented by that object's client. When a client calls IPersistPropertyBag::Load on an object, the client passes in pointers to its own IPropertyBag and IErrorLog interfaces. The object uses IErrorLog to report back any errors that occur while it loads properties. IPropertyBag is more interesting. Its two meth- ods, Read and Write, are used by the object to load and save its properties, respectively. When the object's client calls IPersist- PropertyBag::Load, the object's implementation of this method actually makes one or more calls back to its client, each invoking the client's IPropertyBag::Read method. On each call, the object specifies the name of a property it wants to read. The client sup- plies a value for this property from some persistent storage that it maintains—how this is done is not the object's concern. Similarly, when the object's client calls IPersistPropertyBag::Save, the object hands its properties to the client one at a time, each passed via a separate call to the client's IPropertyBag::Write method.

How a client actually stores an object's properties is entirely that client's concern—the object has no voice in this decision. If the client is Visual Basic, it might store those properties as text strings in a program file it maintains. Another client might choose to store an object's properties in a web page as part of the HTML text. It's even possible (though not very likely) for a client to store an object's properties in a stream. (The interfaces discussed previously are better choices for storing in a stream, however.) IPersistPropertyBag and its associated interfaces offer a convenient way for an object to provide its persistent data structured as a group of named properties. The object's client is free to store them in any way it chooses.

The client, not the object, controls how and where an object's properties are stored

Illustrating IPersistPropertyBag and its associated interfaces.

Figure 5-6

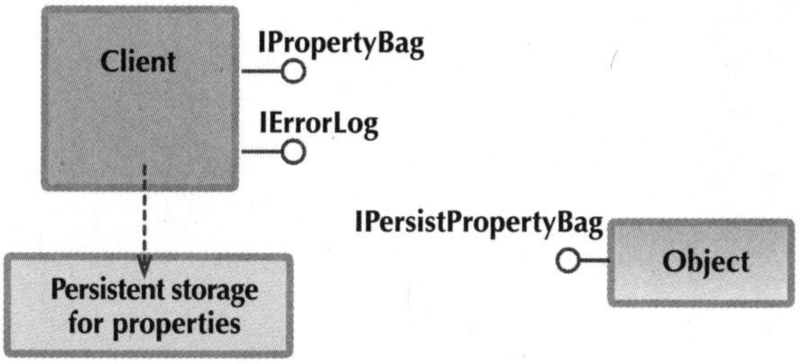

The IPersistMemory Interface

Calling an interface IPersistMemory seems oxymoronic—after all, persistence means storing data in a nonvolatile way, such as on disk, not keeping it in memory. In fact, however, objects that support the IPersistMemory interface can sometimes make life easier for their clients.

Imagine, for instance, that a client is maintaining persistent data for several objects using its own proprietary file format. To store each object's data, the client first must extract that data from the object and then write it to this file. With a compound file, the client could simply pass each object a pointer to its own stream using IPersistStream and let each object save its own data. Alternatively, with each object's persistent data organized into properties, the client could extract it via IPersistPropertyBag. But what about a client that wants to get an object's persistent data directly and then store that data in a proprietary way?

An object that supports IPersist-Memory can pass its persistent data to a client in a chunk of shared memory

IPersistMemory was created for just such a situation. This interface's methods are identical to those in IPersistStreamInit except that the client passes in a pointer to a fixed-size chunk of memory rather than a pointer to an IStream interface.[2] As illustrated in Figure 5-7, the object implements IPersistMemory, and the object's client uses this interface's Load method to pass in a pointer to a chunk of shared memory. When asked to load its persistent data, the object simply reads that data from shared memory. How the data got into that shared memory, as well as how the data was stored persistently, is invisible to the object.

Figure 5-7 *Illustrating the IPersistMemory interface.*

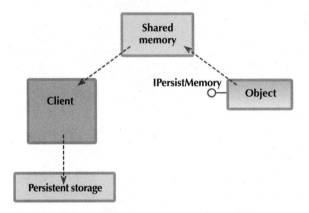

When asked to save its persistent data, the object writes its data into this memory. The client is then free to save that data in whatever persistent way it chooses—for instance, as a record in a file or database. As with IPersistPropertyBag, it's the client rather than the object that actually makes the data persistent. And since the size of the memory block is fixed, the client can rely on the object's data not to exceed known limits.

---

2   Instead of using IPersistMemory, an object could implement IPersistStream on a chunk of memory rather than a stream on disk. Implementations of IPersistStream, however, require that the stream be able to grow as needed. With IPersistMemory, the allocated memory can never change size, a limitation that can improve performance.

Chapter Six

Monikers

In any kind of object-oriented system, it's useful to have a way to identify a specific object instance. A client might want to access a particular bank account, for example, or one document might need to contain a link to another document. In each case, an instance of an object must be specifically named. And that name should identify the same object instance whether or not that instance is currently running.

Naming an object instance generally requires identifying two elements: the object's methods (its executable code) and its persistent data. For objects that have no persistent data, naming only the methods is enough. But for most objects, both methods and data must be designated. To identify your bank account object, for example, it's necessary to indicate where the account balance and other information are stored and also to specify what code should be used to work with that information—that is, the code that implements the object's methods. Similarly, identifying a linked OLE document requires identifying both the data and the application that knows how to work with that data.

COM by itself does not provide a way to name an object instance. In COM, a client can instantiate a generic instance of an object by calling CoCreateInstance with the object's CLSID. If this object has persistent data (as a bank account, a linked document, or many other kinds of objects would), the client can then use one of the IPersist* interfaces (or perhaps another interface) to ask the object to load that data. To do this, however, the client must know

Naming an object instance requires identifying its methods and data

COM alone offers no way to name an object instance

the object's CLSID, know how to locate where the object's persistent data is held (such as in a storage, stream, or file), and be willing to go to all this trouble. COM itself offers no simple solution for the client.

For some kinds of objects and clients, this is entirely acceptable. For others, however, having all this information available within the client is too much to expect. In situations like these, it's better to give a client a single reference to a specific object instance and let the client make one simple request. Something else can then do all the work required to instantiate and initialize that object instance, taking the burden off the client. This help can be provided by a moniker.

Defining Monikers

A *moniker* is a name (in fact, the word *moniker* is a slang term for *nickname)* for a specific object instance, one particular combination of a CLSID and persistent data. Each moniker identifies only one object instance. For example, if you and I have accounts at the same bank and that bank represents our accounts as COM objects, two separate monikers would be needed to identify these two distinct objects.

But monikers are more than simply names. Monikers are themselves COM objects, and they support an interface called IMoniker. Each moniker has its own persistent data, which contains everything the moniker needs to start and initialize the single object instance the moniker identifies.

For example, a moniker that names your bank account might consist of persistent data that specifies where to find your account's persistent data (perhaps the name of a file containing your balance) and a reference to the code required to get your account object up and running (a CLSID, for instance). A typical request made by a client via the IMoniker interface is "Create and initialize the object you refer to, please." A moniker responds to this request by creating

A moniker names a specific object instance

A moniker is an object that supports the IMoniker interface

and initializing the object, returning a pointer to a client-specified interface on the newly running object, and then (typically) dying once its client has decremented its reference count to 0.

This process is illustrated in Figure 6-1. As shown in the figure, a client can invoke the BindToObject method in IMoniker (more on IMoniker's methods later). The client passes as a parameter an IID identifying the interface on the target object for which it wants a pointer returned (interface A in the figure). The client does not, however, pass a CLSID or any indication of where the target object's persistent data is stored—the moniker can learn both pieces of information from its own persistent data. The moniker then starts and initializes the object and passes back the requested interface pointer. With this pointer, the client can now happily invoke methods on the newly running object. The moniker is no longer needed, and it typically dies. (This process of establishing a connection between the client and the object referred to by the moniker is called *binding to the object*.)

A client can ask a moniker to bind to the object the moniker names

Using a moniker.

Figure 6-1

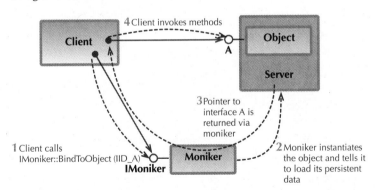

You might want to compare Figure 6-1 with Figure 2-5 on page 58. In the earlier figure, the client called CoCreateInstance, and the COM library instantiated the object and returned the first interface pointer. Here, in Figure 6-1, the client calls IMoniker::BindToObject, and the moniker instantiates the object and returns the first interface pointer. Although the moniker very likely relies on the COM library (specifically CoCreateInstance) to do this, as described next, the monitor does more than create the object—it also initializes the newly created object instance. All this work is wrapped up inside the moniker itself, shielding the client from messy details.

A moniker can do anything it likes to create and initialize the object it names

To start the object it refers to (step 2 in Figure 6-1), a moniker might follow the same steps any other client would to create and initialize an object. For example, since a moniker's persistent data contains either the CLSID of the object it references or information that can be translated to that CLSID, the moniker can create an uninitialized instance of that class by calling CoCreateInstance from the COM library, requesting a pointer to one of the IPersist* interfaces (as described in Chapter 5). The moniker's persistent data also contains an indication (a filename, for instance) of where to find the target object's persistent data. Once it has a pointer to an IPersist* interface on the running but uninitialized target object, the moniker can use this IPersist* interface to ask the target object to initialize itself from its own persistent data. The moniker can then use QueryInterface on the object to acquire the interface pointer the client requested and return it. This scenario is common, but a moniker might also do something entirely different to start the object instance it names. How a moniker accomplishes this is its business; no rules dictate the details of this process.

Monikers can greatly simplify a client's life

A big question remains: why bother with monikers? What does all this buy you? Since the client needs to create the moniker object anyway, why not just skip this whole business and create the target object directly? What does the client gain? In fact, in many cases, a client would gain nothing by using a moniker. In situations where the process of instantiating a moniker (described in "Creating a Moniker," page 137) is nearly as complex as the process of directly instantiating and initializing the object the moniker refers to, using the moniker offers no real benefit. In many other cases, however, using a moniker can make a client's life significantly simpler. In general, any client that knows how to call IMoniker::BindToObject can use monikers to create and initialize many kinds of objects, each of which might have radically different creation and initialization requirements. Encapsulating such requirements in a moniker lets the client avoid any specific knowledge of the binding and initialization process because, to a client, all monikers look the same. To show how valuable this can be, let's look at a couple of examples of how monikers are really used.

A Compound Documents Example

When one document is embedded in another using OLE, the embedded document's data is actually stored in the same file as the container document's data. In the example described in Chapter 5, for instance, a Microsoft Excel spreadsheet was embedded in a Microsoft Word document, and the spreadsheet's data was assigned its own storage object below the root storage of the Word document.

An embedded document's data is stored in its container's file

If the Excel spreadsheet is linked to the Word document rather than embedded in it, however, things look a bit different. A linked document's data is stored in its own file, not in the file of its container. This implies that the container's file (the Word document here) must contain some kind of reference to the linked file. What should this link be? What is the appropriate mechanism for linking documents together?

The container's file stores only a reference to a linked document's data

One obvious possibility is to store a filename in the Word document. Although this would correctly identify the file containing the Excel data, what if the data being used for the link isn't the entire spreadsheet but is instead only a subset of the spreadsheet—say, a specific range of cells within the file? Clearly, a filename by itself isn't enough.

The solution is to use a moniker. Excel and the data the user has linked comprise a specific object instance, made up of the linked data and the methods implemented by Excel. Storing a moniker in the container document means storing a reference to this instance. Figure 6-2 on the following page shows a model of this relationship.

That reference is a moniker

Figure 6-2   *The container's file stores the persistent data for a moniker that refers to a linked document.*

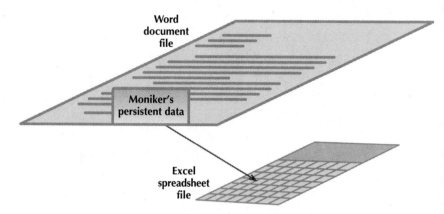

What's actually
stored is the
persistent data
for a moniker

What's actually stored in the Word document (in its own stream) is the persistent data for this moniker. This data includes information such as the name of the file in which the Excel spreadsheet is stored and the range of cells in the spreadsheet that are actually linked. (A more detailed example of this persistent data appears later in this chapter; see "Working with Monikers," page 136.) When a user loads the Word document and activates the link, Word must somehow cause Excel to be started and initialized with the correct information. It does this by instantiating the moniker whose persistent data is stored in the stream in the Word document. The moniker then performs all the work required to instantiate Excel and initialize it with the proper data.

Why is this better than having Word itself start and initialize Excel? Because Word can use links to many kinds of information managed by many kinds of software, not just to Excel files. To make these links, Word might need to store references to specific objects whose data and methods are provided in all sorts of ways. Instead of being required to understand how to create and initialize all of these disparate objects, Word can simply instantiate a moniker and ask it to create the appropriate object. One simple request—IMoniker::BindToObject—can be used to link to all kinds of objects, freeing Word from having to implement the messy details required to make the links work.

A Database Example

OLE Database defines a group of COM objects and interfaces that can be used to access all sorts of data.[1] Among the COM objects it defines are a Command object, which represents a command such as an SQL query that can be executed against a source of data, and a Rowset object, which contains the data that results from executing that command. Rowset objects support the IRowset interface. Once a client has a pointer to this interface, it can use the interface's methods to examine the data in the Rowset object.

Clients often want to run a particular command many times. Frequently executed queries might be hard-coded into a system, but it can also be useful to define a command dynamically and then store it to be repeatedly executed later. In the language of OLE Database, a client should be able to "materialize" a Rowset object, bringing it into existence by executing the correct Command object.

To accomplish this, the client could re-create the Command object and explicitly run the query. A simpler path to the same result, however, is to use a moniker. Once a Rowset object has been created—that is, once a given command has been executed—the client can acquire a moniker to that Rowset object. From then on, the client can simply ask the moniker to instantiate and initialize the Rowset object. Here the moniker does much more than just call CoCreateInstance and initialize the object through an IPersist* interface. To rematerialize a Rowset object, the moniker must actually execute the correct command again, initializing the Rowset object with the current results of running the command's query. The data in the Rowset object can change each time the moniker brings it into existence, since the underlying data source from which the object is created might change. The result is that the client doesn't need to remember the details involved in creating a particular Rowset object—instead, the moniker remembers.

OLE Database provides COM-based access to various kinds of data

A moniker can create an object and then initialize it with results from a database query

---

1   *OLE Database* is the original name of this technology. At the time this book is being written, it appears very likely that the technology will be renamed.

Working with Monikers

Because they can be used to name any kind of object, monikers must be quite general. Sadly, generality and simplicity seldom go together. This section delves a bit more deeply into how clients create monikers and how monikers actually perform their task.

Classes of Monikers

Several standard moniker classes have been defined

Various standard classes of monikers have been defined. Among the most important are *file monikers, item monikers,* and *composite monikers* (also called *generic composite monikers*). Figure 6-3 shows examples of the persistent data for all three classes. These examples are for a moniker used in OLE to identify a linked Excel spreadsheet.

Figure 6-3   *Examples of persistent data for the most important moniker classes.*

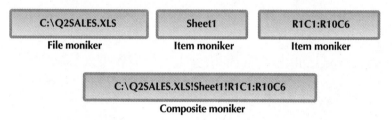

It's easy to imagine using these two item monikers together with the file moniker to precisely identify the data for a linked document. All that's needed is a container in which these various lesser

A file moniker's persistent data is a filename, while an item moniker's persistent data is a character string

A file moniker's persistent data is, not surprisingly, a filename. In Figure 6-3, the example's filename extension is XLS, indicating that this file contains an Excel spreadsheet. An item moniker's persistent data is a character string of some sort. Exactly what that string is and how it's manipulated are the province of the object to which the moniker refers, not the moniker itself. Figure 6-3 shows two item monikers. The first identifies a particular sheet in a spreadsheet file, while the second identifies a specific range of cells within that sheet. The object each moniker names will determine exactly how to use this information to correctly set up its state.

It's easy to imagine using these two item monikers together with the file moniker to precisely identify the data for a linked document. All that's needed is a container in which these various lesser monikers can be packaged into a whole. A composite moniker provides this container, a box into which other monikers (even other composite monikers) can be placed. In Figure 6-3, the composite moniker's data is the data from the monikers it contains, separated with exclamation points. This *display name* is what users see when they examine links directly.

In OLE, what's actually stored as the link for an Excel spreadsheet is the persistent data for a composite moniker, data like that shown in Figure 6-3. When the client activates this link, several different monikers are used: a composite moniker, a file moniker, and a couple of item monikers. The process of binding to the correct initialized object requires traversing this list, asking each moniker in turn to perform its task.

<aside>A composite moniker acts as a container for packaging other monikers</aside>

Creating a Moniker

Where do monikers come from? How does a client get what it needs to use a moniker? To answer these questions, we need to look at three issues: first, the source of a moniker's persistent data; second, the source of the code that implements a moniker's methods; and third, how a moniker object itself is instantiated and initialized.

In some cases, a moniker's persistent data can come from the object the moniker identifies. For example, a user who creates a link using OLE must somehow copy the link information over to the container document. To link an Excel spreadsheet to a Word document, for instance, the user might copy part of the spreadsheet to the clipboard and then paste it into the Word document using the appropriate option for creating a link. What really happens here is that Excel supplies Word with the persistent data for a moniker to that spreadsheet, data such as that shown in Figure 6-3. When the user pastes in what appears to be the spreadsheet itself, Word is actually storing the persistent data for a moniker referring to that spreadsheet object.

<aside>The object a moniker names can supply the moniker's persistent data</aside>

| A client can acquire a moniker's persistent data in other ways | In other cases, the client can acquire a moniker's persistent data in some other way. For example, a client might be given a filename or a URL by a user and then be asked to connect to the object this name identifies. In this situation, the client can convert the name to a moniker and then ask the moniker to create the object it refers to. ("A Generalized Approach to Naming," page 151, explains how a client can easily convert names like these to monikers.) |

| Implementations are provided for standard moniker classes | On to the next issue: where do a moniker's methods come from? These methods are executable code, code that must exist somewhere in the environment. Since monikers are COM objects, they have classes and CLSIDs, and their implementations, like those of other COM objects, must be available. Implementations are provided for the standard moniker classes, and, in addition, anyone is free to create a new moniker class and assign it a new CLSID. |

| Standard monikers are instantiated using system-provided functions | Finally, how are monikers themselves instantiated? Although the obvious answer is that they're instantiated like other COM objects, using CoCreateInstance and a CLSID, this answer is usually wrong. By far the most commonly used moniker classes are the standard classes described earlier. Although each standard class is assigned its own CLSID, system-provided functions also let clients instantiate and initialize monikers of these classes. For example, to instantiate a file moniker, a client can call the CreateFileMoniker function, while an item moniker can be created using CreateItemMoniker. |

Typically, the client passes as a parameter to the function the appropriate persistent data for that class of moniker and in return gets a pointer to the IMoniker interface on the newly running moniker object. For example, a client passes a filename to Create-FileMoniker and in return gets a moniker that knows how to create and initialize the object whose persistent data is stored in that file. (The moniker binding example in the next section describes how the moniker determines what the class of this object should be.) The client can then use the moniker to instantiate and connect to the object that the moniker names. In some ways, each of these library functions acts like a customized version of CoCreate-Instance that works only for a particular standard moniker class.

What about nonstandard moniker classes? How do you instantiate a moniker class that you've invented? Here the answer is more traditional: use CoCreateInstance and the moniker's CLSID, together with a custom scheme to initialize the moniker. Library functions such as those just described are available only for the standard moniker classes.

Library functions aren't available for nonstandard moniker classes

An Example of Moniker Binding

How does all this actually work? The best way to understand monikers is to walk through an example. Imagine that the persistent data of the composite moniker shown in Figure 6-3 is stored in a Word document and that the user has asked Word to connect to the linked object this moniker identifies. Word needs to re-create only the composite moniker from that persistent data. During its initialization, the composite moniker sees that it contains other monikers, so it internally calls the system-provided functions that will create instances of a file moniker and two item monikers, initializing each with the appropriate data. As shown in Figure 6-4, W ord maintains a pointer only to the composite moniker's IMoniker interface, whereas the composite moniker itself internally maintains pointers to the IMoniker interfaces of its constituent file and item monikers.

A composite moniker maintains a pointer to each of its constituent monikers

A composite moniker with pointers to its three constituent monikers.

Figure 6-4

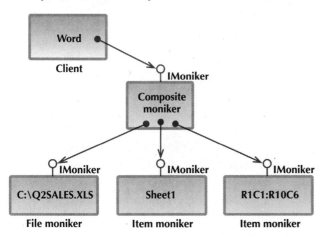

The client sees only the composite moniker

Once all these monikers are running, Word calls the BindToObject method in the composite moniker's IMoniker interface (the only IMoniker interface it knows about), passing in the IID of IOleObject, the interface on Excel to which it needs a pointer. ("The IOleObject interface and verbs," page 184 describes how this interface is used.) The composite moniker's implementation of BindToObject in turn calls IMoniker::BindToObject on one of the three constituent monikers, and the process begins.

Composite monikers bind from right to left

Counter to what you might expect, the composite moniker does not start with the leftmost moniker (the file moniker, in this example). Instead, it calls BindToObject in the rightmost item moniker's IMoniker interface, passing along a pointer to the IMoniker interface of the moniker to the left. The rightmost item moniker, which references the range of spreadsheet rows and columns, then attempts to bind to its object.

If an object is already running, binding can be more efficient

Why start by asking the rightmost moniker? This might seem puzzling since this moniker obviously can't bind to its object until the objects named by the monikers to its left, those for a spreadsheet page and for Excel itself, are active. It's possible, though, that Excel is already running. And if it's running, it might also be maintaining an active object representing exactly the right page of the spreadsheet. It's even possible that this running copy of Excel is maintaining an object that contains exactly the right range of rows and columns—that is, the precise object that the composite moniker names. If any of these scenarios are true, the process of binding this moniker can be made faster, since one or more of the monikers can simply connect to the running copy of the object rather than doing all the work required to start a new copy.

The running object table lets a moniker determine whether the object it names is running

To allow this kind of optimization, the system maintains a *running object table* (ROT), which is described later in this chapter ("The running object table," page 145). For now, think of it as a place where a moniker can check to see whether the object it names is running. If it is, the moniker can get a pointer to that running object directly from the table. If not, the moniker must take a deep breath and actually start the object.

The composite moniker, then, starts with the rightmost moniker in the hope that its object and those named by all monikers to its left are already running. For the purposes of this example, however, let's assume that the object named by the rightmost moniker is not running. The rightmost moniker will then invoke IMoniker::Bind-ToObject on the moniker to its left. This middle item moniker checks the running object table. If its object is running, it returns a pointer to the object. If not, this moniker too must invoke IMoniker::BindToObject on the moniker to its left.

If its target isn't running, an item moniker invokes BindToObject on the moniker to its left

This last moniker, the file moniker, makes its obligatory check of the running object table. Again, we'll assume that it finds nothing. It's this moniker, the leftmost in the composite moniker, that must instantiate its object first. This process, with each moniker asking the one to its left for a pointer to its object, is shown in Figure 6-5.

Each moniker relies on the moniker to its left, hoping to avoid doing more work than necessary.

Figure 6-5

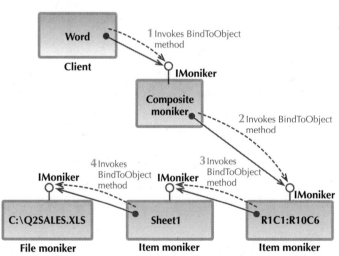

The file moniker uses only its own persistent data to determine the class and locate the persistent data for the object instance it names. The file moniker contains as its persistent data the filename C:\Q2SALES.XLS, which identifies the file containing the spreadsheet's data. But since monikers are supposed to identify both data and methods, where's the indication of the object's class? The

A moniker can use a filename extension to determine an object's CLSID

answer is that the file moniker can use the filename to determine the CLSID of the object that knows how to work with this data. Using the library function GetClassFile, the moniker first determines whether the file is a compound file. If it is, the moniker looks for a stream with a standard name immediately below the file's root storage that contains the CLSID of the object that knows how to work with the data in this file. If this fails, the file moniker next tries to determine the correct CLSID by examining the file's extension. Using the system registry, the moniker can translate a filename extension such as XLS into the CLSID of the code that knows how to work with files of this type. In this example, for instance, the registry indicates that files with the extension XLS are owned by Excel, and the file moniker gets Excel's CLSID. If this fails too, the moniker uses other techniques in a last-ditch effort to determine the CLSID. Once the moniker has somehow acquired the CLSID, it uses it in a call to CoCreateInstance, and the COM library starts Excel.

An object named by a file moniker must support IPersistFile

If a COM object can be referenced using a file moniker, the object must support the IPersistFile interface. (See "The IPersistFile Interface," page 124.) On the call to CoCreateInstance, the file moniker requests a pointer to this interface. It then calls IPersistFile::Load, passing in the moniker's persistent data (the filename C:\Q2SALES.XLS), as shown in Figure 6-6. Excel loads the file, and the object this file moniker names is now active.

It's possible, of course, that someone has moved the file. If so, the file moniker might be able to locate it, depending on exactly how the file was moved. If it can't find the file, the file moniker fails to bind, and the link breaks.

Item monikers rely on IOle-ItemContainer

If an object can be named using only a file moniker, it need support only IPersistFile. Excel, however, supports objects whose data is a specific range of cells on a specific sheet in a spreadsheet file. In this example, the two item monikers identify the sheet object and the range object. To allow those monikers to pass in their persistent data and thus to identify the objects they name,

File and item monikers initializing their objects.

Figure 6-6

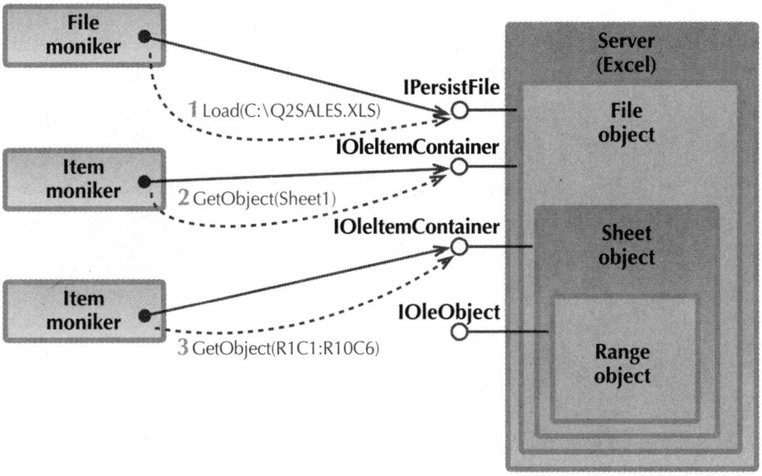

Excel must support IOleItemContainer on the file and sheet objects, as shown in Figure 6-6. The key method in this interface is Get-Object, which allows an item moniker to pass in its persistent data.

Once the file moniker has started Excel, it uses QueryInterface to ask Excel for a pointer to the IOleItemContainer interface on its file object and then passes this pointer back to the item moniker to its right. As shown in step 2 in Figure 6-6, this item moniker uses that pointer to invoke IOleItemContainer::GetObject, passing in the moniker's persistent data. Excel now knows not only which spreadsheet file contains the data for this linked object but also which sheet in that file holds the data. All that's left is to tell Excel what range of cells on that sheet contains the linked object's data.

An item moniker uses IOleItemContainer::GetObject to create and initialize its target object

This is the job of the rightmost moniker. This moniker was the first to have its BindToObject method invoked, but it's the last to actually carry out its task. The previous call to IOleItemContainer::BindToObject returned a pointer to the IOleItemContainer interface on the sheet object in Excel representing the correct sheet within this spreadsheet, and the rightmost file moniker received this pointer from the item moniker to its left. It now uses this pointer to perform the final task in this long process, invoking

IOleItemContainer::GetObject on the sheet object in Excel, as shown in Figure 6-6. This moniker passes in its persistent data, identifying a precise range of cells. This last call accomplishes two important tasks. First, Excel now knows exactly which data comprises the state of the linked object, finally completing the composite moniker's job of instantiation and initialization. Second, this last call to IOleItemContainer::GetObject also returns a pointer to whatever interface the client originally requested when it called IMoniker::BindToObject. In this example, it returns a pointer to Excel's IOleObject interface.

One final but important note: monikers were first applied to the problem of linking in OLE, the problem described here. But keep in mind that they can have far broader application. Since item monikers can contain any character string, for example, they can be used together with the IOleItemContainer interface to identify any kind of object. And the URL monikers discussed later in this chapter ("Asynchronous Monikers," page 147) allow the naming of objects that have nothing to do with compound documents. Don't be misled into viewing monikers as a technology applicable only to linked documents—monikers can be used in a much more general way.

The bind context Throughout the process of binding, any of the monikers involved might need access to certain globally relevant information. To store this information, the client of the moniker creates an instance of a *bind context object*. In the OLE linking example just described, for instance, the bind context keeps a pointer to every object that has been bound so far in the process. With URL monikers, the bind context is used to pass the moniker a pointer to its client. Instantiated via the library call CreateBind-Ctx, every bind context object implements the IBindCtx interface. A pointer to this interface is passed to every moniker that's involved in a specific instance of binding. All of the monikers pictured in Figure 6-5, for example, would have an interface pointer for the same bind context object. The goal is to allow moniker objects to share information that's useful to all of them as they perform their tasks.

The running object table As mentioned earlier, when a client wants to use a moniker to bind to an object instance, it's possible that the object instance is already active. In this case, the moniker should bind to this active object. To allow this, the system supports the running object table (which itself is an object). This object can be accessed via the IRunningObjectTable interface, some of whose methods are listed here:

- The **Register** method registers a running object in the running object table.
- The **Revoke** method removes an object from the running object table.
- The **GetObject** method returns an indication of whether an object with a particular moniker is currently running. If it is, the call returns a pointer to this running object.

By querying this table, a moniker (or anything else) can greatly speed up the process of connecting a client to an object when the object is already running. For instance, if Excel had been running with the correct file loaded when the binding process in the previous example began, the file moniker would have simply returned a pointer to Excel after finding Excel in the running object table.

The running object table is an object that supports the IRunningObjectTable interface

But just what is stored in this table? And how does the table determine that an object named by a particular moniker is running? When a running object registers itself in the table, it passes in a pointer to its IUnknown interface and a pointer to the moniker that identifies it. To determine whether the object it names is currently active, a moniker calls IRunningObjectTable::GetObject, passing in a pointer to itself. The running object table then compares this moniker to each moniker stored in the table: does the persistent data of this moniker match the persistent data of any moniker for a currently running object? If it does, the two monikers must identify the same object instance. If it finds a match, the running object table returns the IUnknown pointer of the matching object in the table to the moniker that called IRunning-

A moniker can query the running object table for the object that moniker names

ObjectTable::GetObject. Using this, that moniker can acquire a pointer to any other interface on the object. If no match is found, the running object table returns a null pointer.

The IMoniker Interface

IMoniker is a relatively complex interface

At long last, it's time to look at the IMoniker interface. For such an apparently straightforward idea, monikers can be surprisingly complex, and that complexity is reflected in this interface. Here are a few of the more important methods in IMoniker:

- The **BindToObject** method instantiates the object the moniker refers to and returns a pointer to a specified interface on that object.

- The **BindToStorage** method returns a pointer to an object's storage rather than to one of its interfaces. (The term *storage* is used in a generic sense here—it can actually mean a storage or a stream or something else.) It's possible, even likely, that the object the moniker names need not actually be instantiated in carrying out this method.

- The **Reduce** method converts the moniker to a more efficient moniker that performs the same task (useful with composite monikers).

- The **ComposeWith** method returns a new moniker that's a composite of the two existing monikers supplied as arguments to this method. This is how composite monikers are created.

- The **IsRunning** method returns an indication of whether the object the moniker names is currently running. The moniker typically determines this by invoking the corresponding method in the running object table.

IMoniker inherits from IPersistStream

Somewhat atypically, the IMoniker interface inherits from IPersistStream. This means that a client can also invoke the methods in IPersistStream through any pointer to an IMoniker interface. Since monikers save their own persistent data in a stream, this makes sense (although it would also have made sense for monikers to support both interfaces separately, a more typical approach for COM-based technologies).

Asynchronous Monikers

When a client calls IMoniker::BindToObject, the moniker instantiates the named object and returns a pointer to one of its interfaces. As described so far, the client has no choice but to patiently wait for this call to return. If the moniker refers to, say, a linked document on the local system, this is no problem—the call returns relatively quickly. But what happens when monikers refer to objects that aren't on the same machine as the client?

If the remote object is accessible via a fast network, it might still be reasonable for the client calling IMoniker::BindToObject to simply wait for the call to return. If the remote object is accessible only via a relatively slow network, however, the client might not be willing to wait for the entire binding process to be completed. In this case, it might make sense to let the client ask the moniker to begin instantiating the object (or retrieving its storage with IMoniker::BindToStorage) and then inform the client when it has finished. An important example of such a case is when a moniker references an object stored on the Internet. Although one day we'll all have lightning-fast connections to this global network, that day isn't here yet. For now, we have to put up with relatively slow links. To allow the use of monikers on this kind of slow network, *asynchronous monikers* were created.

An asynchronous moniker doesn't make its client wait while it starts and initializes an object

While many kinds of asynchronous monikers are possible, only one has been defined so far. Called a *URL moniker*, it can be used to name an object whose data is referenced by a Uniform Resource Locator, the ubiquitous naming scheme for pages on the World Wide Web or an intranet. A client can create an instance of a URL moniker by passing a URL—say, *http://www.acme.com/info*—to the library function CreateURLMoniker. URL monikers are a full-fledged moniker class, just like file and item monikers,

URL monikers are asynchronous monikers

with their own CLSID. Using them, applications can reference an object on the web just as they can reference any other object: through a moniker.

A URL moniker can load an object's data in pieces rather than all at once

With an asynchronous moniker such as a URL moniker, a client can call IMoniker::BindToObject or IMoniker::BindToStorage, as it can with other monikers. The big difference is that these calls might take a long time to complete. Asynchronous binding can mitigate this pain. In the case of BindToObject, for example, the object itself might become active (as seen by the user, anyway) long before all its data has arrived. With BindToStorage, the persistent data of the object the URL moniker points to (that is, the web page) might arrive in pieces rather than all at once. The client that called BindToStorage could display this information to the user as it arrives rather than waiting for the end of the binding process.

How Asynchronous Monikers Work

An asynchronous moniker's client implements IBind-StatusCallback

To make asynchronous monikers work, both the moniker and its client must implement an extra interface. As shown in Figure 6-7, the client implements the IBindStatusCallback interface on a distinct callback object within itself. It gives a pointer to this interface to the bind context object. (Recall that the bind context stores information that's useful to all the participants in the binding process.) The asynchronous moniker in turn retrieves this pointer from the bind context and uses the methods in IBind-StatusCallback to communicate with the client during the binding process.

Figure 6-7   *Interfaces supported by an asynchronous moniker and its client.*

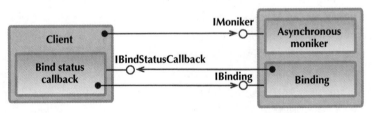

       C h a p t e r   S i x

Once it has the client's IBindStatusCallback pointer, the moniker can invoke this interface's OnStartBinding method to pass the client a pointer to the moniker's own IBinding interface. This interface is typically implemented by a distinct object in the same server as the object that implements IMoniker. The client uses the methods in this interface to communicate with the moniker during asynchronous binding. Figure 6-7 illustrates the situation that results: the client has pointers to IMoniker and IBinding, while the object implementing IBinding has a pointer to the client's IBindStatusCallback interface.

But just what do monikers and their clients have to say to each other during asynchronous binding? Quite a bit, as it happens. First, an asynchronous moniker can call IBindStatusCallback::GetBindInfo to ask its client for details on how it should perform this binding. As the binding process proceeds, the moniker can keep its client apprised of its progress with one or more invocations of IBindStatusCallback::OnProgress. A client can establish the priority of a binding with IBinding::SetPriority or cancel it entirely by calling IBinding::Abort. And, most important, an asynchronous moniker invokes methods in IBindStatusCallback to inform its client that new data is available or that the entire binding process has been completed.

If the client called IMoniker::BindToStorage, the data being retrieved by the moniker might come back in pieces rather than all at once. (Allowing this, after all, is the primary reason asynchronous monikers were created.) To inform its client that a new chunk of data has arrived, the moniker calls IBindStatusCallback::OnDataAvailable. Since an object's data can become available in pieces, the moniker might call this method repeatedly. With a URL moniker, for instance, each call might convey the next chunk of data received from the Web page identified by the moniker's URL. When a client calls IMoniker::BindToObject on an asynchronous moniker, this call doesn't return a pointer to an interface

An asynchronous moniker passes a pointer to its IBinding interface to the client

An asynchronous moniker and its client communicate through methods in IBinding and IBindStatusCallback

An asynchronous moniker informs its client when more data or the complete object is available

on the object as an ordinary moniker does. That pointer is instead returned as a parameter on an IBindStatusCallback::OnObject-Available call that the moniker makes to the client, a call indicating that the asynchronous binding has been completed.

The IPersistMoniker Interface

Imagine an object whose data is stored out on a web somewhere (either on the Internet or in some private intranet) but whose methods (its code) are kept locally. When a client wants to instantiate this object, it can do so by passing the object's CLSID to CoCreateInstance, just as it instantiates any object. But how can the client initialize the object? In the cases we've seen so far, an object can support an interface such as IPersistStorage, IPersist-Stream, or IPersistFile to let a client pass it a storage, a stream, or a file from which to initialize itself. What about the case in which an object's persistent state is kept on another system and identified with a URL?

By supporting IPersistMoniker, an object can identify its persistent data with a moniker

Given a URL, it's possible to create from it a URL moniker. And calling IMoniker::BindToStorage on a URL moniker typically returns the data contained on the web page identified by the moniker's URL. So all we really need is a way to tell an object to initialize itself from a moniker rather than from a stream or a storage or a file. This becomes possible if the object supports an interface called IPersistMoniker. The methods in IPersistMoniker mirror those in IPersistFile, allowing a client to ask an object to load its persistent state, store it, and so on. With IPersistMoniker, however, the client passes in a pointer to a moniker (rather than the name of a file) to tell the object where to find its persistent state. For example, imagine that a client has instantiated an object whose persistent state is identified by a URL. The client can call CreateURLMoniker to convert the URL to a URL moniker. To initialize the object, the client calls IPersistMoniker::Load, passing in a pointer to the IMoniker interface of this URL moniker. The object invokes IMoniker::BindToStorage, asynchronously retrieves its persistent state (for instance, the data from a web page), and initializes itself.

Using a moniker to refer only to an object's persistent state is a little odd; monikers are usually defined as references to object instances, including both methods and data. Nevertheless, the IMoniker interface is flexible enough to allow this variation, which is very useful for some kinds of objects.

A Generalized Approach to Naming

A moniker acts as a name for a COM object. Given a character string such as a filename or a URL, a client can call a function that creates a moniker for an object of the appropriate class, one whose persistent data is stored in that filename or URL. Passing a filename to CreateFileMoniker, for example, returns a pointer to a file moniker for an object whose persistent data is stored in that file and whose CLSID is that indicated by the file. Passing a URL to CreateURLMoniker achieves the same result for an object whose persistent data is stored in the URL.

To use a function such as CreateFileMoniker or CreateURL-Moniker, a client must possess both a character string identifying an object's persistent data and knowledge of what that character string is: a filename, a URL, or something else. In other words, the client must know what kind of moniker it wants to create. In certain situations, however, the client doesn't know this. In some cases, it's useful to be able to transform an arbitrary string into a moniker without being aware of what kind of moniker will be created. Turning character string names into monikers is the job of the library functions MkParseDisplayName and MkParseDisplay-NameEx.

A client can use one of two library functions to turn generic character strings into monikers

Given a name expressed as a string of characters, these functions return a pointer to the IMoniker interface of a moniker that knows how to bind to the named object. A client can pass a name to one of these functions and then call IMoniker::BindToObject on the returned IMoniker pointer to create the object and acquire its first interface pointer. These two functions act as a generalized alternative to the set of specific calls for moniker creation. The only difference between MkParseDisplayName and MkParseDisplayNameEx is that the latter understands a slightly larger set of name formats.

Naming a COM object requires specifying its class and its persistent data (if any). Because this can be done in many possible ways, many kinds of names are used. So far in this chapter, for example, we've seen objects specified with filenames, URLs, and more. Both MkParseDisplayName and MkParseDisplayNameEx can potentially work with a broad range of name formats. Since the algorithm required to instantiate an object with a name can vary quite a bit, however, how can one function know how to start objects identified with so many types of names? The answer is that it doesn't. Instead, these two functions are themselves relatively simple: they know only how to locate and run code to handle each specific kind of name. That code does the work required to create a moniker for the named object and then returns that moniker's IMoniker pointer. MkParseDisplayName and MkParseDisplayNameEx return that pointer to the caller, the client that wants to access this named object.

Both functions can rely on name-specific code to create the appropriate moniker

Both calls, for example, can accept legal filenames, returning pointers to file monikers. Both also support a more general syntax, allowing the process just described to work. The newer of the two functions, MkParseDisplayNameEx, accepts a generalized URL-style format, in the form *ProgID:Name*. The *ProgID* portion is a program identifier (see "A Visual Basic Example," page 95), a character string that is translated to a CLSID using the registry; while the *Name* portion can be anything at all. MkParseDisplayNameEx turns the ProgID into a CLSID and then typically creates an object of that class and hands it the entire string. This object in turn knows how to create a moniker for the object referred to in the *Name* portion. MkParseDisplayName works in a similar fashion, but it uses a different syntax: this function expects a general name to

The newer of the two, MkParse-DisplayName, accepts URL-style names

begin with *@ProgID* rather than using the *ProgID:Name* format. MkParseDisplayNameEx also accepts this syntax, however, so it effectively makes MkParseDisplayName obsolete.

Not only is naming objects this way very general, it's also extensible. Imagine that someone (someone other than Microsoft) wants to add support for naming COM objects that are identified using a distributed directory such as the OSF Distributed Computing Environment's Cell Directory Service (CDS). All that's required is to create the code that knows how to work with this kind of name and install it together with a ProgID such as *cds* and a CLSID for that code. When a client calls MkParseDisplayNameEx with a string such as *cds:/.:/servers/math_server*, this third-party code is loaded and passed that string. The Name portion of this string, */.:/servers/math_server*, is a legitimate CDS name, so the code uses the CDS protocol (which it presumably knows) to locate what's needed for the named object and return an IMoniker pointer for that object. The client can treat this name, one that relies on third-party software installed on the system, exactly as it treats any other kind of name. For software that is capable of working with a particular set of names (commonly referred to as a *namespace),* MkParseDisplayName and MkParseDisplayNameEx can convert a name from that namespace into a moniker that references the object with that name. By making this possible, these functions act as a single entry point into a potentially infinite set of namespaces.

These functions provide a single entry point into virtually any namespace

Chapter Seven

Uniform Data Transfer and Connectable Objects

Frequently, one piece of software needs to transfer data to another. A Microsoft Windows user, for example, might copy text from one program and paste it into another using the clipboard. Networking software might get data from the network by reading it from a device driver. And, in the more complex scenario of a Microsoft Excel spreadsheet embedded in a Microsoft Word document (by now this book's standard example), Excel and Word must exchange data as defined by OLE.

Traditionally, several different ways of moving data between applications have been available, each focused on a particular kind of problem and each with its own idiosyncratic rules. The rationale for this diversity has more to do with history than with reason, however. Why not define a common approach that works in all cases? And why not create that approach using COM, modeling it as a client making requests of an object?

Traditionally, there have been many different ways to move data between applications

Uniform Data
Transfer provides
a single scheme
for moving
data between
applications

This new approach is called *Uniform Data Transfer*. By implementing an object with the standard interface IDataObject, any chunk of software can provide data to any other chunk that knows how to act as a client for this interface. The result is a single scheme for moving data between all kinds of applications, a scheme that can be used in all the cases just described and more.

Connectable
Objects
technology
allows an
object to
send events
to its client

Allowing a client to request data from an object is useful as far as it goes. Sometimes, however, it's not reasonable to expect a client to continually ask an object for new or changed data. An object whose data changes over time must be able to autonomously notify its client of a new occurrence—that is, the object must be able to send its client an event. This event might indicate the addition of new data, the removal of an old value, a change in the data, or the fact that the data value has passed a threshold. Uniform Data Transfer through IDataObject addresses this problem, but only in a limited way. A second technology, known as *Connectable Objects*, offers a more general mechanism for an object to send events to its client. This chapter introduces both the Uniform Data Transfer and Connectable Objects technologies.

Uniform Data Transfer

Most operating systems provide a way to move data between applications. For example, a Windows user who wants to copy a few lines of text from a word processing program into a terminal emulation program can use the clipboard, a designated area in memory. One application copies data from the data area it manages to the clipboard, and another copies it from the clipboard to its own memory area. Windows also provides Dynamic Data Exchange (DDE), a more complex way for applications to exchange data while they're running. For applications to use either the clipboard or DDE, programmers must implement the appropriate series of calls—that is, they must follow the appropriate protocol for data exchange.

Clearly it makes more sense to define one standard means of transferring data between software, and to use COM to do it. Uniform Data Transfer, with its IDataObject interface , accomplishes this.

Among other things, this technology changes a Windows-based application's view of the clipboard and essentially makes DDE obsolete (although it's likely that this widely used data transfer mechanism will be supported indefinitely).

Data Objects

Any COM object that implements the IDataObject interface is considered a *data object.*[1] Data can be transferred into and out of all data objects in a standard way. The software that supports IDataObject might be an application such as a word processor, a part of the operating system, or even a device driver for specialized hardware such as a card connecting a computer to a heart monitoring system. Regardless of what the software in question does, supporting IDataObject can make its data available to any client who understands this interface.

An object implementing IDataObject is known as a data object

Figure 7-1 illustrates a data object with several possible sources of data. An object's data might reside in a file, in a storage or a stream, or in memory; or it might be supplied in another fashion,

IDataObject allows access to data from any source

Through IDataObject, a client can access data from many sources.

Figure 7-1

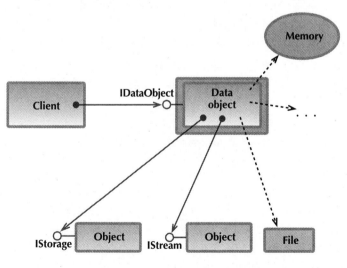

---

1   The object is free to implement other interfaces as well. A data object must implement at least IDataObject but is not restricted to that one interface.

such as through a device driver. IDataObject's goal is to provide one standard interface with one set of methods that allows access to data from any source.

A FORMATETC structure describes data being transferred

Describing data: FORMATETC and STGMEDIUM Defining a standard interface for transferring data implies the creation of standard formats for representing data. To describe the data being exchanged, the methods in IDataObject use a data structure called FORMATETC (pronounced as "format, etc"). This data structure is essentially a superset of the type used by the Windows clipboard to identify data. This clipboard antecedent, however, is very simple, providing only a 16-bit integer value to identify the data type being exchanged. A value of the type FORMATETC allows much more information to be passed, including the following:

- The data format. The standard data formats defined here are the same as those defined today for the Windows clipboard, but organizations can also define and register their own.
- Information about the device for which the data was created. For example, a user might have created a bitmap for a printer with a specific resolution.
- An indication of the role for which this data is designed. For example, the data might be in a form suitable for display to a user, or it might be intended for use as an icon or a thumbnail image.
- An indication of how the data should be conveyed in a particular instance of data transfer. The choices include global memory, a disk file, and storage or stream objects.

A STGMEDIUM structure describes where the data is stored

In the basic Windows clipboard, all data being copied between applications must exist in global memory. This is fine for transferring a few lines of text, but it makes no sense at all for applications that need to exchange data stored largely on disk. With data objects, a STGMEDIUM structure is used to specify where the data is stored. Far from restricting the data's location to global memory, a value of this type can reference data stored in memory, in a disk file, in a storage or stream object, and so on. The STGMEDIUM value also passes a reference to the actual data itself and can optionally include an interface pointer to an object that knows how to free the data. Along with improving the situation in the Windows environment, this generality also makes the STGMEDIUM structure usable for data transfer on the variety of non-Windows systems that can support COM.

Examining the IDataObject interface Here are some of the more important methods in the IDataObject interface:

- **GetData** transfers data from a data object to its client. The client invoking this method provides a FORMATETC structure indicating the format in which it would like the data, and the object passes back a reference to the data (if available) in a parameter of the type STGMEDIUM.

- **SetData** transfers data to a data object from its client. The key parameters are the same as those for GetData, but data is transferred in the opposite direction.

- **QueryGetData** allows a client to ask a data object whether it supports a particular data type for transfer (a particular FORMATETC).

- **EnumFormatEtc** returns an indication of the available formats (described as FORMATETCs) the data object can provide.

- **DAdvise** establishes a connection between a data object and an advise sink object. (Advise sink objects and the use of DAdvise and DUnadvise are discussed in "Notifications," page 160.)

- **DUnadvise** releases a connection established with DAdvise.

Using IDataObject with drag and drop Before invoking any of the methods in IDataObject, a client must acquire a pointer to this interface on the data object. As always, the client can simply

Using IDataObject's methods, an object can read data, write data, and perform other tasks related to data transfer

use QueryInterface to ask for the pointer, but it can also be obtained in other ways. One of them is via drag and drop.

To understand drag and drop, think about how people using a graphical user interface move data between applications. Traditionally, the most common way to do this has been to copy data from one application to the clipboard and then paste the clipboard's contents into another application. This certainly works, but a simpler mechanism (simpler to the user, anyway) would let the user select data in one application, drag it with the mouse to the desired location in another application, and then just drop it in. This sort of easy-to-use interface for data transfer is exactly what COM's support for drag and drop allows.

An application that is a drag-and-drop *source* (an application from which data can be moved using drag and drop) must implement the IDataObject interface, which is used to actually get the data. The application must also implement the IDropSource interface, through which it exposes the functionality needed to implement drag and drop. An application that is a drag-and-drop *target* (one to which data can be moved) must implement the IDropTarget interface. Between the source and the target sits system-provided code, which both parties rely on to carry out the necessary functions. All this works together to implement what a user sees as a very simple way to move data between applications. What really happens, though, is that a pointer to the source's IDataObject interface is moved to the target. The target then uses the methods in this interface to copy whatever data the user has selected.

Notifications

Imagine an object whose data changes over time—for example, an object that tracks the prices of various stocks. As those prices change, the data available from the object changes, too. A client interested in these fluctuations could query the object regularly, asking whether specific stock prices have changed, but this isn't very efficient. If the object itself could send an event to notify the

Drag and drop lets users easily move data between applications

Drag and drop transfers a pointer to IDataObject

An object can inform its client of changes to data via a notification

client of data changes—a *notification*—the client wouldn't need to waste time repeatedly querying the object. To do this, the object needs both the ability to notify the client of changes and a way to get the new data to the client. Also, the client might require a mechanism to tell the object exactly which data it cares about. If the relevant set of data is fixed (for instance, prices for an unchanging set of stocks), object and client might have an a priori agreement and thus forgo such a mechanism. But if the client wants to vary the contents of this set over time, determining dynamically which stock prices the object reports, the object must offer an interface through which this can be done. Some of this functionality can be achieved using IDataObject, but not all of it. More is required.

Using the IAdviseSink interface To support notifications of changes in a data object, the standard interface IAdviseSink is defined. Figure 7-2 illustrates what's needed to carry out the process just described. The object (the source of the data) must support the by-now familiar IDataObject interface. This source might also support an interface that allows the client (the consumer of the data) to tell the object which data changes the client cares about. No standard interface is defined for this purpose—it might be a specially created vtable interface, or it might be a dispinterface accessed via IDispatch. In Figure 7-2, this interface is the fictitious ISpecifyData.

A data object can send notifications to its client via the methods in IAdviseSink

Using IAdviseSink with IDataObject.

Figure 7-2

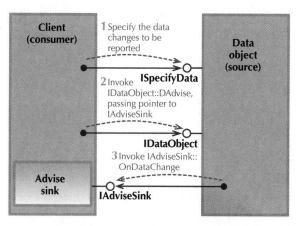

The consumer (client) in turn must implement an interface allowing the source of the data to notify it when a change occurs. This notification can carry with it a reference to the changed data, a reference the client can use to access that data. But to receive that notification in the first place, the consumer must also implement an object that supports the IAdviseSink interface. An object that supports this interface is called, reasonably enough, an *advise sink object* (or simply an *advise sink*).

Invoking the OnDataChange method informs the client of data changes

Most of the methods in the IAdviseSink interface are used in concert with other interfaces defined by OLE for compound documents; only the OnDataChange method is relevant to our discussion here. This method is invoked by a source to inform a consumer that the data in which it's interested has changed. The parameters of this method are a FORMATETC structure describing the changed data and a STGMEDIUM structure indicating where the data can be found.

A consumer invokes IData-Object::DAdvise to establish a connection with the source

Receiving notifications The complete picture, then, is this: A consumer of data (a client) uses an appropriate interface to specify to the source (a data object) which data should be reported. (Alternatively, the consumer and the source might have an existing agreement, allowing them to skip this step.) Next the consumer invokes the source's IDataObject::DAdvise method, with the following parameters:

- A FORMATETC structure indicating the format to use when reporting changes to the data.
- An interface pointer to the consumer's IAdviseSink interface.
- An identifier for this particular consumer/source connection. (A single source of data that has connections with several consumers can use this identifier to distinguish among them.)

When the specified data changes (for example, when a particular stock reaches a particular price), the source uses the IAdviseSink pointer it received from the consumer to invoke that interface's

OnDataChange method. The consumer can then access the changed data. To stop receiving notifications, the consumer invokes the source's IDataObject::DUnadvise method, passing in the connection identifier returned on the earlier call to DAdvise. This breaks the logical connection between the two objects.

A consumer invokes IDataObject::-DUnadvise to break a connection with the source

OnDataChange is the only method in IAdviseSink that's useful for sending generic event data. The other methods in this interface, some of which are described in the next chapter, were created to convey specific notifications needed for implementing compound documents. But the idea of allowing an object to autonomously send an event to its client is important in many situations, not only with compound documents. Furthermore, it's impossible to define one set of events that will suffice for all kinds of applications. What's needed is a way to define and send any sort of event from an object to its client. Providing such a generalized event mechanism is the goal of Connectable Objects.

IAdviseSink is useful only in specific settings

Connectable Objects

An object provides services to a client by allowing the client to invoke methods in the object's interfaces. But what if the object wants to talk back to the client? The object might want to make a request of the client, for example, or simply tell it that an event has occurred. How can general two-way communication between client and object be achieved?

Objects may sometimes need to invoke methods in their clients

The previous section supplied one answer: allow the object to send events to the client using the methods in the IAdviseSink interface. The client passes the object a pointer to this interface using IDataObject::DAdvise, and when the object has something to say (when data has changed, for instance), it invokes the IAdviseSink::OnDataChange method. This scheme is fine for the somewhat specialized worlds of Uniform Data Transfer and compound documents. But the broader problem of allowing an object to talk back to its client in all kinds of settings demands a broader solution.

The Connectable Objects technology provides such a general solution. If an object needs to talk back to its client, the interfaces defined by Connectable Objects offer a standard way to establish a logical connection between the object and its client, no matter what interface the object uses. Because all that's specified are the mechanics of setting up and tearing down this relationship, the Connectable Objects interfaces can be used for all kinds of two-way communication.

Connectable objects provide a generic way to establish two-way communication between object and client

Connection Points and Sinks

To talk back to its client, an object must support one or more *outgoing interfaces*. Supporting an outgoing interface simply means that the object knows how to act as a client for that interface. From the point of view of a data object, for instance, IAdviseSink is an outgoing interface, since the data object knows how to invoke IAdviseSink's methods. That same interface is an *incoming interface* from the point of view of the client that implements it. Although this terminology is used only with connectable objects, one might argue that every client of every COM object supports one or more "outgoing" interfaces, since every client knows how to invoke the methods in those interfaces. An object can describe its outgoing interfaces using IDL and can store descriptions of outgoing interfaces in a type library. (See Chapter 3 for a discussion of IDL, type libraries, and type information.)

An object that supports an outgoing interface knows how to act as a client for that interface

To qualify as a connectable object, an object must support an interface called IConnectionPointContainer. Through this interface, the object's clients can learn which outgoing interfaces the object supports. Each of those interfaces is represented within that object by a separate *connection point object*. Each connection point handles only one type of outgoing interface, and each supports (at least) an interface called IConnectionPoint. Finally, given that a connectable object supports an outgoing interface and thus knows how to invoke that interface's methods, some other object must actually implement this interface. This other object, called a *sink*, is part of the connectable object's client.

A connectable object must support IConnection-PointContainer

All of these components—a connectable object, its connection points, and their sinks—are illustrated in Figure 7-3. Although it's not shown in the figure, it's perfectly legitimate for the connection points in a single connectable object to invoke methods in sinks implemented by different clients. It's also legitimate and quite common for a single connection point to be aware of several different sinks simultaneously. This allows the object to send the same event to many different clients, which can be very handy.

A connectable object can invoke methods in several different sinks

A connectable object, its connection points, and the client's sinks.

Figure 7-3

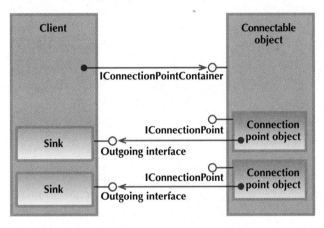

Interfaces for Connectable Objects

Two main problems arise in setting up a connection that allows an object to talk back to its client. First, how does the object (or, more precisely, the appropriate connection point inside the object) acquire a pointer to the sink's implementation of an outgoing interface? To solve this, the client needs a way to pass that connection point a pointer to the correct outgoing interface. The second problem is a bit more existential: how does the client know which outgoing interfaces the object supports (and thus which pointers the object might need)? Both of these problems are solved in a quite general way by the two interfaces IConnectionPointContainer and IConnectionPoint.

A client must pass a connectable object pointers to the client's sink for outgoing interfaces

The IConnectionPointContainer interface This interface is supported by every connectable object. A client can acquire a pointer to IConnectionPointContainer in the usual ways—invoking QueryInterface on the object using a pointer to another interface, for instance. Through IConnectionPointContainer, a client can learn what outgoing interfaces the connectable object supports. This isn't really a very difficult problem, and IConnectionPointContainer isn't a very complicated interface. In fact, it contains only two methods:

- **FindConnectionPoint** allows a client to ask whether an object supports a particular outgoing interface. In other words, the client is asking whether the object knows how to invoke the methods in that interface. The client identifies the interface in question with an interface identifier (IID). If the object supports the interface, it returns a pointer to the IConnectionPoint interface for the appropriate connection point object. The client can then use a method in that interface to pass a pointer to the sink that implements the corresponding outgoing interface.

- **EnumConnectionPoints** allows a client to retrieve a list of all the IConnectionPoint pointers for all the connection points this connectable object supports. The client can look through this list and, using a method in IConnection-Point, can learn the IID of every outgoing interface the object supports.

The IConnectionPoint interface Using the methods in IConnectionPointContainer, a client can both determine what outgoing interfaces an object supports and acquire a pointer to the connection point for each of them. The client is then ready to establish a connection with the connectable object—that is, the client must pass a pointer to the correct sink to one or more of the object's connection points. Once this is done, the connectable object can talk back to the client, making requests and sending events (both of which are accomplished in the same way, by invoking the outgoing interface's methods).

Connections are established and released using the methods in the IConnectionPoint interface, which is supported by every connection point object:

The methods in IConnectionPoint are used to establish and release connections

- **Advise** allows a client to establish a connection with a particular connection point in a connectable object, as shown in Figure 7-4 on the following page. The client passes in a pointer to the interface implemented by the appropriate sink, and the object passes back an identifier for this connection.

- **Unadvise** allows a client to break a connection. The client identifies which connection to break (since the connection point can have connections with many clients) by passing in the identifier it received from the Advise method used to establish the connection.

- **EnumConnections** returns a list of every connection currently active for the connection point.

- **GetConnectionPointContainer** returns a pointer to the IConnectionPointContainer interface for the connection point's connectable object.

- **GetConnectionInterface** returns the IID of the outgoing interface this connection point supports. When a client calls IConnectionPointContainer::EnumConnectionPoints to get a list of all connection points in a connectable object, only the pointers to the IConnectionPoint interfaces are returned. What the client really wants to know, however, is what those interfaces are. This method lets the client translate from an IConnectionPoint pointer to an IID, which precisely identifies the interface.

This process is quite reminiscent of IDataObject and IAdviseSink, discussed earlier in this chapter. Like IDataObject's DAdvise method, IConnectionPoint's Advise method lets a client pass an object a pointer to an outgoing interface. Unlike IDataObject's method, however, which can pass a pointer only to IAdviseSink, IConnectionPoint's Advise method can pass a pointer to any outgoing interface. The Connectable Objects technology provides

Connection points can be seen as a generalized version of how IDataObject and IAdviseSink provide notifications a general solution to the problem of an object acquiring the interface pointers it needs to invoke methods in outgoing interfaces.

Figure 7-4   *Establishing and using a connection.*

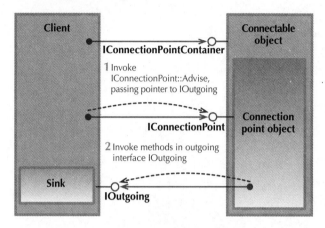

The Future of Connectable Objects

Connectable objects were originally designed for ActiveX Controls (called OLE Controls at the time) because it's essential that this kind of software component be able to both make requests of and send events back to a client. Since then, connectable objects have been adopted by other COM-based technologies. And because the interfaces defined by the Connectable Objects technology provide a general solution to a common problem—allowing two-way communication between an object and its client—it's likely that they will be pressed into service in still more situations. That a technology created for ActiveX Controls can be so easily reused provides a fine example of the generality of COM.

Chapter Eight

OLE Compound Documents

In the beginning, OLE was a technology focused on one problem: creating compound documents. Before long, however, the term *OLE* was being attached to anything built using COM. During this phase, the original COM-based compound-document technology was known as *OLE Documents*. Today both that term and the use of the word *OLE* to refer to a wide range of COM-based technologies are obsolete. The name has returned to its roots, and *OLE* once again refers only to a technology for creating compound documents.

Today the term *OLE* refers solely to a technology for creating compound documents

As this chapter demonstrates, the technology for OLE compound documents relies on many other COM-based technologies, including Structured Storage, monikers, and Uniform Data Transfer. While the end result is a straightforward, natural user interface, providing that simplicity is not simple at all. To understand how this technology works, it's useful to first examine it from a user's point of view. Once that's clear, we can look at the underlying mechanics that make it all possible.

OLE compound documents rely on many other COM-based technologies

A User's View

Figure 8-1 illustrates what a simple compound document looks like to a user. Once again, the example shows a Microsoft Excel spreadsheet inside a Microsoft Word document.[1] The user views this as a single document. In reality, though, Word and Excel must cooperate to present this seamless appearance. This cooperation is achieved, naturally, by each application supporting the appropriate COM objects with standard interfaces.

Figure 8-1 **An example compound document as seen by a user.**

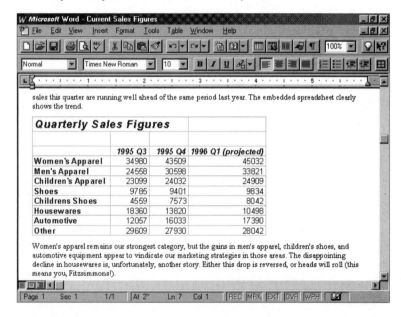

A server can embed its data in a container or link its data to the container

When information from two separate pieces of software is combined in a compound document, one piece of software acts as the *container* and the other as the *server*. OLE allows a server to either *embed* its data in the container or *link* its data to the container. *Embedding* means that the server's data is stored in the same file as the container's data. With *linking*, however, the server's data remains in its own file; only a reference to that data is stored in the container's file.

---

1   Although it's convenient to use these two popular Microsoft products as examples throughout this book, it's worth reemphasizing here that many other applications from many different vendors also support OLE.

The developer of a piece of software decides whether that software should be able to act as a container, a server, or both. Excel and Word, for instance, can act in either role. In our example compound document, Word is acting as the container, Excel as the server. But this arrangement could be reversed, with Excel acting as the container for an embedded or linked Word document. To make the situation even more involved, a developer can write a container application that will allow a server to only embed data in it, only link data to it, or both. Similarly, the creator of a server application can make its data available to containers only through linking, only through embedding, or through both processes. Word and Excel support all these options as both container and server, but many other applications don't.

An application can act as a container, a server, or both

Creating a Compound Document

In Microsoft Windows and Microsoft Windows NT, a user has several choices for how to create a compound document. To create our example document, for instance, the user could open both the Word document and the Excel spreadsheet in their separate applications, copy all or part of the spreadsheet to the clipboard, and then use Word's Paste Special command to paste the copied spreadsheet into the Word document. The Paste Special command lets the user choose whether to embed a copy of the spreadsheet in the Word document or create a link to the spreadsheet in its own file.

A user can create a compound document in different ways

Another choice is to use the COM-based drag-and-drop service that was briefly described in Chapter 7 ("Using IDataObject with drag and drop," page 159). The user selects the relevant spreadsheet data in Excel and simply drags it over to the Word document, inserting the Excel data as either an embedded or a linked document, depending on what options the user chooses. Still another approach is to use Word's Insert Object command, which can insert an embedded or linked Excel spreadsheet directly into a Word document. Regardless of how the user does it, the result is the same: a compound document, with a server's data embedded or linked inside a container.

The choices include copying and pasting via the clipboard and drag-and-drop

Editing a Compound Document

An embedded
document can
be edited in
place or in a
separate window

If the Excel spreadsheet in our example is embedded, the user has two choices for how to edit it. The first choice, editing the spreadsheet exactly where it is, smack dab in the middle of the Word document, is called *in-place activation*, or *visual editing*. When the user double-clicks on the embedded spreadsheet, Excel becomes active. As shown in Figure 8-2, the column and row headers typical of Excel are added to the spreadsheet's embedded image, and the Excel toolbar and menu bar are substituted (partly, at least) for those of Word. The user can then edit the embedded spreadsheet using ordinary Excel commands.

Figure 8-2   ***Editing an embedded Excel spreadsheet in place.***

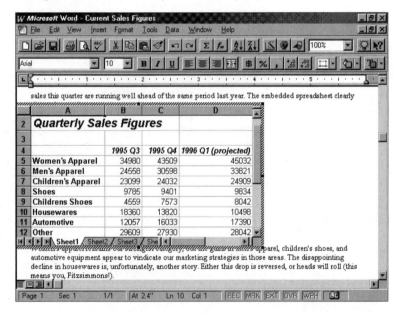

The second option is to edit the embedded spreadsheet in its own window, as shown in Figure 8-3. Here the user specifies an option that causes Excel to open a separate window. The user edits the spreadsheet inside that window and then closes it when done. Throughout the process, any changes the user makes are reflected in the view of the spreadsheet shown in the Word document.

Editing an embedded Excel spreadsheet in its own window.   *Figure 8-3*

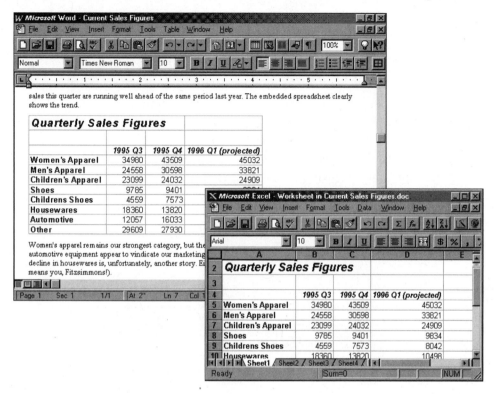

If the spreadsheet is linked to the Word document rather than embedded in it, in-place activation isn't available.[2] Instead, double-clicking on the linked spreadsheet always opens a new window owned by Excel, similar to that shown in Figure 8-3. (When an embedded document is edited in its own window, the view of the embedded data in the compound document is usually overwritten with a light cross-hatching, not shown in Figure 8-3. This is not the case for a linked document edited in its own window.) If the user has chosen to have the link updated automatically, any changes made to the spreadsheet in its new window are immediately reflected in the version that appears inside the Word document, just as they are with embedding.

A linked document must be edited in a separate window

---

2   More correctly, in-place activation is prohibited by the user interface guidelines for compound documents. In-place activation certainly could be implemented for linked documents, but it would be confusing to users because a linked document might be shared by several different containers.

An Implementor's View

To a user, the OLE technology that creates compound documents blurs the distinction between different applications, allowing a more "document-centric" view. An implementor, however, remains well aware that the container and the server are distinct applications and that each has its own duties.

An Aside: Complexity vs. Tools

The available tools make it relatively easy to support compound documents

Before launching into a more detailed discussion of OLE compound documents, there's an important point to be made: it's not as hard as it looks. True, if every application developer were required to explicitly write the code for every method in every one of the necessary interfaces, it would indeed be hard. But the available tools make it much easier. Using Microsoft's Visual C++ and Microsoft Foundation Classes (MFC), for example, the programmer need only choose specific options that these tools provide to have basic support automatically included for various compound-document features. While it's useful and interesting to know what's really going on, the level of knowledge required of an implementor seems to shrink every day—the tools do a lot of the work.

Containers

Both containers and servers must support standard interfaces

The most common examples of containers are stand-alone applications that users can start and work with, such as Word and Excel. (Remember, however, that both of these examples are also capable of acting as servers.) Building a basic OLE container is not terribly difficult—it requires supporting only two interfaces, described in "Embedding Containers," on page 180. Because the interfaces are entirely generic, a container need never know what kinds of servers are providing linked or embedded data for its documents. The container simply supports the standard container interfaces, while the server supports the standard server interfaces. Neither is aware of what kind of application the other is. In our example, for instance, Word knows only that it's interacting with some server that follows OLE's rules for servers; it doesn't know, or care, that the server is Excel.

Servers

Servers aren't quite as straightforward as containers. They support more interfaces than containers do, and some of these interfaces are fairly complex. Servers also come in different configurations, and the creator of an OLE server must decide which one is right for that application.

The choices mirror the options for building a server for any COM object. One choice is to implement a server for compound documents as a local server, running as an entirely separate process. Excel takes this approach when it's acting as a server. In our example, Word and Excel run as two separate processes, yet they cooperate to present the user with one compound document.

A local server runs as a separate process

A second choice is to implement a server for compound documents as an in-process server. Here the server can't run on its own but is instead a DLL, dependent on being loaded into a container. This is absolutely the right choice for some kinds of servers. One common (and important) example of an in-process server that uses some parts of the technology for compound documents is an ActiveX control, discussed in the next chapter.

An in-process server runs as a DLL in the container

There's a complication, however: even a local OLE server, one like Excel that runs in a separate process, needs to maintain a representative in the container's process. To understand why, look back at Figure 8-3. When the user edits the Excel spreadsheet in a separate window, the changes can also be reflected in the view of the spreadsheet that's part of the compound document. Excel itself can reflect the changes in the window it controls, but Excel doesn't control the compound-document window. That window is owned by the container, Word, and only something in the container's process can write to that window. To show the user's edits in the compound-document window, then, Excel (or any local server) must tell its representative in the container about changes to its data and then let that representative actually reflect those changes on the screen.

A local server
relies on an in-
process handler
in the container

This representative, called an *in-process handler*, can take a couple of different forms. If the server is implemented entirely in a separate process, it can rely on the default handler, a standard implementation provided by Microsoft. Alternatively, if the server implements some of its functionality in a separate process and some in an in-process server linked to the container, it can provide its own handler, which is typically built on top of the default handler implementation. Whichever choice is made, a good deal of the work involved in making this Word/Excel example happen revolves around communication between a local server and its in-process surrogate.

Cooperation Between Containers and Servers

Suppose that a user opens our example compound document and edits the part of the document owned by Word. As Figure 8-4 illustrates, all user input—everything that the user types, all mouse clicks within this window, and so on—is sent directly to Word, and Word reflects the changes being made by writing directly to its part of the window. Although it's shown in the figure, it's possible that Excel isn't even running yet. (More on this later.)

Figure 8-4   *Editing the Word part of the compound document.*

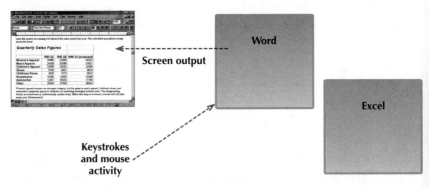

Now suppose that the user decides to edit the Excel spreadsheet in a separate window. The situation becomes a little more complicated, as shown in Figure 8-5. In this case, all of the user's input to the spreadsheet is sent directly to Excel. Excel carries out commands just as it would if the user were editing a stand-alone Excel spreadsheet rather than one that is embedded or linked. The challenge for Excel is to make the view of the spreadsheet within the compound document reflect the changes as they are made. Because Excel can't write directly to that view, it must instead inform its surrogate, the in-process handler loaded by Word, about the user's edits. The in-process handler can then work together with Word to ensure that those changes appear in the view of the spreadsheet seen by the user. (When the user chooses in-place activation rather than editing in a separate window, the situation illustrated in Figure 8-5 is only slightly different. See "In-Place Activation," page 189.)

Changes to a local server's data are sent to the in-process handler

Editing the Excel spreadsheet in its own window.   **Figure 8-5**

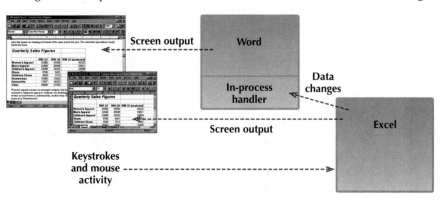

The dynamics of getting the right information to the right place at the right time and then correctly displaying this information to the user are the central problems to be solved in implementing compound documents. The remainder of this chapter is devoted to a closer look at how this is done, beginning with embedding.

The central problem is making the user's changes appear correctly everywhere

How Embedding Works

Embedding, in which the server's data is physically stored in the same file as the container's data, is typically accomplished using Structured Storage (discussed in Chapter 5). If we assume that the

Excel spreadsheet in our example is embedded in the Word document, the compound file would resemble the somewhat simplified picture shown in Figure 8-6.

Figure 8-6   *A simplified picture of a compound file containing a Word document with an embedded Excel spreadsheet.*

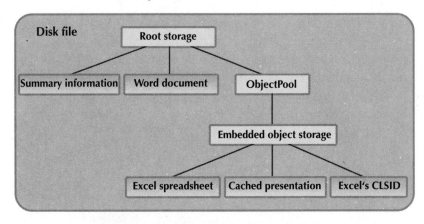

Word creates a storage called ObjectPool to store embedded objects

The text of the Word document is stored in a stream just below the compound file's root storage. The document summary information, described in Chapter 5, also has its own stream below the root. Immediately below the file's root storage is a storage called ObjectPool.[3] Because many objects can be embedded in a single file, embedding even one object causes Word to create an ObjectPool storage. Each object instance that's embedded in this Word file gets its own storage below ObjectPool (labeled *Embedded object storage* in the figure). This example includes only one embedded object, the Excel spreadsheet, so only a single storage is shown below ObjectPool.

An embedded document is stored beneath its own storage object

This single storage belongs to the embedded Excel object. Below this storage, one stream contains the data for the Excel spreadsheet, and another contains Excel's CLSID. (Without the CLSID, how would the container know which application to start to work with the embedded object's data?) Several more streams exist here,

---

3   This is how Word stores embedded objects, but there are no hard-and-fast rules for how this must be done. Many container applications do follow a similar model, however.

too, storing various other information. One of these, shown in Figure 8-6, contains a cached picture of the spreadsheet's presentation—that is, a picture of the way it last looked to the user. Caching, described next, plays an important part in how compound documents work.

Caching

When opening our example compound document, the user expects to see both the Word text and the information in the embedded Excel spreadsheet. Opening the document means that Word itself is active so it can display the Word text. But what about the Excel spreadsheet? Should Word start Excel, too, just to display the spreadsheet? If the user doesn't plan to modify the embedded spreadsheet just yet, having to wait for Excel to load seems like a lot to ask. And what if this Word document contained many embedded objects, created by different applications? Should they all be started, too, simply to display the information they contributed to the compound document?

With compound documents, the answer is commonly no. When the user starts the container application, it usually loads alone. No servers are loaded until the user activates an embedded or linked document by, for instance, double-clicking on it.[4] But something must be loaded to fill the space in the container's window previously occupied by the embedded or linked document. Fortunately, the server application has prepared for this eventuality by storing the document's presentation, a snapshot of how it most recently appeared to the user, and it's this snapshot that is loaded when the compound document is opened. As shown in Figure 8-6, this cached presentation is stored in its own stream in the compound document's file. The embedded data itself is accessed and its application started only when the user decides to modify this data.

A container can load a cached picture of an embedded or linked document's presentation

---

4   A server can indicate that it always wants to be loaded immediately, but applications, such as Excel, don't do this. ActiveX controls, however, do commonly ask to be loaded right away; see Chapter 9.

A data cache manages presentations

Every server for a compound document must be able to store a presentation in a cache, and every container needs a way to request that the cache's data be displayed. These tasks are accomplished by relying on a *data cache object,* which knows how to write a presentation to a cache, how to retrieve it, and how to perform a few more useful actions as well. A cache can even contain several versions of an object's presentation—for instance, one version for display on the screen along with one for each of several printers.

Because a data cache object writes directly to the container's window, it must be implemented in either an in-process server or an in-process handler; it can't be part of a local server like Excel. In fact, the default handler described earlier is built on a standard implementation of a data cache object, explored in more detail later in this chapter ("Using a data cache object," page 182).

Embedding Containers

A container implements one client site object for each embedded document

To support embedding, a container must implement one *client site object* for each embedded document. As shown in Figure 8-7, this relatively simple object supports only two interfaces (plus the omnipresent IUnknown, of course, which isn't shown). Using the methods in these interfaces, a server for an embedded document can communicate with an embedding container.

Figure 8-7   *A client site object in a container.*

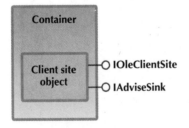

The first interface, IOleClientSite, allows a server to make various requests of its container. For example, when a server needs to make its presentation visible to the user, it calls IOleClient-Site::ShowObject, and the container ensures that the server's display to the user isn't scrolled out of view or otherwise obscured.

A server makes requests of its container primarily through methods in IOleClientSite

The second interface supported by the container's client site object is a familiar one: IAdviseSink. Chapter 7 described using one of its methods, OnDataChange, to inform an object that pertinent data has changed. (See "Notifications," page 160.) Servers can use this method to do exactly this, and they also rely on other methods in this interface to let their containers know what's going on in their world. For example, an in-process server or an in-process handler invokes IAdviseSink::OnViewChange when the server's data has changed and it needs to redraw its screen image. A server can't autonomously redraw its presentation, so a container responds to this method by asking the server to redraw itself. (To do this, the container calls the IViewObject2-::Draw method, discussed in the following section.)

A server informs its container of interesting events through IAdviseSink

As explained later in this chapter (see "Communicating with a local server," page 185), an in-process handler within the container also implements IAdviseSink. The local server uses the methods in the IAdviseSink interface to inform the handler, and the data cache object in the handler, of important occurrences.

Embedding Servers

Describing an embedding server is more complicated than describing an embedding container. An embedding server must implement a *content object*, which acts as the server-side analog of the container's client site object. As seen by a container, an embedding server presents one content object for each embedded document, an object that supports all the interfaces shown in Figure 8-8 on the following page.

Embedding servers must support more interfaces than embedding containers do

Figure 8-8   *A container's view of a content object in a server.*

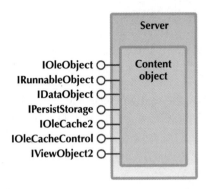

Both a local server and an in-process handler must implement specific interfaces

In reality, though, what the container sees as a single object is typically implemented using several different objects. Furthermore, all of those objects might be running in the same process as the container (for an in-process server), or they might be split between an in-process handler and a local server process. With Excel, for example, support for some of these interfaces is split between the in-process handler and the local server. (Recall that the in-process handler is required because a local server like Excel can't write directly to its container's window.) Figure 8-9 shows a more complete picture of a typical implementation using a local server.[5] As the following sections explain, each object in the figure and each interface has a role to play in providing the user with the perception of a seamless compound document.

An in-process handler or server is typically implemented using a data cache object

Using a data cache object   Although a container sees the content object as implementing all the interfaces shown in Figure 8-8, many of these interfaces are in fact typically supplied by another object. This object is one you've already heard about: a data cache object, responsible for storing and retrieving a cached version of an object's presentation. As Figure 8-9 shows, every data cache object implements several interfaces, two of which, IPersistStorage and IDataObject, are familiar from earlier chapters

---

5   Although it's not shown in the figure, both the in-process handler and the local server also implement a class factory object supporting IClassFactory.

in this book. Through its IDataObject interface, the data cache object's client (the container) can send data to and retrieve data from the cache. Via the IPersistStorage interface, the client can pass the data cache object a pointer to the storage used to store and load its cached presentations.

A typical split between an in-process handler and a local server.   ***Figure 8-9***

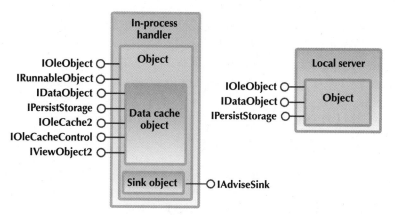

A data cache object also implements the IOleCache2 interface, which the container uses to indicate which presentations should be cached. And, to allow interactions with a local server (if one exists), the data cache object implements IOleCacheControl. Using this interface, a client of the data cache object is able to indirectly cause it to establish and tear down connections with a local server.

Finally, every data cache object implements an interface called IViewObject2. This interface includes several methods, but its Draw method stands out as most useful. When a client wants a data cache object to show an image such as a cached presentation on the screen, it calls IViewObject2::Draw. The method's parameters indicate where on the screen the presentation should be drawn, allowing the container to control where the embedded object is displayed to the user. For instance, when a user loads our example compound document, the initial image of the Excel spreadsheet that the user sees isn't really put there by Excel.

A container calls IViewObject2::Draw to ask a server to display an image

Instead, Word calls the Draw method in the data cache object's IViewObject2 interface. It's this object that actually writes the cached Excel data to the screen.

Data cache objects can do much of what any embedding server needs to do. An in-process embedding server must present several interfaces directly to its container, and since a data cache object already implements some of them, it's typically reused (via containment and aggregation as described in Chapter 2) to provide at least part of what's needed. Of course, an in-process server is free to reimplement some or all of the interfaces and methods provided by the data cache object, but it can use at least some of them as they are. (This means that the arrangement shown in Figure 8-9 can vary because interfaces such as IPersistStorage and IViewObject2 might have some of their methods implemented by the outer object, with the remainder delegated to the data cache object.)

The content object itself must present IRunnableObject and IOleObject to the container

The IOleObject interface and verbs Every content object must present two additional interfaces to its container, and there's no way to push these off onto the data cache object. The IRunnableObject interface allows a content object to know when to enter the running state. (Content objects can exist in a range of states. In the running state, the object's code, including the local server if one exists, is available.) Every content object must also implement the IOleObject interface. This complex interface lets a container ask a content object to perform many different actions. Using IOleObject::SetClientSite, for example, the container can pass the content object a pointer to the container's corresponding IOleClientSite interface. Or a container can use IOleObject::DoVerb to ask the content object to execute a *verb*.

A container can ask a server to perform an action by sending it a verb

Verbs are the way a container tells a server to perform an action. To understand how verbs work, think again about our example: an Excel spreadsheet embedded in a Word document. In this scenario, Excel offers a verb called *Open* to its container (Word). When the user clicks the right mouse button over the spreadsheet part of the compound document, a pop-up menu appears. If the user chooses Open Worksheet from this menu, Word invokes IOleObject::DoVerb on the content object for the spreadsheet. As a parameter to this method, it passes the verb *Open*. When it receives this verb, Excel becomes active and lets the user begin editing the embedded spreadsheet in a separate window.

Excel also supports the *Edit* verb. The user can cause Word to send this verb to Excel either by choosing it from the pop-up menu or by double-clicking on the spreadsheet part of the compound document. When it receives the *Edit* verb, Excel makes itself ready to edit the embedded spreadsheet in place. Other kinds of servers can support other kinds of verbs. The Windows sound recorder, for example, supports verbs called *Play* and *Edit*, which let a user listen to and modify an embedded sound clip.

The verbs a server supports depend on what functions that server provides

Communicating with a local server If embedding is implemented entirely by an in-process server, the preceding discussion pretty much sums up the interfaces that server must support. But if a local server is involved, as is the case with Excel, the in-process handler must provide all the interfaces described so far, and it must also have a way to communicate with the local server. How else could requests the container makes using IOleObject::DoVerb find their way to the local server? And how could changes made by the user when the local server is active be reflected back to the in-process handler and then to the screen?

The local server's interfaces allow an in-process handler to communicate with it

As shown in Figure 8-9, these problems are solved by having the local server implement three of the interfaces supported by the in-process handler and the in-process handler implement one more, IAdviseSink. By using the methods in these interfaces, the in-process handler can pass requests it receives to the local server for processing, and the local server can inform its in-process representative of changes in its data.

As you might expect, requests that the container makes via methods in the handler's implementation of these interfaces can sometimes be passed on by the handler to the corresponding method in the local server's interface. When a container invokes

IOleObject::DoVerb, for example, it actually invokes the method implemented by the in-process handler. This method eventually delegates the call, invoking the same method in the local server's implementation of this interface and passing along the verb it received from the container.

Embedding, especially when a local server such as Excel is involved, can get a little complex. To get a sense of how all this works, it's best to walk through an example.

An Embedding Scenario

This scenario presents an example of creating and using an embedded document with a container, an in-process handler, and a local server. Remember that although the container sees only a single content object for each embedded object, the reality, especially with a local server, is more complicated. Since this example assumes a local server, it will help to keep in mind Figure 8-9 on page 183.

A document can be embedded using Word's Paste Special command

Imagine that a user opens an existing Word document and then starts Excel and creates a new spreadsheet. To embed the spreadsheet in the Word document, the user copies it to the clipboard, returns to Word, and chooses the Paste Special command from Word's Edit menu. In the Paste Special dialog box, the user chooses to insert the spreadsheet as an embedded Excel object.

Word stores the embedded Excel information in a compound file

When this happens, Word creates the appropriate storage in the compound file that contains the existing Word data. As shown earlier in Figure 8-6, it stores the spreadsheet's data, its CLSID, and a cached snapshot of how it looks on the screen in streams below a storage that is set aside for this embedded object. Word doesn't know that it's working with Excel data—Word sees Excel simply as a server that supports embedding.

Suppose that the user now closes Excel, saves the compound document, and exits Word. Returning the next day, the user again starts Word and opens the compound document. When Word loads the document, it notices the storage containing the Excel spreadsheet. Rather than starting Excel, however, Word loads an in-process handler that's built on top of a data cache object. Word uses the data cache object's IPersistStorage interface to pass it a pointer to the storage containing the embedded document's cached presentation, and the data cache object loads that information from the disk. Word then calls IViewObject2::Draw on the data cache object, telling it where to draw, and the data cache object draws the cached Excel presentation to the screen. Word itself fills in the rest of the compound document.

When Word is started again, it loads only the embedded document's cached presentation

As long as the user edits only the Word part of this document, nothing else changes—Word performs its usual functions. But when the user decides to edit the embedded Excel spreadsheet, Word must allow this to happen. To edit the spreadsheet in a separate window, the user right-clicks on the spreadsheet in the compound document and chooses Open Worksheet from the pop-up menu. This causes Word to invoke IOleObject::DoVerb, passing the *Open* verb as a parameter. But Word invokes this method on the implementation of IOleObject provided by the in-process handler, not the one provided by the local server, that is, Excel. (Because Excel isn't running yet, there's no way Word can invoke one of its methods.)

Excel isn't started until the user tries to edit the embedded document

The in-process handler's implementation of the IOleObject::DoVerb method first starts the local server (Excel) by calling CoCreateInstance with Excel's CLSID, retrieved from a stream below this Excel object's storage in the compound file. On the call to CoCreateInstance, the handler indicates that the first interface pointer it wants on the newly created object is to IPersistStorage. Next, the in-process handler uses the local server's IPersistStorage interface to pass in a pointer to the correct storage for this embedded object in the compound file. The local server—Excel—then loads the embedded object's data from the correct stream in this storage. Once Excel is running and initialized, the in-process handler calls DoVerb in Excel's implementation of the IOleObject interface, passing along the *Open* verb it received from the container. Excel now becomes active, opening a new window that contains the embedded spreadsheet data, which the user can now

When necessary, the in-process handler starts and initializes Excel, the local server

happily edit. Keystrokes and mouse clicks from the user now go directly to Excel, completely bypassing Word, and Excel reflects the results of that input in the spreadsheet visible in the newly created Excel window.

The user's changes are reflected back to the container through IAdviseSink

But Excel must somehow make the compound document's spreadsheet reflect the user's input, too. Excel can't write directly to that area because Word owns that window. Instead, Excel passes the user's changes to the in-process handler, which implements the IAdviseSink interface for this purpose.

The in-process handler writes those changes to the screen

To do this, however, the local server needs a pointer to IAdviseSink, which it gets as described in Chapter 7: the handler passes the pointer as a parameter on a call it makes to the local server's IDataObject::DAdvise method.[6] Given the pointer to IAdviseSink, Excel can let it know about changes the user makes to the spreadsheet by invoking the handler's IAdviseSink::OnDataChange method, passing it the changed data. The in-process handler examines this data and decides whether the changes affect what the user is seeing on the screen. If they do, the handler calls IAdviseSink::OnViewChange in the container's client site object. (The handler obtained a pointer to this interface from the container earlier via a call to the SetAdvise method in the server's IViewObject2 interface.) The container responds to this call to OnViewChange by calling IViewObject2::Draw in the in-process handler, and this method draws the new view directly on the screen in the correct location.

This entire process is illustrated in Figure 8-10. Keep in mind that for this example the container is Word, the in-process handler is the default handler provided as a standard part of the OLE technology (specifically as a DLL loaded by Word), and the local server is Excel.

---

6   The more general mechanism defined by Connectable Objects, also described in Chapter 7, isn't used because it hadn't been invented when the OLE compound documents technology was defined.

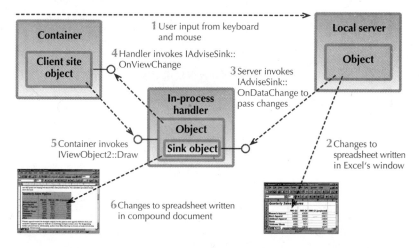

When the user again clicks on the Word part of the document, Excel becomes inactive (although the local server continues to run), and Word regains control. Making all this happen required significant work on the part of the developers of both applications. To the user, however, the process was straightforward and natural—everything behaved as expected.

In-Place Activation

A major goal of compound documents is to present users with a "document-centric" view of computing, allowing them to focus more on their data and less on the software necessary to manipulate that data. In-place activation, also called visual editing, is an important step toward achieving that goal.

In-place activation is allowed only for embedded objects. To make it work, both container and server must implement a few extra interfaces, whose methods focus on negotiating the niceties of the combined user interface. For example, if an embedded Excel spreadsheet is activated within a Word document (as illustrated in Figure 8-2), who owns the menu bar? If the user opens the Help menu, to which application does it refer? Answering questions such as these is central to making in-place activation work correctly.

In-place activation requires the container and the server to implement additional interfaces

To allow in-place activation, a container's client site object must support IOleIn-PlaceSite

In-place active containers As shown in Figure 8-11, a container offers several interfaces that specifically support in-place active objects. As always, of course, a container must implement a client site object, which supports the IOleClientSite and IAdviseSink interfaces, for each embedded object. To make in-place activation work, this client site object must also support IOleInPlaceSite. An embedded object uses the methods in this interface for such tasks as asking the container for permission to activate itself in place, informing the container that in-place activation is happening, and letting the container know that the in-place active object has been deactivated.

Figure 8-11

Interfaces implemented by a container that supports in-place activation.

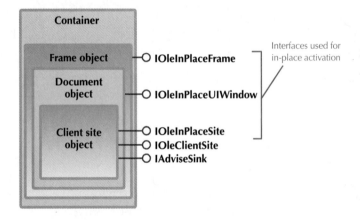

When an embedded object is activated in place, the user can edit it right where it is. In the example shown in Figure 8-2, for instance, the embedded Excel spreadsheet has the row and column headings the user expects. But what about the compound document's menu bar? Clearly, when the user looks for online help or needs to use an Excel editing feature, the Help and Edit menus should contain Excel commands. But is this true for all menus?

During in-place activation, the container and the server share the menu bar

The answer is no. Excel does not take total control here. When an embedded object is activated in place, some parts of the menu are still owned by the container. The commands on the File menu, for instance, such as Save and Print, affect the entire document, so it makes sense that these should still belong to Word (the container). Similarly, the Window menu allows the user to select one of several currently loaded Word documents, so it too must remain under the container's control. Most of the other menus, however, are controlled by Excel.

To make this work, the container and the server must be able to negotiate about the contents of the combined menu bar. To allow this, the container implements the IOleInPlaceFrame interface. While each client site object in the container must support IOle-InPlaceSite, IOleInPlaceFrame is supported by a single frame object within the container, as illustrated in Figure 8-11.

Methods in IOle-InPlaceFrame let the container and the server nego-tiate about the menu bar

If a container allows several documents to be open at once, each in its own window, each document might appear as an object to a server. In this case, each of these objects must support the IOleInPlaceUIWindow interface. The in-place active object uses the methods in this interface to negotiate still more specific details about the user interface, such as the location of the active object's toolbar in a document's window. In practice, this is rarely required, and so IOleInPlaceUIWindow is implemented only occasionally.

The methods in IOleInPlaceUI-Window allow further negotiation

In-place active servers As described earlier, an embedding server always presents the image of a single content object to a container. In reality, this content object might be constructed from several objects that might run in different processes, but the container is oblivious to this. Instead, it sees a single set of interfaces for the embedded object.

Adding support for in-place activation doesn't change this view. As shown in Figure 8-12 on the following page, the server needs to add only two interfaces. The first, IOleInPlaceObject, allows the container to perform such actions as telling the in-place active object how much of its window is visible or deactivating an in-place active object. (Like any embedded object, an in-place object is activated by the container's call to IOleObject::DoVerb.)

An in-place active server must support IOleInPlaceObject and IOleInPlace-ActiveObject

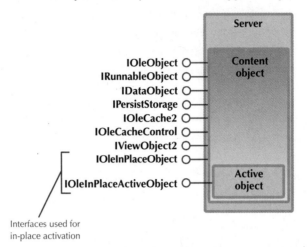

IOleObject

IRunnableObject

IDataObject

IPersistStorage

IOleCache2

IOleCacheControl

IViewObject2

IOleInPlaceObject

IOleInPlaceActiveObject

Server

Content object

Active object

Interfaces used for
in-place activation

A distinct object is created within the content object when a document is in-place active

The second additional interface is actually implemented by a distinct object within the content object, which is called (reasonably enough) an *active object*. This object exists only while the content object is in-place active, and it supports the IOleInPlace-ActiveObject interface. Using the methods in this interface, a container can inform the active object when its window becomes active, when its border has been resized, and more.

An in-place activation scenario Like many problems encountered in working with a graphical user interface, making in-place activation work is not especially simple. It is, however, an essential feature for providing users with a "document-centric" view. It's also essential for creating the powerful software components known as ActiveX controls, which are the subject of the next chapter. Once again, a simple scenario is the best way to make the process clear.

For in-place activation, Excel is activated with the *Edit* verb rather than with *Open*

Imagine that the user from our previous scenario reopens the compound document, a Word file with an embedded Excel spreadsheet. To edit the spreadsheet in place rather than in a separate window, the user either double-clicks on the embedded spreadsheet or right-clicks on it and chooses Edit Worksheet from the pop-up menu. Either action ultimately causes Word to invoke IOleObject::DoVerb, just as in the previous scenario. This time, however, Word passes in the verb *Edit* rather than *Open*. As before, Word invokes IOleObject::DoVerb on the implementation of IOleObject provided by the in-process handler, which starts and initializes Excel and then invokes the local server's IOleObject::DoVerb method, passing along the *Edit* verb.

Receiving the *Edit* verb tells Excel that it needs to activate itself in place (rather than in a separate window). It first ensures that the container in which it's being activated supports in-place activation, by using QueryInterface to request a pointer to an IOleInPlaceSite interface on the container. If this request succeeds, as it will if the container is Word, Excel knows that it's OK to activate in place.

Excel verifies that its container supports in-place activation

In-place activation generally involves three tasks: figuring out what the combined menu bar should look like, creating the appropriate toolbars and other window elements for the in-place active object, and actually creating the window in which the embedded document will be edited. The first two tasks are accomplished using various methods in the interfaces described earlier, those supported by the container and server for in-place activation. Creation of the editing window is a separate process, however, and it's at the heart of in-place activation.

In the previous scenario, the user edited the embedded spreadsheet in an ordinary Excel window, a window that could be positioned anywhere on the screen. But why not constrain this editing window to appear exactly where the compound document's spreadsheet appears on the screen so that the user can view it in the context of the Word document? And why not make the editing window simpler so that it looks more natural to the user?

This is what in-place activation does. As before, Excel creates a new window in which the user can edit the embedded spreadsheet. But this window is much simpler, containing only the spreadsheet's image and row/column labels. Furthermore, Excel positions this window directly over the image of the spreadsheet

Excel creates a new window directly over the spreadsheet's image in the compound document

in the compound document. The original spreadsheet image is hidden by this new window, giving the user the illusion that the embedded spreadsheet has sprung to life.

The user's changes appear in Excel's window and are also sent to the in-process handler

The user's keystrokes and mouse clicks now go directly to this new Excel window, and Excel reflects the results of that input in the new window. Because this window sits on top of the compound document's spreadsheet image, all of the changes appear just where the user expects them. And, as in the earlier scenario, Excel continues to inform the in-process handler about any changes the user makes.

The handler in turn dutifully issues IAdviseSink::OnViewChange notifications to Word. But because Word is aware that Excel has become in-place active, it also knows that the spreadsheet image it's presenting is hidden from view. Accordingly, Word ignores the handler's OnViewChange notifications—why bother repainting its spreadsheet image when the user can't see it anyway?

The in-process handler repaints the screen only when Excel is no longer in-place active

When the user finishes editing the spreadsheet and clicks on the Word document, Excel stops being in-place active and removes its covering window. Only then does Word call IViewObject2::Draw. The handler now repaints the spreadsheet's image, complete with the correct data, back on the screen. Everything seems simple and natural to the user, who remains unaware of the machinations hidden below.

How Linking Works

Linking is in many ways just an extension of embedding

Once you understand how embedding works, linking is easy. To add support for linking, a container that already supports embedding needs no new interfaces (although some existing method implementations might change). More work is required of servers, as usual, but even servers need to support only a handful of new interfaces. In linking, the fundamental mechanisms for getting data to and from the user are the same as in embedding. The main differences lie in where the document's data is stored and how the object that contains the data is started.

When a document is embedded, its contents are stored in its container's compound file. In contrast, when a document is linked, only a reference to its contents is stored in the container's compound file. As Chapter 6 explained, this reference is really the persistent data for a moniker. Figure 8-13 presents a simplified picture of a compound file for a Word document containing a link to an Excel spreadsheet.

Linked documents store only the data for a moniker in the container's file

A simplified picture of a compound file containing a Word document with a link to an Excel spreadsheet.

Figure 8-13

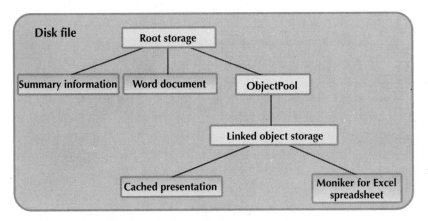

It's useful to contrast Figure 8-13 with Figure 8-6 (page 178), which pictured a compound file with an embedded spreadsheet. In Figure 8-13, the document's data is not stored below the storage for the link. The stream that held an embedded document's CLSID in Figure 8-6 is gone, too. With an embedded document, the container passed this CLSID to CoCreateInstance to instantiate an instance of the correct class of object. In the previous embedding example, for instance, Word used this information to start Excel and then handed Excel a pointer to its embedded storage via IPersistStorage. With a linked document, however, the moniker takes care of all this—passing the CLSID and information about the storage is no longer the container's concern.

Unlike for an embedded document, the data and CLSID for a linked document are not stored in the container's file

The whole idea of linking in compound documents is intimately bound up with monikers. This shouldn't be surprising—a link is really a reference to a specific object instance, and the way

COM-based technologies provide this kind of reference is with a moniker. Compound documents implement links using composite monikers, file monikers, and item monikers, described in Chapter 6.

A container relies on the moniker to start and initialize the linked object

If the moniker data shown in Figure 8-13 contained a reference to a linked Excel spreadsheet, what's actually stored in that stream might look like this:

```
C:\Q2SALES.XLS!Sheet1!R1C1:R10C6
```

This is the persistent data for the moniker, and it identifies the file that contains the linked spreadsheet (and indicates implicitly that this is an Excel spreadsheet), the page of the spreadsheet that contains the linked data, and the exact range of rows and columns the user has selected. When the container needs to launch the application for this link, it creates a moniker containing this data that does the job on the container's behalf. Without monikers or something like them, linking wouldn't be possible.

Linking Containers

Linking containers support the same interfaces as embedding containers

A linking container doesn't need to support any extra interfaces beyond those required of an embedding container. Creating a linking container does require more work on the part of the implementor, however, because the container must know how to use the methods in the new interfaces that linking servers must support. Still, adding support for linking to an existing embedding container is not a big job.

Linking Servers

Linking servers must support a few additional interfaces

As always, servers bear more of the burden, and they must implement a few new interfaces to support linking. Unlike embedding, however, where a server could be either implemented entirely in-process or split between an in-process handler and a local server, linking virtually always uses the second option. The in-process handler typically implements all the interfaces required for embedding plus one more, as shown in Figure 8-14.[7]

Interfaces implemented by an in-process handler for linking.

Figure 8-14

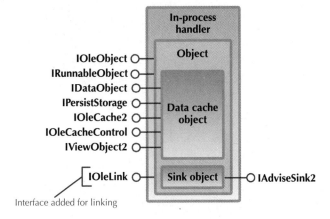

A container uses the new interface, IOleLink, to work with linked objects. Three of IOleLink's more interesting methods are described here:

Containers use IOleLink to start linked objects and to update link data

- The **BindToSource** method causes the in-process handler to instantiate the moniker for this link and then invoke its IMoniker::BindToObject method. The result is a running object containing the data for this link.

- The **SetUpdateOptions** method allows the client to choose whether links will be updated automatically whenever the object's data changes or updated only when the user manually requests it.

- The **Update** method causes the presentation of the linked object's data seen by the user (that is, its image in the compound document) to be updated if the manual update option just described has been chosen.

---

7 As Figure 8-14 shows, an in-process handler that supports linking implements IAdviseSink2 rather than IAdviseSink. This interface inherits from IAdviseSink and adds the function OnLinkSrcChanged. Linking servers use this method to inform their containers that the source of a link has been modified.

Linking to an
embedded ob-
ject is allowed

A server that supports linking to an object that's embedded in yet
another object must also support the IExternalConnection interface (not shown in Figure 8-14). For instance, a user who embeds
an Excel spreadsheet in a Word document might then create a
second Word document and decide to create a link in it to the
spreadsheet embedded in the first Word document. The methods
in IExternalConnection help to control some of the more complicated aspects of this situation. This interface can be implemented
either by a local server or, if no local server exists, by an in-
process server.

Like its affiliated in-process handler, a local embedding server
must implement a few new interfaces in order to add support for
linking. As it does for embedding, the local server must support
IOleObject and IDataObject, and it must also support the interfaces that allow it to be initialized through monikers. What these
interfaces are depends on what style of linking the server supports. If the local server allows linking only to a complete file, it
needs to offer support only for file monikers. Doing this requires
nothing more than supporting IPersistFile alongside IOleObject
and IDataObject, as shown in Figure 8-15.

Figure 8-15   *Interfaces supported by a local server that supports linking only to a
complete file.*

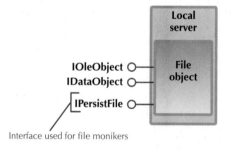

Interface used for file monikers

More likely, though, a link can consist of a composite moniker
built from file and item monikers. A link to an Excel spreadsheet,
for instance, typically uses a file moniker together with item
monikers to identify a particular file, a sheet in that file, and a
range of cells in that sheet. All of this identifies what's sometimes
called a *pseudo-object*, whose data consists of the values in the

specified cell range. (A pseudo-object is a legitimate COM object, but it doesn't have a CLSID and so can exist only as part of some larger entity.) To allow this kind of link, the local server must also support IOleItemContainer, and each pseudo-object must support IOleObject and IDataObject as shown in Figure 8-16. (For a more complete example of this second kind of moniker binding using Excel, refer to Chapter 6.)

Interfaces supported by a local server that supports linking to a pseudo-object.

Figure 8-16

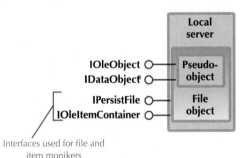

Interfaces used for file and item monikers

One interface that was important for embedding is missing from both Figures 8-15 and 8-16: IPersistStorage. If this local server supports both linking and embedding, it will certainly implement IPersistStorage—how else could its container tell it to load embedded data from the container's compound file? But if the local server supports linking only, it isn't required to support this interface. Instead, the information it receives during the process of moniker binding—a filename and perhaps more—is sufficient to let the server locate and load its persistent data. Because a client of the local server doesn't need to invoke a method in IPersistStorage to initialize the linked object, the object doesn't need to support this interface.

A linking local server need not support IPersistStorage

A Linking Scenario

What happens when a user activates and edits a linked document is much like what happens with an embedded document edited in its own window. The biggest difference is in how the linked object is instantiated and initialized.

A link can be
created using
Word's Paste
Special
command

Imagine that our user opens a Word document and then starts
Excel, creates a spreadsheet, and copies it to the clipboard. Returning to Word, the user chooses the Paste Special command
from Word's Edit menu and decides to insert the spreadsheet as
a linked rather than an embedded Excel object. Let's assume that
the user also sets this link to be updated manually rather than
automatically so that changes to the linked data are shown only
at the user's request.

The persistent
data for a
moniker is
stored in the
Word file

As it does for an embedded object, Word creates the appropriate
storages in its compound file. This time, however, rather than
storing the actual data, Word simply stores the persistent data for
the moniker, data that was passed to it via the clipboard. The
Excel document's data remains in its own separate file.

For a manually
updated link, a
cached Excel
presentation is
loaded

Suppose that the user saves everything and then closes Excel and
Word. The next time the user starts Word and loads this compound document, what happens depends on the options that
were selected for this link. With the manual updating option, as in
this example, the process initially is the same as for an embedded
document: Word reads its document and then loads an in-process
handler and a cached presentation for the linked Excel document.
The local server code for the linked document (that is, Excel itself)
isn't loaded until the user decides to edit the spreadsheet or
specifically requests that the link be updated.

For an automa-
tically updated
link, Excel itself
can be loaded

With automatic updating, the process is a little different. A cached
presentation for a link maintains a timestamp indicating when it
was created. When the user opens the compound file, this timestamp is compared to the last modification time of the linked file.
If the cached version is newer—and thus contains the most recent
presentation—there's no need to start the application. If the
cached version is older, however, Excel must be started and initialized with the real data from the linked file. The spreadsheet
image the user sees in the compound document is then produced
on the spot from data supplied by Excel rather than being read
from a cache. Throughout this process, however, Excel never
becomes visible.

With an automatically updated link, Excel might or might not be started when the compound document is loaded. With a manually updated link, Excel definitely isn't started until it's needed. In either case, the moniker whose persistent data is stored in Word's compound file is used to instantiate and initialize Excel.

Assuming a manually updated link, let's suppose that our user double-clicks on the linked spreadsheet to start Excel and begin editing the spreadsheet. The double-click causes Word to invoke IOleObject::DoVerb, passing it the *Edit* verb, just as in the embedding scenario. Word invokes this method on the implementation of IOleObject provided by the in-process handler—again, just as it does for an embedded object. This time, however, the in-process handler's implementation of the IOleObject::DoVerb method winds up instantiating the composite moniker for the linked Excel object. (Recall that with an embedded object this method was itself responsible for starting and initializing Excel.) It then invokes the moniker's IMoniker::BindToObject method, requesting a pointer to the IOleObject interface of the object named by this moniker (Excel). The moniker starts and initializes the object as described in Chapter 6 and then returns the requested pointer.

The user can initiate the editing of linked and embedded documents in the same way

Once the local server is running and initialized, the in-process handler calls DoVerb in Excel's implementation of the IOleObject interface, and, as it does with an embedded object, it passes in the *Edit* verb it received from the container. Excel is now active, and the user can edit the linked spreadsheet, with keystrokes and mouse clicks sent straight to Excel.

According to the rules of OLE, linked objects can't be edited in place, so Excel displays the spreadsheet in a separate window. If this is an automatically updated link, the user's changes will be reflected in the spreadsheet's presentation within the Word document. This happens through the same process illustrated earlier in Figure 8-10 on page 189 for an embedded document edited in a separate window rather than in place. As shown in Figure 8-10, the local server notifies the in-process handler of data changes,

The user's changes are reflected as with an embedded document the handler notifies the container, and the container calls the handler's IViewObject2::Draw method to make those changes visible to the user.

Although they're started differently, linked objects have a great deal in common with embedded objects. One key difference to a user, though, is that linked objects don't support in-place activation, an option that is available to embedded objects.

The mechanisms underlying linking and embedding aren't especially simple to understand. Thanks to the available tools, however, building applications that support these features needn't be terribly difficult, since most of the messy details are hidden. And best of all, the user sees only a natural, easy-to-use interface, which is, of course, the point of everything described in this chapter.

Chapter Nine

ActiveX Controls

One of the main goals of COM is to allow the creation of component software, applications that are assembled by wiring together prebuilt parts. It's entirely possible to build effective components using only the conventions defined by COM itself. All that's required is to define interfaces that are appropriate for the component's purpose and then implement them. For example, a text tools component like the one used as an example earlier in this book might support only the interfaces ISpellChecker and IThesaurus (and IUnknown, of course). A component like this could be used by word processors and other applications that work with text.

Most really useful components aren't this simple, however. Providing a few basic methods that their clients can invoke just isn't enough. Instead, components need to allow for a more powerful set of interactions with their clients. For example, why should the text tools component mentioned above be forced to rely on its client to present a user interface for it—say, a dialog box that allows the user to begin spell checking a document? Why not define a standard way for the component to display its own user interface? Components might also need a mechanism to send events to their clients or to let a client examine or modify a component's properties (for instance, which dictionary should be used to look up words). Given that many components are likely to have similar requirements for how they interact with their clients, it makes sense to define a common way to meet those requirements.

It's useful to define standards for components

Such standards also make life much easier for software that uses the components. Rather than having to understand the idiosyncrasies of many different components, that software can support one set of standards followed by all components.

An ActiveX control is a software component that performs common tasks in standard ways

Defining standards for software components is what the specification for *ActiveX Controls* does. By specifying a standard set of interfaces that COM objects can support to carry out particular actions, the ActiveX Controls specification provides a blueprint for building powerful components. And because components need a way to effectively interact with the code that uses them, the ActiveX Controls specification also defines rules for creating *control containers*. A control container is client software that knows how to use an ActiveX control.

Many kinds of control containers are available

Microsoft Visual Basic is a frequent choice for a control container, but many other languages and applications can also play this role. Today, for instance, web browsers such as Microsoft's Internet Explorer are important examples of control containers. With a browser as a container, ActiveX controls can be stored on the browser's system and executed when needed. This allows the creation of web pages with active content, pages that interact with the user. The code for a control can even be stored on a web server and then be downloaded and executed as needed. While the emphasis in this chapter is on using ActiveX controls with a container such as Visual Basic, using controls with web browsers is an important topic as well and is examined in more detail in Chapter 11.

The Evolution of ActiveX Controls

VBXs are an earlier component technology created for Visual Basic

The idea of reusable binary components that provide features to their clients in standard ways didn't originate with COM. Instead, the path that led to ActiveX Controls began with *Visual Basic Extensions*, or VBXs. VBXs are software components that offer many of the same features as ActiveX controls but are designed to work specifically with Visual Basic. An active market in VBXs exists today, with third parties supplying all kinds of services using this software paradigm.

VBXs have several limitations, however, not the least of which is that they are narrowly focused on working with Visual Basic. Creating a more general component mechanism, especially one built using the fundamental abstractions provided by COM, made good sense. The original *OLE Controls* specification met this need. This specification was fairly rigid, requiring a COM object to implement a large set of interfaces to qualify as an OLE control. Under this original definition, every control was able to display its own user interface, send events to a control container, let a container set its properties, and more. But for many kinds of components, this was overkill. Even if part of the definition wasn't relevant to a particular component—if, for example, the component didn't need a user interface—it still had to implement all the required interfaces just to fulfill the mandates of the specification.

VBXs were superseded by OLE controls

This potential for code bloat became an especially noticeable problem once it became clear that components could be loaded from a web server. Downloading from a web server often means downloading over a slow Internet connection. Requiring a control to implement anything at all extraneous to its function can result in longer download times and frustrated users.

To address this problem, the current version of the specification has become much more relaxed. Qualifying as a control now requires only support for IUnknown and the ability to self-register, which means that the control is able to create its own entries in the system registry when requested to do so (for instance, when the control is downloaded from the Internet). If a component supports any of the standard services defined by the specification, however, such as providing a user interface or sending events, it must do so as defined in the specification (and as described in this chapter). At about the same time that Microsoft was amending the definition of OLE Controls to work more smoothly with the Internet, the company also began using the *ActiveX* designation to signify a technology with connections to the Internet or the World Wide Web. To reflect these new capabilities, the OLE Controls technology was renamed *ActiveX Controls*.

OLE controls are now called ActiveX controls

What then is the difference today between an ActiveX control and an ordinary COM object? The answer is simple: not much. Since supporting IUnknown is all that's required to qualify as a COM object, and since that and self-registration are all that's required to qualify as an ActiveX control, the distinction is a little ephemeral. In fact, it's likely that over time the distinction will completely disappear.

This chapter examines ActiveX controls from several perspectives, describes how they are used, and explains how they work. One terminology note before proceeding: for the remainder of this chapter, the word *control* refers to an ActiveX control unless otherwise specified.

Component Categories

As originally defined, an OLE control was required to support a large number of interfaces, including IDispatch, the interfaces defined for OLE embedding and in-place activation, and many more. To advertise this broad support, a control could place the keyword *Control* in the registry. Although these heavy requirements meant that controls tended to be fairly large, they also allowed control containers to safely make certain assumptions. If a software component claimed to be an OLE control, for instance, the container could count on that component supporting the interfaces required for embedding, in-place activation, and all the rest.

Today the requirements for what is now called an ActiveX control have been relaxed, but a container still needs a way to know the capabilities of a component it plans to use. It's pointless for a container to load a control that it can't use, and more detail than a gross generalization like *Control* is necessary. Although it might be possible to define a larger set of terms that identify various feature sets, as more combinations of component capabilities are created, using simple text strings to identify them is likely to be problematic.

Component categories were created to deal with this problem. Component categories let a control advertise its functionality to containers by placing one or more keys in the registry, just as before. Instead of simple text strings, however, these keys are GUIDs known as *category identifiers* (CATIDs). By examining the CATIDs associated with a component, a container can learn what that component can do without actually instantiating it. Component category information can be written to the registry and retrieved from it using the interfaces ICatRegister and ICatInformation.[1] And because there's really no distinction between ActiveX controls and COM objects, component categories can be used with any kind of COM object, not only with controls.

A control can now use component categories to specify its capabilities and requirements

A component category defines a specific area of functionality. For example, a category might specify that the object supports a particular set of interfaces, or even a specific subset of methods in one or more interfaces. A component category can indicate not only what interfaces an object supports, but also something about how those interfaces should be used. A category definition, for example, might specify both that all components of that category support IDataObject and that they support specific kinds of text conversion through that interface. A single component might support many different interfaces and uses of those interfaces and so might legitimately qualify as a member of several categories. For an object like this, the registry would contain several CATIDs, each identifying a particular area of functionality. It's also worth noting that component categories aren't required to have any special relationship to one another. One category, for instance, doesn't inherit from another, and thus no standard category hierarchy exists. Instead, the creator of a new category is allowed to include whatever functions are appropriate.

A component category can be used to identify any collection of functionality

---

1 At the time this book is being written, component categories aren't yet widely implemented. For example, Visual Basic 4 doesn't support them, relying instead on the older *Control* flag in the registry.

A component might also require certain functionality from its container. Just as a container should avoid loading components that don't provide the right functions, a component should do its best to avoid being loaded by containers that can't use it correctly. To allow this, a component can place CATIDs in the registry that indicate the functionality it requires of a container. By examining these values, a container can tell whether it's capable of correctly using a component. For example, if a container allows its user to insert controls into it, the container can display to the user a list of candidates limited to only those controls the container is able to use.

Finally, it's important not to confuse CATIDs with CLSIDs. Although both are GUIDs and both are used to categorize objects, they are not the same. A CATID guarantees that a COM object is capable of performing certain functions, which can imply support for specific interfaces or for specific uses of those interfaces. A CLSID, on the other hand, simply identifies a particular implementation of a COM object. In fact, it's entirely possible for two objects with different CLSIDs to support an overlapping or identical set of CATIDs, each providing a different implementation of those functions. For example, suppose that someone has defined a standard component category and CATID for a spell checker. Different components might exist, each with a different CLSID, that support the interfaces and functionality required by this category. Each of those components might also support other functionality, identified by other CATIDs, along with that for the spell checker category.

Three Views of ActiveX Controls

ActiveX controls can be complicated beasts. To understand what they are and how they work, it's useful to examine them from the perspectives of three different groups: end users, developers who build applications that use ActiveX controls, and the implementors who actually create the controls.

An End User's View

End users generally aren't aware that they're using a control. Instead, they see a typical graphical user interface, which displays various buttons to click on, sliders to drag, text boxes to fill in, and so on. Most modern operating systems allow applications to present this kind of interface to the user. In the past, the code necessary to display and work with these user interface features has been an integrated part of the system or of a specific application.

An end user isn't aware that ActiveX controls are being used

In a component world, this is no longer true. Increasingly, what a user sees as an integrated whole is in fact a control container that includes a number of ActiveX controls. A control container is like an OLE compound documents container, but it supports a few extra interfaces for working with ActiveX controls. Each control is plugged into the container, and each commonly presents its own user interface as an embedded object supporting in-place activation. A particular button on the screen, for example, might be the user interface of a specific ActiveX control. A user who clicks on that button and interacts with the code that executes is actually triggering an ActiveX control. What the user sees as one application, presenting one integrated user interface, is in fact a control container populated with various discrete ActiveX controls, each providing part of the complete solution.

A control container and the controls it uses look like a single application

Figure 9-1 on the following page provides a simple illustration. The user is presented with a window that contains a large button with up and down arrows and the label *Click An Arrow.* Imagine that when the user clicks the up arrow, the message *Up arrow clicked* appears; clicking the down arrow produces the message *Down arrow clicked.* The user sees a single (though in this case entirely useless) application. In reality, however, this application consists of a control container with one ActiveX control plugged into it. To understand what the control does and how it does it, it's useful to next examine the perspective of the developer who created this simple application.

Figure 9-1   *A user's view of a simple application built using an ActiveX control.*

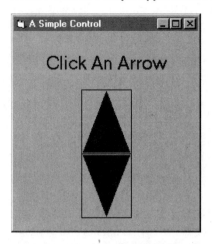

An Application Developer's View

An application developer plugs controls into a control container

The end user sees one application, but someone must have created this application by plugging the ActiveX control into a control container. An application that is more realistic than our example uses more than one control, and so the application's creator must plug several controls into the container and probably write some code, too. Building an application that's constructed largely with controls is quite different from building an application from scratch. Using controls makes the process much quicker—after all, building a house from existing bricks is much faster than making the bricks yourself and then building the house. Using controls is also easier and thus requires less programming skill. This is the promise of component software: quicker, easier application development.

Available control containers include Visual Basic, web browsers, and more

To create an application using ActiveX controls, the developer must first decide on a control container. As mentioned earlier, there's no shortage of choices today. Popular tools for creating containers include Microsoft's Visual Basic and Visual C++, along with plenty of options from other vendors. It's also possible to use a web browser as a container, an option that's explored more fully in Chapter 11.

Let's assume that the developer of our example application has chosen to use Visual Basic as a container. The next problem is to decide which ActiveX controls need to be included to supply users with the expected functionality. Beginning with version 4, Visual Basic itself includes a number of ActiveX controls, so the developer might well find the right control there. If not, an alternative source is the large and rapidly growing third-party market for ActiveX controls, with products from hundreds of companies. Among the available options are controls that offer speech recognition, spreadsheet functions, mainframe connectivity, numerical analysis, and imaging support; there are even controls to help organize and search your collection of controls. Virtually any kind of functionality can be provided by an ActiveX control.

A wide variety of ActiveX controls are available for purchase

If the application developer can't find the appropriate control in Visual Basic or through the third-party market, the control might need to be developed in-house. The skills required to build an ActiveX control are quite different from those required to create an application that uses it. For instance, although Visual Basic is a fine choice for a control container, version 4 can't be used to build an ActiveX control.[2] Today, at least, ActiveX controls are typically written in C++. This application developer might have the skills required for this task, but in a component-based environment, it's more likely that software developers are divided into two distinct groups: one group focuses on developing specialized ActiveX controls, while the other is concerned with assembling those controls into complete applications. Sometimes called creators and assemblers, these two groups perform complementary functions in a component-based development shop.

Organizations can also create their own controls

Figure 9-2 on the following page shows some of what a Visual Basic programmer would see during development of our example application. This is the *design-time* view of the control, as opposed to the *run-time* view the user sees. On the left is a set of

At design time, a developer chooses from an array of controls

---

2   As of this writing, however, the next version of Visual Basic is slated to support such development.

controls from which the programmer can choose. Some of these are ActiveX controls, potentially usable in a variety of containers, but others are purely for use within Visual Basic. For example, the control whose icon is an uppercase *A* (in the top righthand corner) allows the developer to create labels. This control is used only in Visual Basic. On the other hand, in the lower righthand corner of this set (identified by a small picture of up and down arrows) is an ActiveX control called a *spin button*. This control, which is included with Visual Basic 4, is the one used to create the up and down arrows in the example application. Although this control is provided with Visual Basic, it can be used with any ActiveX control container. (In Chapter 11, for instance, we'll use this control with a web browser; see "Loading Controls into a Web Browser," page 290.)

Figure 9-2　*A developer's view of creating a simple application using Visual Basic and an ActiveX control.*

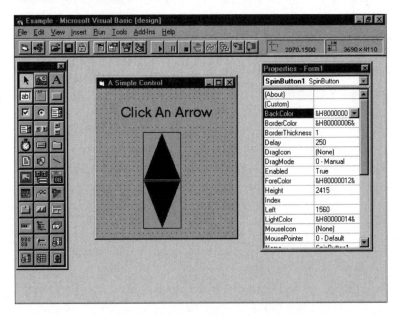

The developer positions controls on a form

To create the application, the developer simply selects a control and then sets its location and size on the form shown in the middle of Figure 9-2. In this example, the developer creates the label *Click An Arrow* with the Visual Basic text control just mentioned and then uses the spin button ActiveX control to add the up and down arrows. What the end user sees when the application is running is determined by the various controls the developer uses to create this form.

Virtually every ActiveX control defines a set of properties. To examine or modify a control's properties in Visual Basic, the developer first selects the control on the form. Its properties then appear in a window like the one on the right in Figure 9-2, which shows the properties of the spin button control. Setting these properties allows the developer to determine the control's color, the color and thickness of the border around the control, and so on. More powerful controls, of course, have more powerful and complex properties to set, but they're presented to a Visual Basic programmer in the same way.[3]

> Controls can have properties

In addition to its properties, a control typically defines a set of *events*. For instance, the spin button control defines an event called SpinUp and one called SpinDown. When a user clicks on the control's up arrow at run time, a SpinUp event is sent from the control to its container. Similarly, clicking on the control's down arrow sends a SpinDown event to the container. These events are sent and received using a COM-based mechanism (see "Events," page 223), but how this happens is of no concern to the Visual Basic developer assembling the application.

> Controls can also send events

Control containers commonly allow a developer to specify an action that should occur in response to an event received from a control. In our example, clicking on either arrow produces a message box indicating which arrow was clicked. To implement

> Control containers typically allow a developer to attach code to events

---

3 A web authoring tool can also be used to create forms containing ActiveX controls. Here, too, the developer can drag controls onto a page, position them, set their properties, and so on, with the results stored in an HTML file. Chapter 11 describes how an HTML file stores a control and its properties; see "Loading Controls into a Web Browser," page 290.

this, the developer need only write the appropriate subroutines in Visual Basic. For the up arrow, this code might look like this:

```
Sub SpinButton1_SpinUp()
    MsgBox ("Up arrow clicked")
End Sub
```

Similarly, the Visual Basic code to output a simple message when the user clicks on the down arrow might look like this:

```
Sub SpinButton1_SpinDown()
    MsgBox ("Down arrow clicked")
End Sub
```

At run time, a control can take several actions in response to a mouse click

Figure 9-3 shows what happens when the user clicks on an arrow in the control. The control itself writes its own user interface, the up and down arrows, directly to the screen. (Like most ActiveX controls, this one is an embedded object that supports in-place activation.) When the user clicks on an arrow, the mouse click is sent directly to the control. The control then visually confirms the mouse click for the user by changing the arrow's image briefly to white and then back to black. Next the control sends an event to its container. If the user clicked on the up arrow, for instance, the control sends a SpinUp event. In general, the container is free to do anything it likes with this event, including ignore it. In this example, the container executes the code that the developer has associated with the event (the first Visual Basic subroutine shown above). This code generates the message box the end user sees, containing the message *Up arrow clicked*.

An ActiveX control can be very simple or very complex

From this example, one might get the impression that ActiveX controls are useful only for simple elements such as buttons and arrows. Don't be misled, however. Controls can be arbitrarily complex, and they can have many kinds of properties and events. Remember, too, that Visual Basic is by no means the only possible choice for a control container. It's used as an example here because of its popularity and because its approach to application development has in some ways driven the requirements for ActiveX controls.

In response to a mouse click, a message box appears.

Figure 9-3

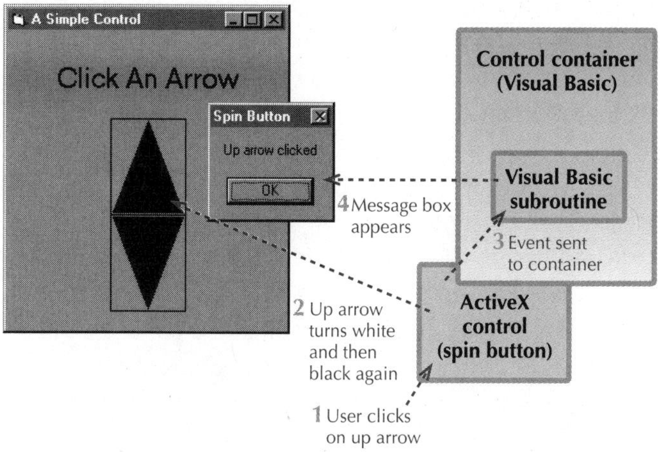

In addition to a defined set of properties that it supports and events that it can send to its container, a typical ActiveX control also has methods. Because ActiveX controls are COM objects, it's reasonable to expect that their clients, the control containers, should be able to make requests of them. Exactly what a container can request from a control is determined by the methods the control supports.

Controls can have methods

The spin button control in our example doesn't offer much in the way of interesting methods—it's just too simple. Among the straightforward methods it offers are Move, which allows a control container to change the location of the spin button's arrows, and Refresh, which lets the container ask the spin button control to redraw its user interface (the up and down arrows).

More complex ActiveX controls have more interesting methods. For instance, the RichTextBox control, a standard ActiveX control included with Visual Basic, essentially implements a simple word processor that can be plugged into an application. The RichText-Box control has properties such as Font and TabStop to set various characteristics of the text. It also offers its container methods such as Find, which searches for a given text string in the text being edited; LoadFile, which loads a file into the control's edit buffer;

More complex controls typically offer a more powerful set of methods

and SaveFile, which saves the control's edit buffer to a file. A container might provide its own user interface in which the user can specify a string to search for or the name of a file where data can be saved. Once the user has entered the information, the container can invoke the appropriate method in the control to carry out that function.

Controls expose
their methods via
dispinterfaces

ActiveX controls always provide access to their methods via a dispinterface and IDispatch (although a control might optionally support a dual interface). From the point of view of an application developer using an ActiveX control, invoking the control's methods looks just like invoking the dispinterface methods of any COM object. Using the methods of an ActiveX control doesn't require anything special—the process is the same as with any COM object.

To an application developer working with ActiveX controls, then, these three elements—properties, events, and methods—define what a typical control can do. As described in the following section, it's the job of the control's implementor to make them work correctly.

A Control Implementor's View

How a control looks to an implementor depends on the kind of tools that implementor is using to build the control. Both a container and the controls it contains implement COM objects, each of which supports a particular set of interfaces. That set can be quite large, and each of those interfaces contains several methods. Clearly, writing a full-featured control entirely from scratch is a fairly complex endeavor.

A developer has
several choices
for how to build
a control

For a simple control that implements only a few features, developing it entirely by hand might be the best approach, since it's likely to lead to the smallest, fastest code. But if the developer chooses to work with a powerful set of tools for control development, implementing even a complex control can be quite straightforward. Microsoft's Visual C++, for example, includes a Control Development Kit (CDK) and a Control Wizard, which, taken together, make it possible for competent C++ programmers to develop controls without even being aware of, much less expert in, most of the detail presented in this chapter. Other tools also exist, allowing control creators to choose the one best suited to their needs.

Understanding how controls work can also appear complex, although this complexity dissolves when it's examined systematically. The functionality defined by the ActiveX Controls specification breaks down into four main aspects, each implemented by its own group of interfaces:

The ActiveX Controls specification defines four main aspects of a control's functionality

- Providing a user interface
- Allowing the container to invoke the control's methods
- Sending events to the container
- Learning about properties of the container's environment and allowing the control's properties to be examined and modified

These four tasks are illustrated in Figure 9-4. The next section explains how each task is accomplished.

The four main aspects of an ActiveX control's functionality.

Figure 9-4

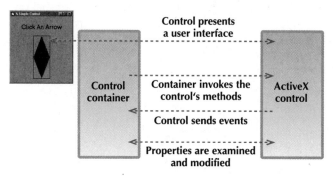

How Controls Work

To describe the standard services that ActiveX controls can provide, this section first presents the large set of interfaces that have been defined for controls and control containers and then examines the interfaces relevant to each of the four aspects of a control's functionality. The section ends with a discussion of licensing, an important control-related topic.

Interfaces for Controls and Control Containers

Figure 9-5 shows an example set of interfaces implemented by an ActiveX control. Although most of these interfaces have been described earlier, a few are new—and controls sometimes work with the familiar ones in interesting ways. The original OLE Controls specification required all controls to implement all of these interfaces. Today this set of interfaces represents a smorgasbord of choices from which ActiveX control developers can select what they need. The interfaces shown in Figure 9-5 include those used to support a complex control's functionality: a user interface, methods, events, and properties. ActiveX controls that omit one or more of these features can also omit support for the interfaces that feature requires.

Figure 9-5   *Standard interfaces for an ActiveX control.*

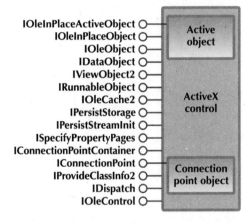

Every control container must implement certain interfaces

Compared to the number of controls, there are relatively few control containers. Plenty of people write controls that work with Visual Basic, but how many write Visual Basic itself? Still, understanding how ActiveX controls work also requires understanding the interfaces that control containers support. Figure 9-6 shows an example of these interfaces. Bear in mind that this is only an example—control containers have options, just as controls do. The ActiveX Controls specification, however, is more rigid about the stipulations for control containers than it is about controls themselves. Control containers are required to support certain interfaces, such as those for embedding and in-place activation.[4]

Standard interfaces for an ActiveX control container.

Figure 9-6

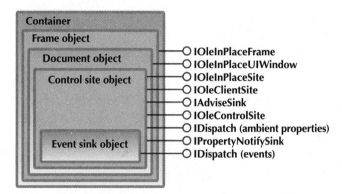

It's worth pointing out that an application needn't be a full-fledged control container to make some use of an ActiveX control. By querying the registry to learn what a control supports (using either CATIDs or the character-based registry keys), a simpler client might be able to use the control in some capacity. If an ActiveX control provides everything required to act as an embedding server, for example, it can be plugged into an ordinary OLE embedding container (and its registry entry will likely contain the key *Insertable*).

Even applications that aren't control containers can use controls

---

4   As described so far, an ActiveX control plugs into a control container, and both together present a seamless interface to their user. It's possible, though, and often useful for a control to act as a container for other controls. An ActiveX control that's capable of having other ActiveX controls plugged into it is called a *container control* (which should not be confused with a control container). Imagine, for example, a control that provides an on-screen box containing buttons and sliders produced by other controls. This container control looks like a control to its container, but it acts in the role of container for the controls that are in turn plugged into it. For this to work, the container itself must support the ISimpleFrameSite interface, whose methods are invoked by the container control as needed.

Similarly, because a control's methods are accessed through IDispatch, any client capable of invoking methods via this interface can call them. In both cases, though, the client probably won't be able to use the control's full functionality. It will instead see the control as a simpler COM object supporting the interfaces it knows about.

A control container must function correctly even with simple controls

Just as a full-fledged ActiveX control can be used in a somewhat hobbled fashion by a client that isn't really a control container, a true control container must be able to work sensibly with even stripped-down ActiveX controls. Since the strict definition of an ActiveX control requires support only for the IUnknown interface, a control container might find itself working with an object that supports very few of the interfaces shown in Figure 9-5 on page 218. In this case, the control container must degrade sensibly, rather than failing in some catastrophic way, when it uses this simple control. To ascertain a control's capabilities before loading it, a container can look in the registry to learn what component categories that control supports.

Providing a User Interface

Controls provide a user interface using OLE embedding and in-place activation

For the most part, a control can provide a user interface simply by supporting the interfaces defined for embedding servers and in-place activation in OLE compound documents. Figure 9-7 shows the interfaces supported by both the control and its container for this purpose. In a typical control, these interfaces are used exactly as described in Chapter 8. Although not much is new here, it's useful to mention a few points about how these interfaces are implemented in an ActiveX control.

ActiveX controls are usually in-process servers

First, the overwhelming majority of ActiveX controls are built as in-process servers. This means that they're implemented as DLLs, with no separate local server. Unlike Microsoft Excel (our example of an embedding server in Chapter 8), controls typically don't need to pass data between separate server and container processes. Instead, the control runs entirely within the address space of its container. Because it's in the same process, the control itself can write directly to the screen without the interprocess complications we saw in Chapter 8's local server example.

Figure 9-7

Interfaces used by a control and a control container for providing a user interface.

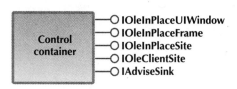

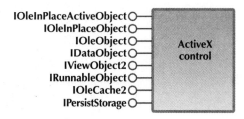

Second, all controls don't necessarily support every embedding and in-place activation interface shown in Figure 9-7. For instance, the example control in Figure 9-7 supports IOleCache2, implying that it saves a cached picture of the last image the user saw, but some kinds of controls don't need to do this. Imagine, for instance, a control that presents only a single button as its user interface—what is there to save? In a case like this, the control doesn't need to provide a cache or to support IOleCache2.

Third, controls can support what is called *inside-out activation.* A typical compound document, by contrast, relies on *outside-in activation.* In Chapter 8's Word/Excel example, for instance, the user double-clicked on the embedded Excel spreadsheet to activate Excel and was then free to use the services Excel provides via its user interface. If yet another object had been embedded in the Excel spreadsheet, that object couldn't have been activated until the Excel object that contained it was activated. With outside-in activation, it's not possible to activate a nested embedded object just by clicking on it directly—the embedded objects that contain it must be activated first.

Controls can support inside-out activation

This model wouldn't work very well for controls. From the user's point of view, an ActiveX control is part of the container application. When the user clicks on a control's user interface, that control must become active and respond immediately regardless of what it's nested in. To allow this, controls can support inside-out activation. Wherever an inside-out control might be in an embedding hierarchy, a single click on the control causes it to become active and respond to that click. Unlike outside-in activation, in which the user must double-click to activate the embedded object and then click again to have the object perform an action, inside-out activation lets an embedded object both become active and respond with a single click. Another option lets a control mark itself as activate-when-visible, which means that the control can immediately process mouse clicks whenever it's visible.

A control's code isn't loaded until it's needed

Even with inside-out activation, the in-process server for an ActiveX control isn't loaded until the first time it's needed. If a control maintains a cached presentation, for example, the control's code typically isn't loaded until the user decides to work with the control. Think of a container with many embedded controls—loading them all when the container itself is started might take quite a while, and the user might not even use them all. Controls that have a user interface but don't maintain a cached presentation, on the other hand, must always be loaded when their container is started—it's the only way the container can make available a presentation of the control's user interface.

Methods

A control's methods are defined in an ordinary dispinterface

There's nothing unique about how a control implements its methods or how a container invokes them. A control's methods must be defined in a dispinterface and are typically invoked with IDispatch::Invoke. As shown in Figure 9-8, the control's IDispatch is the only interface directly involved when a container invokes a control's methods. A control's implementor is free to make its methods available through a vtable interface as well, by supporting a dual interface. (For details, see "Dual Interfaces," page 99.)

But the ActiveX Controls specification requires only that a control's methods be accessible via IDispatch.

Figure 9-8

Interfaces used by a control and a control container for invoking a control's methods.

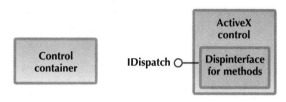

An ActiveX control can also support a type library. By querying this type library, a control container can learn about a control's methods and their parameters. Visual Basic, for instance, allows an application developer to browse through available controls and find the correct syntax for calling each method in those controls. This browser relies on the controls' type libraries for information about what the controls have to offer. A programmer must still typically rely on a control's documentation to completely understand what each method does, but the availability of the type library makes it easier to locate information about methods. Type libraries also play an important part in allowing controls to send events to their containers, as discussed next.

An ActiveX control commonly supports a type library

Events

Methods allow a container to make requests of a control. To make a request of its container, a control must send it an event. When a user clicks on either arrow in the spin button control described earlier, for instance, an event is sent to the container. A control can define a set of events appropriate for its function, and containers typically provide a way to specify what should be done when each event is received. In the spin button example, a Visual Basic subroutine executes, causing a message box to appear when a SpinUp or SpinDown event is received. Events are a critical part of ActiveX controls, and understanding how they work is key to understanding controls.

A control can send events to its container

An event is a
method the
control invokes
on its container

How events work Events are really just methods that a control invokes on its container. When a container invokes a control's methods, the container is acting as the client. When a control sends an event to its container, the control is playing the role of the client. To make this work, the control must acquire a pointer to an interface supported by its container, and the methods in that interface must match the events that the control wants to send. Put another way, the control must support an *outgoing* (or *source*) interface for events, while its container must provide a *sink* for that interface.

By now, bells of recollection should be ringing in your head—this is a job for connectable objects. As Chapter 7 explained, the Connectable Objects technology provides a generic way for a client to establish a logical connection with its container and thus to invoke methods in that container. In fact, connectable objects were first used with ActiveX controls, although they're now used in other COM-based technologies, too.

A container
implements an
interface for a
control's events

A control must support an outgoing interface for its events—that is, it must know how to invoke methods in its container for those events. (The events that a control can send are sometimes referred to as its *event set*.) The container has a somewhat harder problem, though—it must support the event interface itself. It's reasonable to expect a control to know how to invoke methods representing its own events, but how can a control container know how to implement that interface? For events to work, each control container must be able to implement a sink with methods for any outgoing event interface supported by any control. But how can a container conceivably implement interfaces with methods for all possible events that might be sent by any control?

The container
builds its event
interfaces
dynamically,
relying on the
control's type
library

The solution depends on dispinterfaces and type libraries. Both a control's events and its methods are defined in dispinterfaces, accessed via IDispatch. Every ActiveX control that can send events must provide a type library describing both its incoming and outgoing interfaces. A container can read the library's incoming interface descriptions to learn what methods a control supports. More relevant here, however, is that a container can read the type library's outgoing interface descriptions to learn what events the control supports, because those events are simply methods that the control knows how to invoke. Once it learns the methods that a control expects to invoke to send its events, the container must then dynamically create an implementation of IDispatch::Invoke that supports those methods. Given the information in a control's type library, any container is able to construct while it's running an implementation of the dispinterface required to allow that control to send it events.

Event-related interfaces Figure 9-9 shows the event-related interfaces that controls and control containers typically implement. To let a container learn about its outgoing interfaces for events, a control can support the IProvideClassInfo2 interface, which, as its name suggests, is the successor to the earlier IProvideClassInfo. IProvideClassInfo's only method, GetClassInfo, returns a pointer to an ITypeInfo object describing the control's coclass.

A control can support IProvide-ClassInfo2 to give a container access to its type library

As you might recall from Chapter 3 ("Describing IDL," page 77), type libraries contain a coclass element that lists all the interfaces, both disp-interfaces and vtable interfaces, that an object supports. An object's outgoing interfaces are labeled as *source* interfaces in the IDL for its coclass. Once it has called GetClassInfo, the container can examine the coclass to learn which interface is marked as an outgoing interface and so must contain the control's events. If the control has more than one outgoing interface for events, one of them, known as the *primary event set*, must be marked as the default (and an IDL attribute exists for this, too). In IProvideClass-Info2, another method is added: GetGUID. Rather than going

Interfaces used by a control and a control container for sending events. **Figure 9-9**

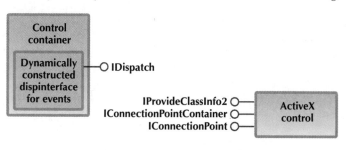

through all the steps just described to find the IID for a control's primary event set, the container can simply call IProvideClassInfo2::GetGUID, which returns that IID directly.

A container uses connection points to pass an event dispinterface pointer to a control

Once the container has learned about the control's event interface, it can dynamically build a dispinterface implementation of that interface. To send an event, the control can then invoke a method in this dispinterface via IDispatch. The last remaining problem is to pass the control a pointer to that dispinterface in the container.

To allow this, the control supports the IConnectionPointContainer and IConnectionPoint interfaces. (For details about these interfaces and their methods, see "Interfaces for Connectable Objects," page 165.) To begin the process, the container calls IConnectionPointContainer::FindConnectionPoint, passing in the IID of the control's event interface. In return, the control gives back a pointer to the IConnectionPoint interface for this outgoing interface. The container then invokes IConnectionPoint::Advise on this pointer, passing as a parameter a pointer to its implementation of the control's event dispinterface. From now on, whenever the control needs to send an event to the container, it can use this pointer to invoke the method in the container that corresponds to the event.

Properties

Although it's not strictly required, the great majority of controls have properties. The spin button control described earlier, for example, has properties that determine the color of its arrows and border. Both a control and its container commonly support certain interfaces related to properties, shown in Figure 9-10.

A control's properties are accessed via dispinterface methods

Chapter 4 first introduced the notion of properties, as part of the discussion of Automation. As described there, the IDispatch::Invoke method can be used to read or write (get or set) the values of an object's properties—and this is also true for an ActiveX control's properties. As Figure 9-10 shows, a control implements a dispinterface that allows access to its properties. The control's container can get or set a property's value by calling the appropriate dispinterface method via IDispatch::Invoke.

Figure 9-10

Interfaces used by a control and a control container for working with properties.

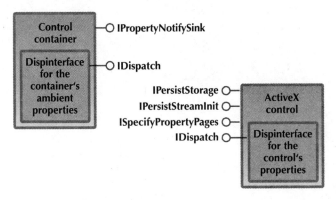

Property pages Some control containers provide a direct, obvious way to examine and modify a control's properties. Visual Basic, for instance, provides the Properties window shown in Figure 9-2 (on page 212) that lets an application developer directly see and set a control's properties. Not all control containers provide this kind of access, however. In such situations, a control needs another way to display its properties.

Rather than letting each control solve this problem in its own idio-syncratic way, providing its own kind of user interface, the creators of the ActiveX Controls specification instead relied on the notion of *property pages*. With property pages, the properties of any ActiveX control can be examined and modified in a standard way using a standard user interface. Figure 9-11 on the following page shows an example of that interface—it's a tabbed dialog box familiar to Windows 95 users, and in this example it displays the properties of the spin button control. Visual Basic allows an ActiveX control's properties to be displayed on property pages, as shown here, as well as in the Properties window. Although they're organized a little differently, the properties available here are essentially the same as those available through the Properties window. For some other container that doesn't already support an alternative scheme like a Properties window, the property pages interface might offer the only way to set and change a control's properties.

Property pages provide a standard way to examine and set a control's properties

Figure 9-11 *A user's view of an ActiveX control's property pages.*

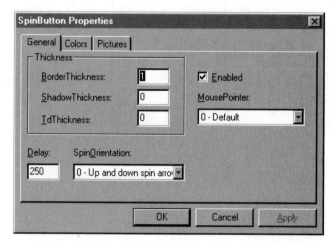

Each property
page is handled
by a separate
COM object

Producing the simple, easy-to-use interface in Figure 9-11 is actually a fairly complex task. In reality, each page in the tabbed dialog box is provided by its own *property page object*. A property page object is just a COM object, complete with its own CLSID, that supports the IPropertyPage interface. To allow its container to learn about the property page objects it supports, a control implements the ISpecifyPropertyPages interface, which has only one method: GetPages. When a user asks to see a control's properties, the control container can call this method. In return, the container gets a list of CLSIDs, one for each property page object the control supports.

Once it knows what property pages a control supports, the container then creates a *property frame*, which in turn instantiates each property page object using CoCreateInstance. For each property page object, the property frame provides a *page site object*, each of which supports the IPropertyPageSite interface. Using this interface, a property page object can learn about the property frame that created it. Each property page object presents its page to the property frame, which assembles them into a tabbed dialog box like the one shown in Figure 9-11.

When this edifice of objects is in place, the user can directly examine or modify the control's properties. Any changes are communicated first from the property frame to the property page objects via IPropertyPage and then by the property page objects directly back to the control itself through its IDispatch interface. Figure 9-12 illustrates this entire process and the objects involved.

Using property page objects to modify a control's properties. **Figure 9-12**

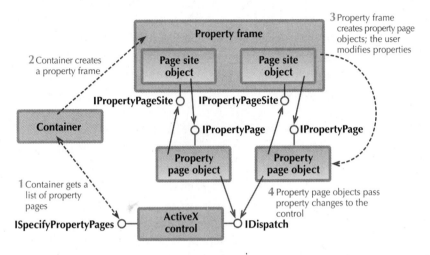

Involving the container in changes to properties After it has created a property frame and passed it the appropriate CLSIDs for the control's property page objects, the control container no longer needs to be involved in this process. The user's changes are communicated from property frame to property page object to control with no container involvement. But if, for example, the container itself needs to take some action in response to a change to some property, it can stay apprised of what's going on by supporting the IPropertyNotifySink interface. Using the methods in this interface, the control can request permission to change a property or inform its container that a property has been changed. The container passes the control a pointer to its IPropertyNotify-Sink interface using connection points, in much the same way

A container can also learn about changes to properties

that connection points are used with events. (The interfaces for connection points are not shown with the other property-related interfaces in Figure 9-10, however.)

One last point about property pages: although ActiveX Controls was the first COM-based technology to specify use of this generic mechanism, property pages are not only for ActiveX controls. Any kind of object that needs to let a user see and change its properties is free to do so in this standard way.

Making properties persistent When a control is first loaded into a control container, the control's properties typically have initial values. Where do those values come from? The answer is that, like any object, a control must store its data in a persistent way between instantiations. There are lots of choices for how to do this. One option is for the container to maintain a compound file. Just as with any embedded document, the container can assign a storage or a stream in this file to each ActiveX control that's been plugged into it. The control can then use this storage or stream to persistently store its properties.

A control might, for example, support IPersistStorage. The control's container can use a method in this interface to pass the control a pointer to a storage, and the control can then use one or more streams below this storage for its persistent data. This is overkill for the average control, however, which typically needs only a simple stream for its persistent data, not several streams below its own storage. To allow this, the control needs to support only IPersistStream or, more likely, IPersistStreamInit. (The latter has one extra method, InitNew, that lets a control know when it's being initialized for the first time.) Then the control's container can pass it a pointer to a stream that the control can use to load and save its persistent data, including information such as the values of the control's properties. A control can also store its persistent data in other ways and thus might support other IPersist* interfaces as well. One important example of this is the IPersistPropertyBag interface, introduced in Chapter 5 ("The IPersistPropertyBag Interface," page 125).

A control can store its properties in many ways

Which of the IPersist interfaces a control supports depends on how it stores its persistent data*

Ambient properties Controls aren't the only ones with properties—control containers have them, too. When an ActiveX control is plugged into a container, it needs to fit smoothly into the environment. For example, the control might need to adopt the current background color of the container or cause its own text to appear in the container's default font. Allowing a control to arbitrarily select such settings is guaranteed to destroy the user's illusion of a single application, an illusion this technology works so hard to maintain.

To allow a control to learn about the environment in which it finds itself, control containers support *ambient properties*, which include default background color, default font, and more. A control can learn about these properties in the same way a container learns about the control's properties: via IDispatch. As shown in Figure 9-10 on page 227, every control container must support a dispinterface that allows a control to query it for the values of standard ambient properties, each of which is assigned a standard, unchanging DISPID. Once it has discovered the values of its container's ambient properties, a control can set its own properties to these same values, allowing it to better fit into the neighborhood.

A control learns about its environment through its container's ambient properties

Containers can also support *extended properties*. To an application developer, these properties look like they belong to the control; but in reality they're maintained by the control container, and the control is unaware of them. Examples of extended properties include the control's position on a form and the (optional) text name assigned to it by an application developer.

A container can support extended properties

The IOleControl and IOleControlSite Interfaces

ActiveX controls commonly support IOleControl, and every control container must provide a control site object supporting IOleControlSite for each control that's plugged into it. (Remember, the rules for what containers must do are stricter than the rules for controls.) Neither of these interfaces is especially big or complicated, and both are in some ways holdovers from the original, tightly prescriptive definition of controls. The methods in IOleControl, for example, allow a container to tell the control that an ambient property has changed or that the container will ignore its events for a while. Similarly, the methods in IOleControlSite allow the control to look at the container's extended properties and more.

Licensing

Although it wasn't shown in Figure 9-5, every control implements a class factory. As described in Chapter 2 (see "Creating Multiple Objects of the Same Class: Class Factories," page 60), class factories support the IClassFactory interface, whose most important method, CreateInstance, allows a client of the factory to create a new instance of the object. A simple control can get away with using only this straightforward mechanism. More likely, though, a control's creator will choose to support IClassFactory2 instead, an interface that inherits from and extends IClassFactory. The extensions in IClassFactory2 concern licensing, a critical topic for control developers and their customers.

Controlling illegal software copying poses a difficult problem

It's hard to control the copying of software applications. Pirated software costs its creators lots of money in lost revenue every year. But if it's hard to control the copying of complete applications, imagine how hard it is to control the copying of individual components like ActiveX controls. Just in terms of quantity, it's likely that components vastly outnumber applications. Also, the difficult moral calculus that (some) people undertake when deciding whether to copy an application might be much simpler with components. After all, components are meant to be small and relatively cheap—how evil can copying one be? The answer, at least to the developers of the components, is that it's very evil. Those developers would like nothing more than a way to control who can use their painstakingly developed components. There's no really effective way to control the copying of components—they're just binary data—but there is a way to control a container's ability to use a particular component: licensing.

Suppose that a user buys an ActiveX control for a desktop machine. Perhaps this control has general applicability, and the user intends to plug it into several different applications. In this case, the user needs to acquire a general license for the control, which will allow its use with any container application on the machine. Now suppose that the user buys a complete application that actually consists of a control container and some number of ActiveX controls. Does the license for this application also allow the user to extract one or more of the application's controls and use them with other containers? If the companies that sold those controls have any say, the answer will very likely be no. The licensing scheme for ActiveX Controls provides support for both these scenarios. It does not define what licenses look like or how they are constructed. Instead, it provides a general mechanism for addressing the problem of licensing.

Licensing provides a way to limit the usefulness of a copied control

The time to decide whether a user is licensed to use a control is when an instance of that control is first created. It shouldn't be surprising, then, that license checking is accomplished through the three methods IClassFactory2 adds to IClassFactory, methods called GetLicInfo, CreateInstanceLic, and RequestLicKey.

Licensing relies on IClassFactory2

Before a container attempts to create an instance of a control, it can use IClassFactory2::GetLicInfo to learn whether this control has a global license on this machine that allows it to be used with any container. If it does, the container can call IClassFactory2::CreateInstance as always to instantiate the control. This addresses the case in which a user has a global license to use a control with any container application. If the control's class factory can find this global license, it will let any container create instances of the control.

A global license for a control might exist on a particular machine

If the call to IClassFactory2::GetLicInfo finds no global license for this control, the situation becomes a little more complicated. Instead of simply calling CreateInstance to create the control, the container must instead call another of the IClassFactory2 methods, CreateInstanceLic. This method has nearly the same parameter list as CreateInstance, but it also requires its caller to pass in a license key. This license key is typically stored as part of the container application itself. The control's class factory verifies that the key is

A container can carry with it a license for a control

correct, ensuring that this control is used only by applications that are licensed to do so. This addresses the case in which a control should be instantiated only by a particular container application. If a container doesn't have the correct key, its calls to Create-InstanceLic will fail.

A container can acquire a license for a control before the container is packaged for shipment

For this to work, the container must be able to acquire a license key when it is itself created. To do this, the container can call the third new method in IClassFactory2, RequestLicKey. This method returns the license key that the container saves and later uses in calls to CreateInstanceLic. In general, the machine on which the container makes this call—for instance, the machine on which it's being packaged for shipment—needs to have a global license. When the container is distributed, it carries its own license, which it then uses to create controls on machines that don't have global licenses. Calls to RequestLicKey on a machine without a global license will fail, so containers without prepackaged licenses can't create controls that depend on those license keys.

No standards are defined for describing or storing license keys

The ActiveX Controls specification does not define what license keys look like, how and where they're stored on disk, and many other licensing-related concerns. Control implementors are free to make their own decisions on these issues. In fact, a control isn't required to implement licensing at all—its class factory can support IClassFactory rather than IClassFactory2 if its developer chooses to do so. Note too that it might not be possible to use the COM library function CoCreateInstance to create an object that supports licensing through IClassFactory2. As described in Chapter 2, this function implicitly calls IClassFactory::CreateInstance and thus can't make use of the extra licensing methods in IClassFactory2. To use these methods, clients must acquire a pointer to the licensed object's IClassFactory2 interface and then invoke them directly.

Paranoid readers (and perhaps larcenous ones, too) have probably observed that this licensing scheme might not be foolproof. Depending on the choices a control implementor makes, breaking a licensing scheme can be very difficult or relatively easy. The primary goal of most component developers, though, is to stop end users from casually copying licensed components. While the mechanisms described here probably won't stop a determined pirate, they can prevent a significant amount of casual copying.

Extensions to ActiveX Controls

There's always room for improvement. A set of improvements to the ActiveX Controls specification, collectively referred to as *Controls 96*, defines a number of compatible extensions to the basics described so far. Those extensions include the following:

The Controls 96 specification extends the current definition of an ActiveX control

- Capabilities that allow a control's user interface to be of any arbitrary shape, not only a rectangle
- A new, faster initialization scheme that allows a control and its container to acquire all the initial interface pointers they need from each other through a single exchange
- Enhancements that allow a control to draw its user interface more efficiently and with less on-screen flicker

Another category of extensions to ActiveX controls grows out of the changes wrought by the Internet. As mentioned earlier, the once-onerous requirements for controls have been greatly relaxed, making it easier to create controls that can be swiftly downloaded across a slow Internet connection. To be truly useful in the Internet environment, however, controls also need a way to become active quickly while still downloading their persistent data in the background across a slow connection. And since this data might arrive in pieces, the control also must be able to notify its container that all the data has arrived. As Chapter 11 details, these features and more have been defined to allow the creation of Internet-aware controls. As support for these new features begins to appear in controls and control containers, the potential applications of ActiveX controls will become even broader.

New features have also been added to make ActiveX controls better suited for the Internet

Chapter Ten

Distributed COM

From the start, COM was designed to allow support for distribution, the ability of a client to create and invoke the methods of objects on other machines. This architectural promise was fulfilled by the release of *Distributed COM* (DCOM) in 1996. With DCOM, a client can create and use objects on other systems as well as objects running locally. Even better, the client needn't be aware of the distinction between the two. Just as COM lets clients transparently access objects in libraries and in local processes, DCOM allows transparent access to objects in remote processes. In fact, the hard part of making this transparency work is ensuring that a running object works seamlessly with an object running in another process, regardless of whether the other process is on the same machine or a different machine. In this sense, DCOM, from a design perspective, is a fairly minor enhancement to the original COM release.

DCOM allows objects to be created and used on remote machines

Being able to start remote objects and invoke their methods is an important advance, but more is required. In particular, there must be a way to control who is allowed to create objects on a given machine, along with a way to ensure secure access to those objects across a network that could be teeming with potential attackers. To make this possible, DCOM is built on a set of security services. Applications (including existing pre-DCOM applications) can exploit DCOM and work securely without adding any code to deal with security. On the other hand, applications that are aware of DCOM's new security features can exploit them explicitly.

DCOM provides access to distributed security services

Although it presents a few complications, DCOM is for the most part simple to understand. It adds only three main elements to the familiar basics of COM: techniques for creating a remote object, a protocol for invoking that object's methods, and mechanisms to ensure secure access to that object.

Creating a Remote Object

Among the most important services COM provides are those for creating an object. As this book has demonstrated, clients typically create objects through calls to the COM library or by using monikers. Both of these approaches also work in DCOM, albeit with a few new concerns, as you might expect. This section examines the various options clients have for creating remote objects.

Using CoCreateInstance

A client can create a remote object using CoCreateInstance

Regardless of where an object runs, a client typically creates it and then acquires the interface pointers it needs to use. For most of the objects described in this book so far, those implemented in an in-process server or a local server, this can be done by calling CoCreateInstance and then using QueryInterface to request the required interface pointers. A client can create an object in a remote server by using this same call—the client doesn't even need to be aware that the object is running on another machine. By passing a CLSID along with an IID specifying the first interface pointer it wants, the client can call CoCreateInstance as usual to create a remote object.

Where an object is created can be configured in the system registry

For a remote object, however, one additional item must be specified: the machine on which the remote object should be created. As Chapter 2 described, for an object created on the same machine as the client, the system registry maps the client-specified CLSID to the name of a DLL or an executable file to load for that class. For an object created on another machine, the system registry can map the CLSID to the name of the machine on which to create that object. For the creation of a remote object, that machine is contacted, its registry is searched for the CLSID, and the appropriate server is started on that machine. If the remote object is implemented in a DLL, a surrogate process is executed that simply loads the DLL and then gets out of the way completely.[1] Otherwise, the object's process is started just as it is with a local server. Figure 10-1 shows a slightly simplified picture of using CoCreateInstance to create a remote object.

Using CoCreateInstance to create a remote object.   ***Figure 10-1***

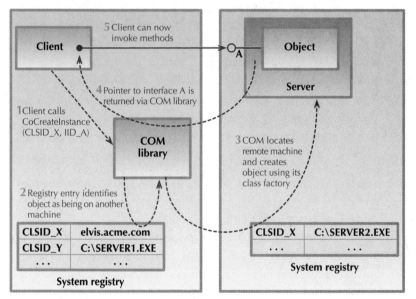

In Figure 10-1, the client asks the COM library to create an object with CLSID X, requesting an initial pointer to interface A on that object. The registry entry for CLSID X on the client's machine contains the name of another machine (in this example, elvis.acme.com). DCOM allows several choices for how remote machines are identified, depending on what network protocols will be used to access the remote system. DCOM supports the domain names used with TCP/IP (such as elvis.acme.com) as well as Internet Protocol (IP) addresses, NetBIOS names, and names used by NetWare's IPX/SPX. However it's identified, the remote

How a remote machine is named depends on the protocol used to access that machine

---

1   Although this particular feature is not supported in DCOM's initial release, plans call for adding it as soon as possible.

machine is contacted, and the object is created there using the information about CLSID X found in the remote machine's registry. In the process illustrated in Figure 10-1, for example, the remote machine launches the server C:\SERVER2.EXE and then asks its class factory to create an object and return a pointer to interface A. This pointer is then returned to the client as usual. To the client, this process looks the same as the process of creating a new object locally.

Remote object creation requires only one round-trip across the network

As you might recall from Chapter 2 ("Creating Multiple Objects of the Same Class: Class Factories," page 60), CoCreateInstance calls CoGetClassObject to retrieve a class factory for this class and then invokes the factory's IClassFactory::CreateInstance method to create an object on the local machine. The process is similar when creating an object on a remote machine, at least as seen by a programmer. In reality, however, the process has been optimized for performance, and all these tasks are accomplished in a single round-trip to the remote machine.

Using CoCreateInstanceEx

Using the familiar CoCreateInstance to create a remote object might not always be the best choice. No matter how fast the network, accessing an object running on another machine is bound to be slower than accessing one that runs locally. And even on high-speed networks, it's better to minimize the amount of data that is sent across the wire. Providing performance that leaves users (and network administrators) happy, then, means minimizing the number of requests required to get a remote object ready for use. An important part of this is avoiding unnecessary calls to QueryInterface on the remote object.

A client can create a remote object with CoCreateInstanceEx

To accomplish this, DCOM provides the CoCreateInstanceEx function, an alternative to CoCreateInstance. Like CoCreateInstance, CoCreateInstanceEx allows the client to specify a CLSID identifying the class of the object it wants to start. But whereas CoCreateInstance allows a client to include only a single IID identifying the initial interface pointer it needs, CoCreateInstanceEx lets the client specify a list of IIDs, as shown in Figure

10-2. Once the object is running, CoCreateInstanceEx requests an interface pointer from the object for every interface in this list and then returns all of them to the client at one time. In contrast to having the client make multiple QueryInterface calls on the object to acquire the necessary interface pointers, returning all of these pointers at once can significantly speed up the process. (Although Figure 10-2 shows only three interfaces in the list, a client can actually specify an arbitrary number of IIDs, getting back an interface pointer for each one.) And even though it was created for use with remote objects, there's no reason why clients can't use CoCreateInstanceEx to efficiently instantiate objects implemented in in-process and local servers, too.

Using CoCreateInstanceEx to create a remote object and request multiple interface pointers.

Figure 10-2

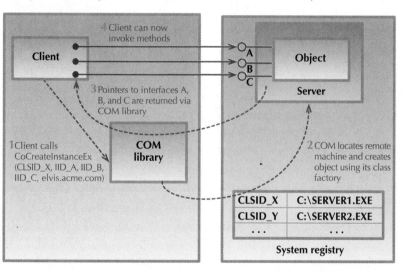

CoCreateInstanceEx also includes a parameter that allows a client to specify the machine on which it wants an object to be created. Rather than relying on the local registry to identify the remote system, a client can dynamically choose that machine at object creation time. The machine's name is specified just as in the previous case—that is, with a domain name, an IP address, or another format that's supported by the underlying protocols in use. Since CoCreateInstanceEx, like CoCreateInstance, relies on

CoCreateInstanceEx also lets a client specify where an object should be created

CoGetClassObject to acquire an interface pointer to the right class factory, the machine name must be passed in the call to CoGetClassObject. A previously reserved parameter is used to do this, which makes it unnecessary to define a "CoGetClass-ObjectEx" call.

Combining Creation and Initialization

A client typically initializes an object after creating it

After a client has created an object, its next step is usually to initialize the object by instructing it to load its persistent data. As Chapter 5 described, a client might invoke the newly created object's implementation of IPersistFile::Load to load the data from a file. If the object stores its persistent data using Structured Storage, the client might invoke IPersistStorage::Load, passing a pointer to the appropriate storage.

Remote objects might also require initialization

This two-step process of creating and then initializing an object is no different when a remote object is involved—a typical client still performs both steps and is free to do so in the traditional way, by calling first CoCreateInstance or CoCreateInstanceEx and then invoking the appropriate IPersist* method to initialize the object. When the object is running on a remote system, however, performing these steps separately requires a series of round-trips that can be unacceptably slow. To improve this situation, DCOM provides clients with two alternative calls, each of which creates and initializes an object in one fell swoop. If the object is running locally, using these calls is mostly just a convenience (although some performance gain results even in that case, as cross-process calls are minimized). But for a remote object, the implementation of these calls is optimized to carry out the necessary functions efficiently.

CoGetInstance-FromFile and CoGetInstance-FromIStorage combine creation and initialization

The first call, CoGetInstanceFromFile, creates a new object and initializes it from a file. The call's parameters include the machine on which to create the object, a CLSID, a filename, and, like CoCreateInstanceEx, a list of IIDs for which the client needs pointers. If no CLSID is supplied, the call's implementation attempts to derive one from the filename, just as a file moniker does. Using this call is similar to calling CoCreateInstanceEx and then invoking the object's IPersistFile::Load method. The second call, CoGetInstanceFromIStorage, works the same way except that the caller passes an IStorage pointer (to identify the appropriate storage) rather than a filename. Using this second call is similar to calling CoCreateInstanceEx and then invoking the object's IPersistStorage::Load method.

Although both calls allow the caller to specify the machine on which the object should be created, neither requires this information. If no machine name is specified, where the object is created depends on several factors. If a remote machine name has been configured in the local registry for a particular CLSID, as described earlier, the object is created on that machine. Alternatively, if the registry entry for this class contains a value called ActivateAtStorage, the object is created on the machine where the specified file or storage exists. For example, if a client calls CoGetInstanceFromFile, passing \\tegan.acme.com\REPORT.TXT as the file identifier, the object is created on the machine named tegan.acme.com and then initialized from the file on that machine named REPORT.TXT.

The Activate-AtStorage value causes an object to be created where its persistent state resides

It's also possible that the machine on which the CoGetInstance-FromFile or CoGetInstanceFromIStorage call is made has no information whatsoever about this class—its registry might contain no entry for the specified CLSID. In this case, an attempt is made to create the object on the machine where the specified file or storage resides. If that machine also has no registry information for this class, the call fails. Otherwise, the object is created on that machine, just as it is when the ActivateAtStorage value appears in the caller's registry.

Using a Moniker

A client can also use a moniker to create a remote object. As Chapter 6 explained, a moniker is an object that knows how to create and initialize one other specific object instance. In most of our discussion so far, both the moniker and the object it references have existed on the same machine. But monikers can also

A moniker can create an object on a remote machine

instantiate and initialize objects on another system. Whether the object a moniker creates is running locally or on a remote machine is invisible to the moniker's client. In fact, where that object is running might even be invisible to the moniker itself.

A moniker might unknowingly create a remote object through a call to CoCreateInstance

When a client calls IMoniker::BindToObject on a moniker, the moniker typically calls CoCreateInstance with a CLSID obtained from the moniker's persistent data. It then initializes the newly created object, again using information from the moniker's persistent data, such as a filename. If a remote machine name is specified in the registry entry for the CLSID that the moniker passes to CoCreateInstance, the object is created on that machine. In this case, even the moniker itself won't know that it has created an object on another machine.

Monikers use the ActivateAtStorage value

Alternatively, the moniker might be aware that it is creating an object on a remote machine. When a client calls the moniker's IMoniker::BindToObject method, it's possible that the persistent storage for the object referenced by the moniker resides on a remote machine and that the ActivateAtStorage value appears in the client machine's registry for the class of this object. If so, the moniker creates the object on the machine where the object's persistent storage exists, just as CoGetInstanceFromFile or CoGetInstanceFromIStorage would.

A file moniker can create an object on the machine where the file it references resides

For example, recall that a file moniker includes a filename that typically identifies both the location of an object's persistent data (in the file) and the object's class (derived from the filename extension or perhaps from the file contents). If that file is stored on a remote file server rather than on a local machine, and if the ActivateAtStorage value appears in the local machine's registry, the moniker creates the object on the file server machine rather than on the local system. Figure 10-3 illustrates this process for a file moniker containing \\tegan.acme.com\REPORT.TXT as the file identifier.

In the same way, a URL moniker contains a URL identifying where an object's persistent storage resides. If the ActivateAtStorage value is set in the local registry for the class of object this URL moniker identifies, a call to the moniker's IMoniker::BindToObject method creates the object on the machine identified by the URL, not on the machine where the moniker and/or its client are running. The moniker then instructs the object to load its persistent data from the information specified by the URL. And like CoGetInstanceFromFile and CoGetInstanceFromIStorage, a file or URL moniker automatically attempts to create the object on the machine where the object's persistent storage resides if the moniker finds no information about the object's class in the local machine's registry.

A URL moniker can create an object on the machine identified by the moniker's URL

Using a file moniker to create and initialize a remote object.

Figure 10-3

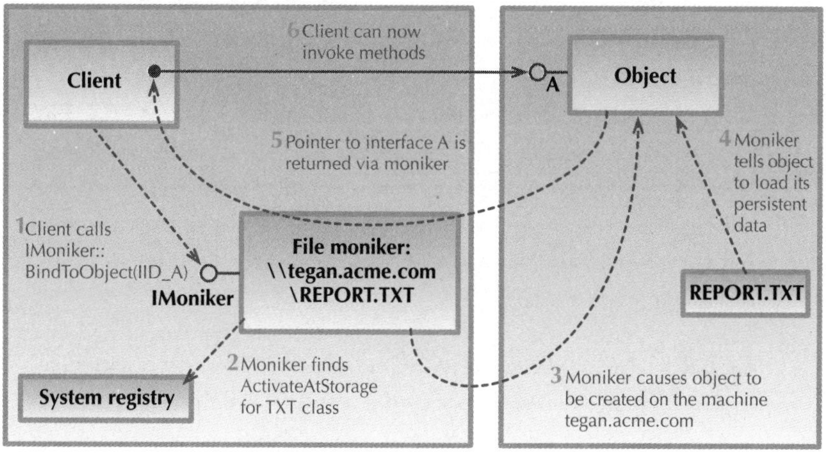

Accessing a Remote Object

Creating a COM object remotely is the first essential for distribution. To a client, this remote object can be accessed just like a local object—there's no difference. The underlying reality is significantly more complex, however, as access to remote methods relies on mechanisms that are quite different from those used with local objects. This section looks at those mechanisms and explains how they work.

Object RPC

Once an object is running and its client has acquired the necessary interface pointers, the client can invoke the methods in those interfaces. As earlier chapters explained, invoking a method in an in-process object really means directly calling the method through a vtable (and, with a dispinterface, going through IDispatch::Invoke). Invoking a method in an object implemented in a local server makes use of a proxy, a stub, and some kind of interprocess communication.

Remote method calls rely on Object RPC

Invoking a method in an object implemented in a remote server also relies on a proxy and a stub, but in this case a remote procedure call (RPC) must be made from client to server. The world is full of RPC protocols, and Microsoft has chosen to adopt an existing one rather than create a new one. This protocol, which Microsoft calls MS RPC, is borrowed from the Open Software Foundation's Distributed Computing Environment (DCE).[2] Both MS RPC and its DCOM usage, known as *Object RPC* (ORPC), send information on the network in the same format as DCE RPC (that is, using the same packet structure). While ORPC includes a number of new conventions for interaction between client and server, adds a few new constructed data types, and uses some packet fields in special ways, it does not change the structure of the packets themselves.

Object RPC includes two different protocols

DCE RPC and MS RPC actually include two different protocols, both of which are also supported by ORPC. One of them, called CN or CO, is used over a connection-oriented transport protocol such as the Transmission Control Protocol (TCP). Because it assumes that the underlying transport protocol will guarantee reliable transfer of data, it doesn't check the accuracy of the transfer. The other, called DG or CL, is used over a connectionless transport service (also called a *datagram service*) such as the User Datagram Protocol (UDP). This protocol assumes that the underlying transport protocol is entirely unreliable, and so it implements its own mechanisms that guarantee reliable transfer of data. To a client making requests, the two appear virtually identical, even

---

2 Microsoft did not, however, borrow the protocol's implementation from OSF. Instead, MS RPC is a reimplementation of DCE RPC based on its publicly available specification.

Chapter Ten

though the underlying transport protocols behave quite differently. Those differences are masked by the RPC protocol that is used with each one.

Whichever protocol is used, a client must possess *binding information* for the destination before it can make an ORPC call. Binding information typically includes data such as the network address of the remote machine (an IP address, for instance) and an indication of what protocol combination should be used (for example, CL RPC and UDP). Binding information can also include a transport endpoint, often called a *port,* that identifies a specific process on a remote machine. One convenient way to represent binding information is a *string binding,* which is a character string that contains all the necessary information.

Making an ORPC call requires binding information

A client acquires binding information for a particular system or object in various ways. When a machine name is passed to Co-CreateInstanceEx, for instance, that name can be used to locate at least some of the required binding information for that system. It's also possible, though, to pass binding information (or a reference to it) from one object to another. Understanding how this works and why it's important first requires understanding the role played by OXIDs and OXID resolvers.

OXIDs and OXID Resolvers

A server implementing one or more COM objects that are accessible to clients on other machines can be thought of as an *object exporter.* By allowing remote clients to access its objects, this server in some sense "exports" the objects, making them usable across machine boundaries. If the server is a single-threaded process with one or more objects, the server as a whole acts as the object exporter. If the server is a multithreaded process with one or more apartments containing various objects, each apartment acts as an object exporter. (For more about multithreaded processes and the apartment model, see "COM and Multithreading," page 54.) In either case, each object exporter is assigned an 8-byte value called an *object exporter identifier* (OXID).

An OXID identifies an object exporter, which might be a process or an apartment

Note that a single process with several apartments can have several different OXIDs.

Every DCOM
machine runs an
OXID resolver

In order to access a remote object, a client must first acquire the object's OXID. (The next section explains how this is done.) Once it has the OXID, the client can rely on an *OXID resolver* to map that OXID to binding information for the object. Every machine that supports DCOM includes an OXID resolver, and every OXID resolver supports an interface called IObjectExporter. [3] Despite its COM-like name, IObjectExporter isn't a COM interface. Instead, it's an RPC interface and is accessed by raw RPC calls rather than by ORPC calls. It contains three "methods": ResolveOxid, SimplePing, and ComplexPing, all of which are discussed later in this chapter.

An OXID maps
to binding
information
for an object
exporter

As Figure 10-4 illustrates, each OXID resolver maintains a table of OXIDs and their string bindings. At a minimum, this table has an entry for every object running on the machine that has a client outside its process or apartment. It also typically includes some OXIDs and string bindings for objects running on other machines. To understand why, we must look next at how interface pointers are passed from one machine to another.

Figure 10-4   *An OXID resolver runs on every machine that supports DCOM.*

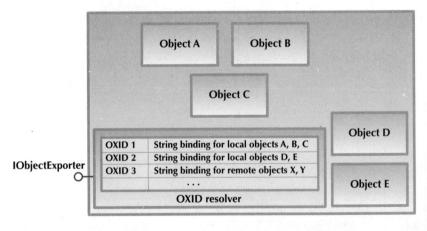

---

3   This interface's name, rooted in DCOM's history, is somewhat unfortunate since the interface is not implemented by an object exporter.

Chapter Ten

OBJREFs: Passing Interface Pointers

When a client calls a method in a remote object, the call can contain parameters, just as a local call can. But different machines sometimes use different formats to represent the same data. Many systems, for example, use ASCII to represent characters, whereas IBM mainframes use EBCDIC. Similarly, different machines use various formats for integers and real numbers. To allow interaction between machines with different data formats, the parameters in an ORPC call are marshaled using a network format called *Network Data Representation* (NDR). NDR is a standard part of DCE RPC (and, of course, of MS RPC), and it provides an efficient way to move parameters of nearly all COM IDL types between machines that might use different representations for those data types. It's up to the machine receiving the call to translate parameters as needed from NDR into its own local format.

ORPC uses NDR to represent a call's parameters on the network

One type of parameter that's frequently passed in ORPC calls is not directly addressed by NDR, however: interface pointers. Objects frequently pass their interface pointers to clients, and a client is allowed to pass any interface pointer it holds to any other object. When that interface pointer refers to an object in the same process, this is no problem: the pointer itself is passed. When the interface pointer refers to an object in another process on the same machine, a reference to that interface in the process is passed. But when an interface pointer refers to an object on another machine, what must be transmitted is a fairly complex construct called an *object reference* (OBJREF).

Object references are used to pass interface pointers between machines

As defined in the DCOM protocol, an OBJREF includes these elements:

- An OXID
- A unique identifier for the interface on the object, called an *interface pointer identifier* (IPID)
- An *object identifier* (OID) identifying the object
- A string binding for the OXID resolver on the machine where the object is running

When an OBJREF is passed from one object to another, the receiving object can start invoking methods on the interface pointer that OBJREF represents.

But how does the object that receives the interface pointer know how to contact the object the pointer identifies? Put more concretely, where does the receiving object acquire the necessary binding information for the object, since that information isn't part of the OBJREF itself? There are two possibilities. If any object on the local machine has recently contacted any object with the same OXID as the object to which the pointer refers, binding information for that OXID will already be stored in the local OXID resolver table. If the binding information is not in the table, it must then be requested from the machine on which the object referenced by this OBJREF is running.

Given an OBJREF, an OXID resolver can locate the binding information for a remote interface pointer

To get the binding information required to use a new OBJREF, then, DCOM, on the client that received the OBJREF, asks the local OXID resolver for help, passing it the new OBJREF. (This is all hidden from the programmer, of course—it's part of the "plumbing" provided by DCOM.) The OXID resolver extracts the OXID from the OBJREF and looks it up in its own table of OXIDs. If any object with the same OXID is in use by any client on this machine, the table will contain an entry for this OXID that contains the necessary string binding. Suppose, for example, that object A in Figure 10-4 (page 248) has been passed an OBJREF to an interface supported by object X in another machine. To acquire the binding information it needs to make requests using this new pointer, the recipient passes the OBJREF to its local OXID resolver and asks for help. In this case, the OXID resolver can hand back the necessary binding information immediately—as shown in the figure, it's already present in the resolver's OXID table.

One OXID resolver can query another to get binding information

Suppose, however, that the OBJREF is for an interface on remote object Q, an object for which the local OXID resolver has no information. This time, the OXID resolver extracts from the OBJREF the binding information for the OXID resolver on the machine where object Q is running and uses it to contact that

OXID resolver. As Figure 10-5 illustrates, the local OXID resolver accomplishes this by invoking the ResolveOxid method in the IObjectExporter interface of the remote machine's OXID resolver. As a parameter on this call, it passes the OXID extracted from the newly received OBJREF. The call returns the string binding associated with this OXID, which the local OXID resolver then adds to its own table. The newly received interface pointer is now ready for use.

To get binding information for a new OBJREF, an OXID resolver queries the machine on which the object identified by that OBJREF is running.   ***Figure 10-5***

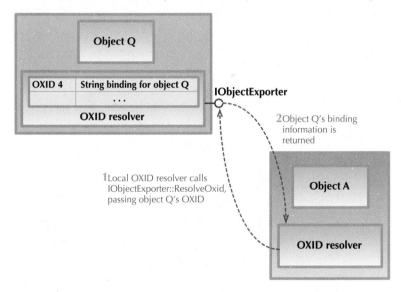

An obvious question arises here: why not pass the string binding for the object itself as part of the OBJREF rather than passing the binding for the OXID resolver on that object's machine? If this were done, the client's OXID resolver would have no need to contact the object's OXID resolver at all—the received OBJREF would contain everything the client needed to contact the object.

To understand why DCOM's designers chose not to do it this way, first recall that DCOM allows a client to communicate with a remote object using different protocols, including TCP/IP, UDP/IP, IPX/SPX, and more. For each protocol an object supports, it might

DCOM's design reduces the overhead incurred by an object

need to load a specific DLL, and it also typically allocates extra threads to listen for incoming requests on that protocol. An object that is communicating using many protocols, then, can incur a significant amount of overhead. Not surprisingly, a goal of DCOM's designers was to minimize this overhead by loading protocols only when needed and loading as few as possible.

Objects do lazy protocol registration

To meet this goal, objects do *lazy protocol registration.* In other words, an object loads the necessary code for a protocol only when it knows that a specific client wants to communicate with it using that protocol. For example, when an object's OXID resolver gets an IObjectExporter::ResolveOxid request from a client machine, that request is made using a specific protocol such as TCP/IP. The OXID resolver on the object's machine can determine whether the object has currently loaded the necessary code for TCP/IP. If it hasn't, the resolver tells the object to load the code, and the client and the object can then communicate using TCP/IP. If another OXID resolver later asks to communicate with this object using UDP/IP, the object is told to load the code for this protocol as well. While all OXID resolvers must listen for requests using every protocol their machine supports, each object loads the code only for protocols that specific clients have requested. Although this approach sometimes requires an extra round-trip at the start of a connection, it allows objects to avoid wasting resources on protocols they're not using.

The Role of the SCM

Creating a remote object relies on IActivation

When an object is created on the same machine as the client, the COM library on that machine delegates the actual work of starting the appropriate server to the Service Control Manager (SCM). When an object is created on a remote machine, the client machine's SCM must in turn delegate this task to the SCM on the remote machine. To allow a standard scheme that lets one SCM talk to its comrade-in-arms on the remote machine, SCMs support an interface called IActivation.

The very simple IActivation interface, illustrated in Figure 10-6, has only one operation: RemoteActivation. This operation is used to activate objects created in any of the ways described earlier in this chapter.

An SCM asks the SCM in another system to create an object through the IActivation interface.

Figure 10-6

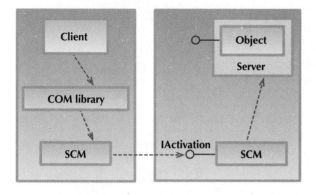

Optimizing IUnknown

Every COM object must support IUnknown—and that's no less true for objects accessed across a network. But if every client's call to an IUnknown method were translated directly into an ORPC to the object, the result would almost certainly be unacceptable performance. Accordingly, DCOM provides optimizations for these important methods.

These optimizations rely on the existence of *OXID objects,* each of which supports an interface called IRemUnknown. Recall that an OXID identifies a group of objects that can be contacted using a single string binding. As shown in Figure 10-7 on the next page, all of those objects are represented by one OXID object and therefore one IRemUnknown. All remote calls on all of those objects' IUnknown methods are first handled by the IRemUnknown interface in their OXID object. (Recall that since every interface inherits from IUnknown, IUnknown's methods can be invoked on any

The IRemUnknown interface allows optimizing calls to IUnknown methods

interface. While it is possible to invoke these methods on an interface pointer to IUnknown itself, it's more common to invoke the IUnknown methods on some other interface pointer.)

Figure 10-7   *An OXID object handles remote IUnknown calls for its objects.*

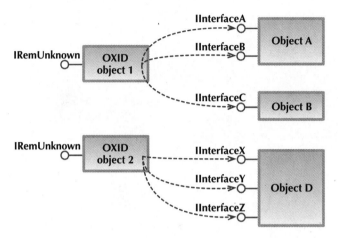

IRemUnknown is similar to, but not the same as, IUnknown. Like IUnknown, it has three methods: RemQueryInterface, RemAddRef, and RemRelease. Unlike IUnknown, however, those three methods allow making multiple requests. For example, RemQueryInterface allows the requesting of multiple interface pointers on multiple objects in a single call. Likewise, RemAddRef and RemRelease allow incrementing and decrementing reference counts for several interfaces on several objects (all of which must be accessible using the same binding information) at one time.

Clients don't call IRemUnknown methods directly

Clients don't directly use the IRemUnknown interface. Instead, they call the ordinary IUnknown methods as always. The standard proxy implementation for those methods groups calls as appropriate and then makes (as few as possible) remote calls to IRemUnknown. For example, client calls to AddRef and Release are typically not translated one-for-one into calls to IRemUnknown::RemAddRef and IRemUnknown::RemRelease. Instead, the IRemUnknown calls are typically made at most once each, after the first call to AddRef and the last to Release. This means that an object could have a reference count of only 1 even though several clients are actually using it. This isn't a problem, however, since the object will stay alive as long as the reference count is nonzero. To both the object and its clients, everything works just as it does in the local case, but this solution is much more efficient in a distributed environment.

While it's certainly useful for the COM infrastructure to optimize calls to the methods in IUnknown, at times the client itself can make smarter choices. When a client needs several interface pointers from the same remote object, for example, getting all of them in a single call is the fastest way to do it. To allow this, DCOM defines the IMultiQI interface. A client acquires a pointer to IMultiQI in the usual way, by calling QueryInterface on an interface pointer. This interface is actually implemented by the local proxy rather than by the remote object, however, so it appears to be supported by every object. This simple interface has only one method (beyond those it inherits from IUnknown), called QueryMultipleInterfaces. Using this method, a client can pass in a list of interface identifiers and in return get the interface pointer for each one. Rather than having the client make several remote requests, all of this information is acquired in a single round-trip to the remote object.

The IMultiQI interface allows a client to request many interface pointers at one time

Pinging

As Chapter 2 explained (see "Reference counting," page 51), all COM objects rely on reference counting to know when it's safe to destroy themselves. An object running on a different machine than its client has a special problem, however: what happens if the client dies unexpectedly? When an object and its client are on the same machine, the object can be directly informed of the client's untimely death. But in the distributed case, the situation is a little more complex.

Fortunately, a time-honored solution to this problem is available: a client can periodically *ping* each object it's using by making an ORPC to it. If a sufficient time interval passes without a ping from a particular client, that client is assumed to have died and the

Pinging lets a remote object learn about a client's untimely death

object can take the appropriate action. Pinging can be a straightforward way to support effective reference counting in a distributed environment.

Pinging can also be incredibly inefficient. Imagine, for example, that one machine contains 10 clients and that each of those clients holds pointers to 30 interfaces on 10 different objects, all of which are on a second machine. A naïve (and very expensive) approach to pinging would require every client to ping every interface on every object individually. A more intelligent solution would be to group those pings together, allowing much more efficient use of the network.

A single packet is sent to ping many interfaces on many objects

This is what DCOM does. Rather than each client being required to ping each object individually, pings are sent and received by OXID resolvers. An OXID resolver determines which interfaces are on the same object and which objects are on the same machine. It then defines a ping set that includes all those interfaces on all those objects by invoking IObjectExporter::ComplexPing on the remote machine's OXID resolver. Once this has been done, a single ping can be sent from one OXID resolver to another for the entire set by using IObjectExporter::SimplePing. This is significantly more efficient than sending one ping per client per object and vastly better than sending one ping for every interface on every object.

Ensuring Secure Access to Remote Objects

DCOM's Object RPC provides a way for clients to create remote objects and invoke their methods. But allowing access to objects on other systems increases the risk of those objects being created or used by unauthorized processes or individuals. To minimize this risk, DCOM defines a standard way to access and use security services.

DCOM provides both activation security and call security

Two problems are involved here. The first is to control who is allowed to launch servers for various classes on a remote machine, a concern that's addressed by *activation security*. The second problem is to ensure that, once an object is running, appropriate security is applied to the method calls clients make on that object, known as *call security*. DCOM addresses both these areas.

Activation Security

Settings in a machine's registry determine exactly who is allowed to launch servers on that machine. The broadest setting enables or disables remote activation as a whole. If this setting is disabled, no remote client can launch servers or connect to any objects on the machine. It's also possible to establish per-class activation security, controlling which remote clients are allowed to launch servers for a particular class. An *access control list* (ACL) determines who is granted this permission. Finally, default activation security can be applied to all classes for which per-class security has not been set. Like per-class security, default activation security relies on an ACL to determine who is permitted to launch a server on the system.

Activation security controls who can launch a server remotely

Whenever an ACL is used, it's necessary to know the identity of the user or object making the request. But this leads to another question: what is an object's identity? Or, in the jargon of the security world, what *principal* is it? A principal is essentially someone (such as a user) or something (such as a running process) that has an account in the environment, whatever that might be. When you log on to a system, you establish your principal identity by typing your logon name and a password. Imagine that, after you've logged on, a client you've started creates an object on a remote machine. What is that object's principal identity? The answer to this question is important because an object's principal identity can determine what that object is allowed to do.

DCOM allows several answers, which depend on the configuration information established for the class. A newly created object can be configured to run as a specific principal, as would a Win32 service on Microsoft Windows NT. Alternatively, it can be configured to run as the same principal as the client that created

Several options exist for setting a new object's principal identity

it or as the same principal as the interactive user who started that client (if different). If nothing is specified in the registry for a class, a newly created object by default takes on the principal identity of the client that created it.

Call Security

Once created, an object is ready to receive method calls from clients. When those clients are running on another system, several security services can be usefully applied. The most important services are listed here:

- Authentication, which proves that you are who you say you are. Authentication allows an object to be certain of its client's identity. If mutual authentication is supported, the client can also be certain that the server is who it claims to be.

- Authorization, which determines what a client is permitted to do. An object can use any scheme it wants to make this decision. On Microsoft Windows NT, for instance, a COM object can make use of the operating system's built-in support for ACLs to determine who is allowed to access that object.

- Data integrity, which ensures that data sent across a network isn't modified in transit. Without this service, an attacker might be able to pull a packet off the network, modify it, and then retransmit it without the packet's recipient detecting the change. If the packet in question contains, say, a request to add money to a bank account, this can cause serious problems.

- Data privacy, which ensures that data sent across a network can't be read while it's in transit. This generally requires encrypting the data, which can significantly affect performance.

Various mechanisms can provide these security services. The security mechanisms included with Windows NT, for example, support all four services. Another alternative is Kerberos, a security mechanism created at the Massachusetts Institute of Technology. Kerberos provides authentication, data integrity, and data privacy but doesn't address authorization (although it does support mutual authentication, a feature missing from Windows NT's distributed security mechanisms). Other security mechanisms offer other combinations of services.

Many distributed security mechanisms are in use today

Given the existence of multiple security mechanisms for providing call security, DCOM's designers faced a problem: which one should they support? Their answer was not to pick only one but instead to define common interfaces that can function over many existing choices. In its initial 1996 release, however, DCOM supports only the security mechanisms provided with Windows NT. Support for Kerberos is planned for a later version.

DCOM allows the use of several security mechanisms

Whatever underlying mechanism is used, DCOM's call security interfaces define two basic options: *automatic security* and *per-interface security.* In automatic security, a client or server process can establish the default level of security for all calls made to or from that process. In per-interface security, different security settings can be established for different interfaces on the same object or on different objects. It's also possible to use both options together, setting basic defaults with automatic security and then fine-tuning with per-interface security.

Automatic security Whether it will act as a client making requests, an object receiving requests, or both, a process can set its automatic security defaults by calling CoInitializeSecurity. As might be expected, this call is not simple, but it allows a process to quickly and completely specify its security requirements. Its more interesting parameters include the following:

Automatic security uses CoInitialize-Security to set security options for an entire process

- An ACL that specifies who is allowed to call the methods of any object in the process as well as who is explicitly denied that right.

- The process's authentication level. The authentication level controls how frequently authentication is done (once per connection, once per call, or once per packet) and also determines whether data integrity and/or data privacy should be used. Calls made from this process will use this level of security, and any incoming calls that don't use at least this level will be rejected.

- A list of the authentication services that can be used to authenticate incoming calls.

An administrator can set system-wide security defaults

By calling this single function, a process can set a broad range of security options. Even if a process elects not to call CoInitialize-Security, however, it nevertheless inherits the default call security settings for that system. In a secure area of the system registry, an administrator can establish machine-wide defaults that apply to all processes that do not call CoInitializeSecurity themselves. These defaults include the ability to set the authentication level and to define an ACL controlling who is allowed to access processes without ACLs of their own.

Per-interface security sets security options for individual interfaces

Per-interface security Automatic security is a blunt instrument. It defines one set of security options to be used for everything a process does, whether it acts as client or server. Automatic security is also straightforward to use, and, for many applications, CoInitializeSecurity is all that's required. Not every process can get by with automatic security, however. For instance, a client might want to use different levels of security for calls made on different objects or even on different interfaces on the same object. A server that implements several objects might want to apply separate authorization schemes to each object or to various interfaces on one object. Per-interface security allows these fine-grained distinctions.

Unlike automatic security, in which a single call sets the options for both client and server security, per-interface security looks different to clients and servers. To use per-interface security, a client must acquire a pointer to the IClientSecurity interface, while a server must get a pointer to IServerSecurity. Using the methods in these two interfaces, each can choose the specific security services and levels it needs to use.

From a client's point of view, every object supports IClientSecurity. To get a pointer to this interface, then, a client can just ask for it in the usual way with QueryInterface. But this apparently simple situation is in fact not quite so straightforward. In reality, the IClientSecurity interface is implemented by COM itself in a library loaded in the client. When the client requests IClientSecurity using QueryInterface, the destination object is never contacted. Instead, a pointer is returned to the local implementation of the interface.

Once it has a pointer to IClientSecurity, the client can use its methods to set security options for each interface on the object. What's really being set, however, are the options maintained by the proxy in the client for the corresponding interface, so calls to IClientSecurity's methods do not disturb the object itself. Among the methods in IClientSecurity are the following:

- **SetBlanket** sets the security information that is used for all calls made using the proxy.[4] The values specified here override any set using CoInitializeSecurity. SetBlanket can be used to specify an authentication service, such as Kerberos (someday) or the Windows NT authentication service (today), along with an authentication-service-specific client name that is passed with each call. This method can also set the authentication level, which is the same parameter used in CoInitializeSecurity.
- **QueryBlanket** returns information about the current values of a proxy's security settings.

Clients use IClientSecurity to set per-call security options

The methods of IClientSecurity set security options maintained by client proxies

---

4   The use of the word *blanket* derives, of course, from the term *security blanket*.

Once a client has set a proxy's security options with IClientSecurity::SetBlanket, all calls made using that proxy are governed by those options. Calls made using other proxies are governed by whatever security options have been set for them. (If no security options have been explicitly established, the default security set with CoInitializeSecurity or the machine-wide default is used.) Helper functions that package common sequences of calls make setting these options a little easier. Rather than querying for IClientSecurity, calling IClientSecurity::SetBlanket, and releasing the IClientSecurity interface pointer, for example, a client can call CoSetProxyBlanket, which wraps all those calls into a neat package.

Whatever security options are used, each call a client makes eventually winds up executing the code in a method implemented by an object. Verification of the client's identity (authentication) is performed by COM, as is any requested decryption and integrity verification of the received data. If any of these checks fail, the call is rejected. If everything succeeds, the method in the object must then determine whether this client is authorized to do whatever it's requesting. In other words, the object must make an authorization decision.

Deciding what the client is allowed to do requires knowing who that client is and what security options it specified for the call. To acquire this knowledge, the object's method code begins by calling the library function CoGetCallContext, which returns a pointer to IServerSecurity, the server-side analog of IClientSecurity. Through the methods in this interface, the object can learn about the client that made the call and then use that information to decide what that client can do. Among the methods in IServerSecurity are the following:

- **QueryBlanket** returns the information that the client set using IClientSecurity::SetBlanket. This information, including the client's name and the authentication level it requested, allows the server to make an authorization decision. It might, for example, first make sure that the client has used a sufficiently high authentication level (whatever that might mean for this object). If so, the object might then check the client's name against an ACL that controls access to this object. Or the method might use a wholly different scheme to make this decision—no hard-and-fast rules exist.

- **ImpersonateClient** allows the object or a thread in the object to take on the client's identity. Various levels of impersonation are possible (all under the client's control), ranging from the ability to impersonate only for ACL checks to allowing the object to make requests of other remote objects under the client's identity, a feature called *delegation*. (Delegation isn't supported in the initial release of DCOM, however.)

- **RevertToSelf** returns the object or a thread in the object to its own identity after a call to IServerSecurity-::ImpersonateClient.

As with IClientSecurity, a few helper functions are provided. An object can call CoQueryClientBlanket, for example, which wraps together calls to CoGetCallContext, IServerSecurity::Query-Blanket, and IServerSecurity::Release.

The Importance of DCOM

The two biggest trends in software development today are the use of object technology and the spread of distributed computing. These trends meet in DCOM. Although it's a relatively simple set of extensions to COM, DCOM provides what is needed to achieve basic distribution of COM objects. While DCOM's first incarnation doesn't contain everything that one might want (it would be nice, for instance, to have a directory service to help locate specific objects), it's a safe bet that Microsoft will continue to expand on this initial foundation. The popularity of Microsoft Windows and Windows NT shows no sign of shrinking, and, as COM continues to spread, DCOM seems likely to play a significant role in the world of distributed computing.

Object technology meets distributed computing in DCOM

ActiveX, the Internet, and the World Wide Web

From its modest beginnings as a U.S. government–sponsored research network, the Internet has developed into a genuine phenomenon. By providing a global network linking millions of computers, the Internet makes possible things that once weren't even conceivable. And as ever-increasing numbers of homes and offices set up high-speed connections to this network, we can expect still more advances that are today inconceivable. The availability of cheap bandwidth—and the ubiquitous global network it makes possible—might prove to be a technical innovation as transforming as the invention of the microprocessor.

Like most new hardware-oriented innovations, the Internet expanded so rapidly because of a "killer" application, attractive enough to motivate people to use it. That killer app was the World Wide Web. The Web today is a major source of information and commerce for millions of people around the world. Web technology has found a receptive home in the business world, too, as corporate intranets based on Internet technologies have proliferated rapidly. Using these technologies, private organizations can build their own internal webs, allowing them to share information inside

The growth of the Internet was driven largely by the World Wide Web

an organization just as the Internet-based Web does externally. With its easy-to-use, easy-to-understand user interface, web technology has broad appeal.

COM is used throughout Microsoft's Internet and Web-related technologies

COM is fundamentally about defining the boundaries between pieces of software. The Internet has a major impact on those boundaries in several ways. The Web's browsing metaphor also affects how applications interact both with data and with their users, two more traditional concerns for technologies built using COM. To address these changes, several new COM-based technologies have been created, and others have been adapted for this new environment. This chapter explores these new and adapted technologies.[1]

ActiveX Documents

Embedded OLE documents, useful as they are, have some limitations

The conventions defined by OLE allow a user to edit an embedded document in place, much as if it were opened in a separate application. With an embedded Microsoft Excel spreadsheet like the one shown in earlier chapters, for instance, the user can activate the embedded object and have access to Excel's commands. Useful as this is, however, an ordinary embedded document doesn't suffice in every situation. Typically, for example, an in-place active document is relegated to whatever area on the screen its container is willing to allot, an area that's usually fairly small. In some cases, the user might want to have the embedded document completely take over the editing area of the user interface. Similarly, when a user prints an ordinary compound document, only the cached presentation appears for any embedded elements—the embedding server's own print functions can't be used. Having a way to access these functions and a few other extra features would let the user see the full functionality of the embedded application rather than just the (admittedly quite large) subset provided by OLE embedding and in-place activation.

---

1 An important note: this discussion is based on a pre-release version of the ActiveX Software Development Kit (SDK). It's possible that some parts will change before these technologies are finalized. Be aware that what's described here might not exactly match what is finally delivered.

The Office Binder, a tool included with Microsoft Office 95, provides a good example of how this can be useful. The idea behind the Binder program is that a user might want to work in a unified way with information created by several Office applications. For instance, imagine a current sales report containing text created with Microsoft Word, quarterly financial data in a Microsoft Excel spreadsheet, and a sales presentation created with Microsoft PowerPoint. To collect these disparate kinds of information in a coherent whole, a user might embed the Excel spreadsheet and the PowerPoint presentation in the Word document. Another solution would be to embed all three in yet another document—in this case, in a binder.

Figure 11-1 shows an example of the three kinds of data just described embedded in a binder document. As shown in the figure, the binder presents a two-part user interface. On the left appears an icon for each embedded document. On the right is the active document, the Excel spreadsheet. Each of the three documents in this binder is embedded, and the Excel spreadsheet is currently in-place active.

The Office Binder lets a user work in a unified way with data from different applications

A binder document with three embedded ActiveX documents.

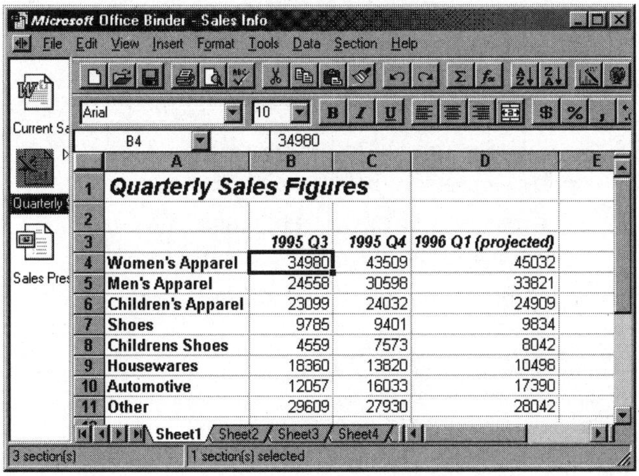

Figure 11-1

The ActiveX
Documents
technology
builds on or-
dinary OLE
documents

This binder document and the applications that have embedded data within it interact using conventions defined by the *ActiveX Documents* technology.[2] The binder is an ActiveX Documents container, while Excel, Word, and PowerPoint are all ActiveX Documents servers. Each application acts like an ordinary OLE embedded document server, although each one also has a little more functionality. For instance, any ActiveX Documents server is able to take over the entire editing area provided by the container. The container, which in this case is the binder document, essentially gets out of the way and lets the ActiveX Documents server completely control what the user sees. In Figure 11-1, for example, the user can have Excel take over the entire editing area by removing the window on the left containing the icons. An ActiveX Documents server presents a user interface that's more complete than the interface of an ordinary embedded document. To the user, in fact, it looks as if Excel is running independently—the limitations imposed on an in-place active embedded document are gone. Excel really is functioning as an embedded document here, as described in Chapter 8, but it can also offer extra features made possible by the ActiveX Documents technology. (And if you're starting to wonder what all this has to do with the Internet and the Web, be patient—it turns out to be very important.)

Describing ActiveX Documents

Supporting
ActiveX
Documents
requires a few
additional
interfaces

All of the things required to present this richer user interface for an embedded document—the ability to take over the container's entire editing window, access to the server's print functions, and so on—are simply extensions to the current embedding and in-place activation features of OLE. Accordingly, containers and servers must first implement embedding and in-place activation

---

2   When Microsoft introduced the *ActiveX* designation, some technologies formerly assigned the *OLE* label were renamed. OLE Controls, for example, became ActiveX Controls. It's tempting to also assume that OLE Documents became ActiveX Documents, but this is not correct. The former OLE Documents technology is now referred to simply as *OLE*. ActiveX Documents describes a technology that builds upon this older technology—it's not just a new name.

and then add a few more interfaces whose methods support the new features. The ActiveX Documents specification defines these extra interfaces.

Containers and servers To qualify as an ActiveX Documents container, an application must support all the interfaces OLE requires for embedding and in-place activation. As shown in Figure 11-2, ActiveX Documents containers must also support the IOleDocumentSite interface. This interface is implemented on a document site object, the ActiveX Documents analog of the client site object in an OLE container. An ActiveX Documents container provides one instance of a document site object for each embedded ActiveX document. A container can also support the IOleCommandTarget and IContinueCallback interfaces, both of which are discussed later in this section ("Commands," page 271).[3]

ActiveX Documents containers must support IOleDocumentSite

An ActiveX Documents container must implement at least one extra interface in addition to those required by OLE.

Figure 11-2

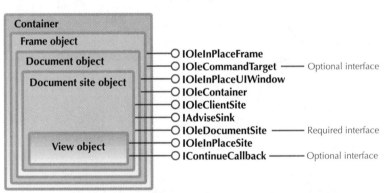

As shown in Figure 11-3 on the following page, acting as an ActiveX Documents server requires support for all the server-side embedding and in-place activation interfaces described in Chapter 8

ActiveX Documents servers must support IOleDocument and IOleDocumentView

---

3   Figure 11-2 includes one other interface, called IOleContainer, which allows a server to enumerate the objects managed by its container. Although this interface is not strictly required for an OLE container, IOleContainer turns out to be quite useful and so is commonly supported in the situations discussed in this chapter.

and more. A server might optionally support IPrint and IOleCommandTarget (discussed later), and it must support IOleDocument and IOleDocumentView. Understanding what these two mandatory interfaces do requires first understanding what the word *view* means in this context.

Figure 11-3 *An ActiveX Documents server must implement at least two extra interfaces.*

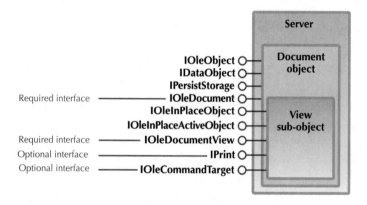

A view acts like a filter for an application's data

An application such as Word or PowerPoint knows how to manipulate a certain kind of data. Word, for instance, works primarily with text, whereas PowerPoint works with slides and their contents. In each case, the application can present different views of its data. In Word, a user can see a document in Normal view, Page Layout view, or Outline view. PowerPoint allows the user to work with a presentation in Slide view, Outline view, Notes Pages view, and so on. Each view acts like a filter through which the user sees the application's data, each showing the same information in a different way.

Each view has its own sub-object

In an ActiveX Documents server, each view is represented by a view sub-object. This sub-object must implement the IOleDocumentView interface and might also implement IPrint and/or IOleCommandTarget. The server must also implement IOleDocument, which can be used to create view sub-objects. The container in turn implements one view object supporting IOleInPlaceSite (and perhaps IContinueCallback) for each view sub-object in the server.

Printing When a user prints a document directly from Word, what is actually printed depends on the view Word is currently displaying. If the user is looking at the document in Outline view, for example, the document's outline is printed. When a user prints a document from Word acting as an ActiveX Documents server, the same thing should occur. To allow this, a view sub-object can support IPrint. Using this interface, an ActiveX Documents container can ask a particular view sub-object in the server to print its view of the data. No longer does printing an embedded document mean that only the document's cached presentation is printed; with ActiveX Documents, the server itself can control exactly what is printed.

A view sub-object can implement IPrint to support printing

Printing can be a lengthy process, and users might get bored or change their minds about the wisdom of their print request. Once an ActiveX Documents container has asked a server to print a document, that server should periodically call the FContinuePrinting method in its container's IContinueCallback interface. This method's parameters include the number of the page currently being printed and the number of pages printed so far. A container might use these to keep its user apprised of the server's progress in printing. If the user tells the container to cancel the print job, the container can pass this information on to the server by setting an appropriate return code on FContinuePrinting. When the call returns to the server, it checks this code and, if necessary, cancels the print job.

A container can support IContinue-Callback to keep informed about printing progress

Commands Both a container and a server can support the IOle-CommandTarget interface. It's easiest to think of this interface as a stripped-down version of IDispatch. Recall that a dispinterface assigns DISPIDs to a group of methods and then lets a client invoke any method in that dispinterface using the single vtable method IDispatch::Invoke. The dispinterface itself is assigned a GUID, allowing the same DISPIDs to be used in different dispinterfaces without fear of ambiguity. With IOleCommandTarget, various *command groups* can be defined, each of which is assigned a GUID. Each command in a command group is assigned an integer value, analogous to the DISPIDs in a dispinterface. To execute

Both container and server can implement IOle-CommandTarget to receive commands

any command, a client of IOleCommandTarget can invoke the Exec method of IOleCommandTarget, providing the GUID that identifies a command group along with an integer identifying a command in that group. It's also possible to pass a command with parameters using variants, the same mechanism used by IDispatch.

IOleCommand-
Target is like a
lightweight ver-
sion of IDispatch

Why invent a new interface when IDispatch would certainly have sufficed? The answer is that the creators of ActiveX Documents felt that IDispatch was too heavyweight for the simple requirements here. The primary reason for using commands at all in this context is to allow a container to ask a server to perform such tasks as displaying its properties and to ensure that toolbar commands work as expected. Accordingly, an ActiveX Documents container and server typically exchange straightforward commands such as Open, Save, and Copy. Using IDispatch for such simple operations was seen as needlessly complex.

How the ActiveX Documents Technology Works

ActiveX
Documents
interactions
are much
like OLE
interactions

Because the interfaces required for using ActiveX Documents are simply extensions of those already used for OLE embedding and in-place activation, the interactions between an ActiveX Documents container and server are very similar to those between an OLE container and server. As in OLE, an ActiveX Documents container (such as a binder document) loads an appropriate server (such as Excel or Word). The container then initializes the server using one of the IPersist* interfaces. A binder stores all its embedded documents' data in a single compound file, each in its own storage. This isn't the only choice, however. An ActiveX Documents container can also initialize a server from a file or from some other persistent storage, assuming that the server supports the appropriate IPersist* interface.

As part of the ordinary initialization process for an embedded document, a container invokes a server's IOleObject::SetClient-Site method. In OLE, the container passes a pointer to its IOle-ClientSite interface as a parameter on this method. In ActiveX

Documents, however, the container passes a pointer to its IOleDocumentSite interface instead. From this, the server can determine whether its container views it as an ordinary OLE embedded object or as an ActiveX Documents object. When the user requests that an ActiveX document be activated by, say, double-clicking on it, an ActiveX Documents container invokes the server's IOleObject::DoVerb method as always. An ActiveX Documents server responds to this differently than an ordinary OLE embedding server does, however. When it receives a call to this method, the ActiveX Documents server invokes the only method in its container's IOleDocumentSite interface, the whimsically named ActivateMe, to request that its container make it active. The container can respond by using QueryInterface to ask the server for a pointer to its IOleDocument interface. The container then invokes IOleDocument::CreateView, which creates a new view sub-object in the server and returns a pointer to that object's IOleDocumentView interface. Using this interface's methods, the container can activate the view, work with it, and close it when it's no longer needed.

ActiveX Documents and the Web

What does all this have to do with the Internet or the Web? Well, initially, nothing at all. ActiveX Documents objects were originally known as *Document Objects*, or just *DocObjects*, and they were first widely disseminated in the Office Binder program. The Binder is a useful tool, but it was created with a desktop-centric focus. What DocObjects provided, though, turned out to be useful in a much broader context. By supporting only a few extra interfaces in addition to those already required by OLE, one application could host another while still allowing a user to access the complete range of the hosted application's features. Those few extra interfaces brought with them the ability to work with everything the embedded application had to offer. The user could see a common frame yet work naturally within that frame with all types of data.

ActiveX Documents objects were originally called Document Objects (DocObjects)

A binder document is one example of a common frame through which a user can access different applications. Another example, one that's much more interesting today, is a web browser. It too

A web browser can provide an ActiveX Documents container

can provide a common frame for accessing and working with all kinds of data and all kinds of applications. It was this realization—the tie to the Web—that prompted the name change from Document Objects to ActiveX Documents. As described next, the result was a complete revamping of Microsoft's web browser and ultimately of the Windows user interface itself.

Microsoft's Internet Explorer and COM

Although COM has since been applied to many other problems, it was originally created as part of a mechanism for creating compound documents. In some ways, the ultimate compound document is the World Wide Web. It shouldn't be surprising, then, that COM has been applied to the problem of web access, too.

Building a Browser from Components

Internet Explorer 3.0 relies on ActiveX Documents

Think for a moment about what happens when a web browser downloads a typical HTML page from a web server. When the information is received, the browser interprets the HTML and displays the page to the user. In older browsers such as Microsoft's Internet Explorer 2.0, the code for displaying HTML pages was built into the browser itself. As browsers came to be used to display more than just HTML, however, they needed a general way to load code on demand to handle any kind of information. If the user downloads a file in Adobe Acrobat format, for instance, the browser must be able to load the correct code to interpret that file and display the information. ActiveX Documents defines this sort of relationship—one application acting as a frame for another. It makes sense, then, to build a web browser using this technology, which is exactly what's done in Internet Explorer (IE) 3.0.

IE 3.0's Web Browser object, an ActiveX Documents container, provides generic browsing functions

IE 3.0 separates generic browser functionality—navigating to a link, going forward and back, and so on—from the intelligence required to load, display, and manipulate particular kinds of information. The user sees one cohesive application, but the browser is actually built from several pieces, as shown in Figure 11-4. (Some of the relationships among the components are slightly simplified in the figure.) The smallest piece is the Internet Explorer *frame*, implemented in IEXPLORE.EXE. This simple piece of code does little more than provide a host process for the Internet Explorer *Web Browser object* (once known as the *shell document viewer*), implemented in SHDOCVW.DLL. This object provides generic browser functionality, and it communicates with the frame through various COM interfaces (the details of which aren't included here). The Web Browser object has no knowledge at all of HTML documents or any other sort of displayable information. What it does know how to do, however, is to act as an ActiveX Documents container. By loading the appropriate ActiveX Documents server, the Web Browser object can let the user see and work with many different types of information.[4]

Microsoft's Internet Explorer 3.0 is built from separate components glued together using COM.

Figure 11-4

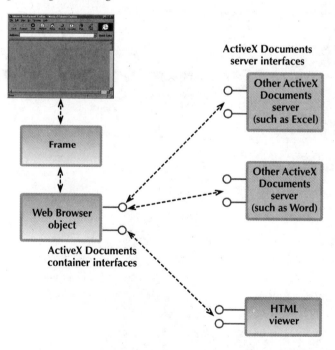

---

4 The Web Browser object also qualifies as an ActiveX control, which means that it can be plugged into any control container.

IE 3.0's HTML
viewer, an
ActiveX Doc-
uments server,
knows how to
display HTML

Its deconstructionist look notwithstanding, IE 3.0 is still a web browser, and a key part of its function is displaying HTML pages. When asked to display an HTML page, the Web Browser object loads the *HTML viewer*, shown in Figure 11-4. This viewer, implemented in MSHTML.DLL, is an ActiveX Documents server that contains all the code required to display and work with HTML documents. Figure 11-5 shows an HTML page displayed using IE 3.0's frame, Web Browser object, and HTML viewer. All these components work together to present the user with the familiar, seamless look of a web browser.

Figure 11-5   *An ordinary HTML page displayed using Internet Explorer 3.0.*

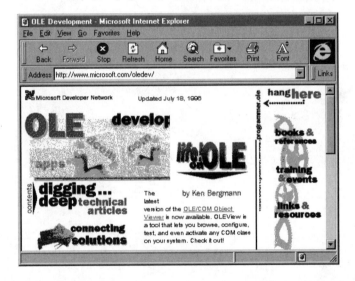

The Web Browser
object can host
any ActiveX
Documents server

Because the Web Browser object is an ActiveX Documents container, it can also load and display anything that knows how to act as an ActiveX Documents server. Why not load an Excel file, for instance, into a web browser? Excel is capable of acting as an ActiveX Documents server, as shown earlier in the Binder example. Accordingly, IE 3.0's Web Browser object can load Excel and a spreadsheet the same way it loads the HTML viewer and an HTML document. Figure 11-6, an Excel spreadsheet displayed using IE 3.0, illustrates how this looks to a user. Because the ActiveX Documents technology exposes the full functionality of an embedded application, hosting Excel within IE 3.0's Web Browser object in no way limits what the user can do. This spreadsheet can be directly edited just as if the user were working with a stand-alone instance of Excel.

An Excel spreadsheet displayed using Internet Explorer 3.0.

Figure 11-6

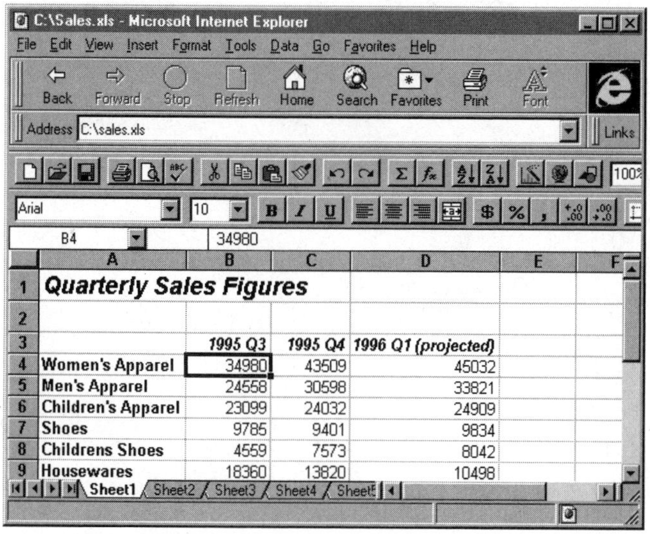

To the Web Browser object, both the HTML viewer and Excel look identical: they're ActiveX Documents servers. This ecumenical approach to browsing means that a web server can store information in various formats (not only HTML pages) and then let the browser load the appropriate code to work with that information. For example, if an Excel spreadsheet is stored on a web server on the Internet, an ActiveX Documents–enabled browser can let its user click on a reference to that page and then automatically load Excel (assuming that Excel or a simpler ActiveX Documents–enabled Excel viewer is available on the browser's machine) and display the spreadsheet as an ActiveX document within the browser. A user can now use one approach—browsing—to access HTML pages on the Web, application-specific files on a local hard drive, and nearly anything else.

The Web Browser object treats the HTML viewer, Excel, and any other ActiveX Documents server identically

Making the Windows Shell a Browser

The Windows
shell provides a
user interface

When you start Microsoft Windows, the user interface you see is provided by an application called the *shell*, which provides you with a way to access other applications and files on your machine. In Windows 95 and Windows NT 4, the standard shell presents a desktop metaphor, allowing you to work with the contents of your machine through folders and files in those folders. A web browser presents a different metaphor. Here you navigate through data and applications by following *hyperlinks* between documents, moving forward and back as needed. Given the popularity of browsing, integrating this new metaphor into the user interface is very desirable.

Given the structure of Internet Explorer, it's also very simple to accomplish. In IE 3.0, a generic browser (the Web Browser object) is loaded into a simple frame. Because that browser is an ActiveX Documents container, it allows users to access all sorts of information using the browsing metaphor. To let users access their systems as a whole using the browsing metaphor, then, all that's required is to modify the Windows shell so that it functions more like IE 3.0 and can then serve as a frame for the Web Browser object. In practice, this means adding support for a few more COM interfaces to the shell, not an especially onerous task. The shell itself can then host the Web Browser object in a natural way, and users can access information using this tool's generic navigation facilities. Files and applications on the local disk, a local network, or the Internet can all be browsed directly from the shell—there's no need for a special web browser application. And through the generic interfaces of ActiveX Documents, other applications can be loaded into that frame to work with other kinds of data, not just HTML pages.

Internet Explorer
4.0 extends
Windows 95

This is exactly what happens in Internet Explorer 4.0. By supplying a new Windows shell, one that is capable of acting as a frame for the Web Browser object, the browsing metaphor can be applied throughout the user's environment. This is more than just a benefit for users—it's also a great example of the power of components. Code originally built for one application, a web browser, can be reused in a very general way.

Truly integrating browsing throughout the Windows user interface requires more than this, however. Browsing depends on the ability to create links among documents and to follow those links from one document to another. A traditional browser allows hyperlinks from one HTML document to another, but applying browsing more generally implies the ability to create more general links as well. A user might want to create a link from a PowerPoint presentation to a Word document, for example, or from a Word document to an Excel spreadsheet. Ordinary HTML hyperlinks aren't enough. To address this problem, the ActiveX family includes a technology called ActiveX Hyperlinks, which allows the creation of hyperlinks between all sorts of documents, not just HTML documents. The ActiveX Hyperlinks technology is already supported by IE 3.0's Web Browser object. (For details, see "ActiveX Hyperlinks," page 305.)

The ActiveX Hyperlinks technology allows the creation of hyperlinks among many kinds of documents

Making a Browser Programmable

Once the Windows shell itself lets you browse the Web, the need for a separate web browser application becomes less apparent. But while web browsers as such might one day fade into the mists of history, that day hasn't yet arrived. And even if browsers per se vanish, components such as the Web Browser object and the HTML viewer will survive. Like spreadsheets, word processors, and other applications, these components provide functions that are useful to other programs as well as to people. All that's required is for these components to expose a set of COM objects with appropriate interfaces that clients can use to access the components' services. In Internet Explorer 3.0, all of these interfaces are defined as dual interfaces, allowing easy access by clients written in Microsoft Visual Basic and similar languages as well as by C++ clients.

A web browser can expose its functions to applications as well as to people

Internet Explorer 3.0 has two components that provide programmability: the Web Browser object, providing generic browsing capabilities; and the HTML viewer, with its HTML-specific functionality. The Web Browser object is typically driven from the outside by, say, a Visual Basic program that uses this object to

The Web Browser object is typically driven from a tool such as Visual Basic

locate a particular document. To make this possible, the Web Browser object exposes methods that correspond to a user's actions, such as the following:

- The **Navigate** method is used to move to a new location specified by a hyperlink.
- The **GoBack** method is used to move to the previous location in the history list.
- The **GoForward** method is used to move to the next location in the history list.
- The **Refresh** method refreshes the current view by reloading the document.

The Web Browser object has methods and properties

Like most objects accessed through dual or dispatch interfaces, the Web Browser object also has properties. This object's properties include the following:

- The **Type** property returns the type of the currently loaded ActiveX Documents server, such as HTML or Excel.
- The **Busy** property indicates whether an activity such as a document load is in progress.
- The **Document** property returns a pointer to the IDispatch interface of the ActiveX Documents server for the currently loaded document. If an HTML document is loaded, for example, this property returns a pointer to the IDispatch interface of the HTML viewer. If an Excel spreadsheet is loaded, it returns a pointer to Excel's IDispatch interface. Using this pointer, a client of the Web Browser object can access the methods made available by the currently loaded ActiveX Documents server, whatever it happens to be.

The Web Browser object also has events

The Web Browser object can also send events, such as OnDownLoadComplete, an event indicating that the current page has been completely received. As with all events, the creator of a program driving the Web Browser object can write a subroutine that is called when this event is received.

Unlike the Web Browser object, the HTML viewer is typically driven from "inside." The viewer might, for example, load an HTML document containing an embedded script. This script then executes, making requests of objects within the HTML viewer as needed. The viewer supports several objects, arranged in a hierarchy.[5] A script can directly access the topmost object in this hierarchy, the Window object, and then acquire access to objects below it through the Window object's properties.

The HTML viewer is typically driven by a script in a loaded HTML file

The Window object represents the browser window that the user sees. Its methods include these three:

- The **Alert** method displays a simple message box.
- The **Prompt** method displays a message and prompts the user for a reply.
- The **Navigate** method causes a jump to a new location identified by a URL.

The Window object also has several properties, some of which return references to objects lower in the hierarchy. These properties include the following:

- The **History** property returns a reference to a History object containing a list of visited locations.
- The **Frames** property returns an array of the window's current frames.
- The **Document** property returns a reference to the current Document object.

Finally, the Window object is able to send two events: onLoad, sent when a page is loaded; and onUnload, sent (not surprisingly) when a page is unloaded.

---

5   The HTML viewer's object model is patterned after the model exposed by Netscape Navigator. This makes it straightforward to create scripts that work with both Navigator and Internet Explorer.

After the Window object, the Document object is probably the most important for creators of scripts. This object, located using the Window's Document property, represents the currently loaded HTML document. Its methods include Write, which writes text such as HTML code, and Open and Close, for opening and closing new documents. Among the Document object's many properties are bgColor, which sets a page's background color; linkColor, which sets the color for links on the page; and vlinkColor, which sets the color for links that the user has visited.

The Window object, the Document object, and all the other objects implemented by the HTML viewer can be accessed by scripts embedded in HTML documents that the viewer loads. If there were only one possible choice for a script language, it might make sense to build support for it into the HTML viewer itself. Several options for scripting languages are available, however, which suggests that a more general solution would be useful. That general solution, called ActiveX Scripting, is what the HTML viewer uses to execute scripts, and it's described next.

ActiveX Scripting

HTML documents can contain scripts written in languages such as JavaScript and VBScript

When the HTML viewer loads a document, that document might contain one or more embedded scripts. Those scripts can make use of the programmable objects exposed by the viewer, along with any objects that are loaded dynamically. Today the two leading languages for writing scripts embedded in HTML are Netscape's JavaScript and Microsoft's Visual Basic Script (formally known as Visual Basic Scripting Edition but commonly called VBScript). JavaScript is syntactically similar to the Java programming language, whereas VBScript is a subset of Visual Basic. It's not hard to imagine that other languages might be used for scripting as well.

A script is executed by a scripting engine under the control of a host

The HTML viewer itself has no reason to either know or care what language an executing script is written in. The script executes in a separate component called a *scripting engine,* while the viewer acts as a generic host for this engine. The viewer can instantiate a scripting engine, hand it a script, and tell it to begin executing the script. As the script executes, it can invoke methods in the viewer's objects and receive events from those objects. The interfaces supported by the HTML viewer and a scripting engine that make all this possible are defined by the *ActiveX Scripting* specification. (ActiveX Scripting was originally known as *OLE Scripting*.)

Furthermore, because the HTML viewer can also act as an ActiveX control container, loading an HTML page can result in loading one or more ActiveX controls as well as a script. Scripts executed by a scripting engine can interact not only with the built-in objects in the HTML viewer but also with any loaded controls. (In fact, an executing script can't distinguish between the two.) The relationships among the HTML viewer (acting as an ActiveX Scripting host and an ActiveX control container), a scripting engine, and a pair of ActiveX controls are shown in Figure 11-7. And finally, although this discussion uses only the HTML viewer as an example of an ActiveX Scripting host, this technology is in no way specific to this application. Any application can become an ActiveX Scripting host and then load and be driven by any scripting engine.

A host can provide built-in objects and might also load ActiveX controls

The HTML viewer is both a host for ActiveX scripting engines and a container for ActiveX controls.

Figure 11-7

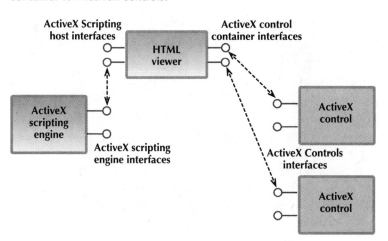

Describing ActiveX Scripting

A script can
access its
host's objects

A scripting engine is a COM object, generally implemented as an in-process server, that is capable of executing a set of scripts—for instance, all those written in a particular language. Internet Explorer 3.0, for example, includes scripting engines for both VBScript and JavaScript. An ActiveX Scripting host typically implements objects whose methods, properties, and events can be invoked, accessed, and received by an executing script. For the HTML viewer, these objects include the Window object and the Document object, described in the previous section. The host can load objects such as ActiveX controls dynamically as well.

Scripting hosts
must implement
IActiveScriptSite
and the host's
objects must
implement
IDispatch

Figure 11-8 illustrates the objects and interfaces that can be implemented by an ActiveX Scripting host. As the figure shows, a host implements a *scripting site object* that supports the IActiveScriptSite interface. Using the methods in this interface, a scripting engine can acquire pointers to the interfaces of top-level objects the host makes available, inform the host of errors that occur, notify the host that the script has completed, and more. If the object supporting IActiveScriptSite provides its own user interface, it can also support IActiveScriptSiteWindow, allowing a scripting engine access to that object's window. Each object in the host, such as the Window and Document objects in the HTML viewer or a loaded ActiveX control, implements its own IDispatch interface, allowing a scripting engine to invoke its methods and access its properties. Each object should also implement IProvideClassInfo (or perhaps IProvideClassInfo2), allowing its client to access its type information. And finally, host objects that generate events also implement IConnectionPoint and IConnectionPointContainer.

Figure 11-9 illustrates the interfaces that a scripting engine can support. Every scripting engine must support the IActiveScript interface. A host uses the methods in IActiveScript to pass the scripting engine a pointer to the host's IActiveScriptSite interface, to tell the script to begin executing, and to perform other tasks. If the scripting engine can load scripts from persistent storage, it also supports one or more of the IPersist* interfaces, such as IPersistStorage, IPersistStreamInit, or IPersistPropertyBag. Scripting engines that

The interfaces that an ActiveX Scripting host and its objects can implement.

Figure 11-8

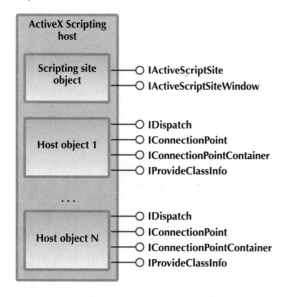

allow script text to be added dynamically can support IActive-ScriptParse, which lets a host such as the HTML viewer pass in a script received as part of an HTML file. If an error occurs during execution of a script, the engine passes its host a pointer to the IActiveScriptError interface, which is implemented by a distinct object in the engine. By calling methods in this interface, the host can learn more about the error. Finally, scripting engines that can accept events sent by a host or that allow a host to access the script's methods and properties must also implement IDispatch.

Scripting engines must implement IActiveScript and more

The interfaces that an ActiveX scripting engine can implement.

Figure 11-9

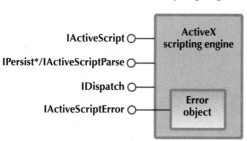

An ActiveX Scripting Scenario

To understand how all this works, imagine that Internet Explorer 3.0's HTML viewer, an ActiveX Scripting host, loads the following very simple HTML document:

```
<HTML>
<TITLE>ActiveX Scripting Example</TITLE>
<BODY>
<H1>Illustrating Scripting</H1>
<SCRIPT LANGUAGE=VBScript>
  document.bgColor = "White"
  document.write "<HR>"
  document.write
    "Hello from the VBScript scripting engine"
  document.write "<HR>"
</SCRIPT>
</BODY>
</HTML>
```

The value of the HTML LANGUAGE parameter determines which scripting engine is loaded

When the HTML viewer loads this document, it happily reads and interprets the first few lines using the HTML tags in the angle brackets. For example, the IE 3.0 viewer renders the line *<H1>Illustrating Scripting</H1>* as a level-one heading (based on the *H1* tag) as shown in Figure 11-10. When the viewer encounters the next line, however, beginning with the *SCRIPT* tag, it knows that it will need to load a scripting engine. Examining the *LANGUAGE* parameter, it determines that a VBScript engine is required. (If this were a JavaScript example, the value of the *LANGUAGE* parameter would be *JavaScript*.) The HTML viewer looks up *VBScript* in the registry—it's a ProgID, which is described in Chapter 4—and finds the associated CLSID. The viewer then calls CoCreateInstance with this CLSID to create an instance of the VBScript scripting engine and get an initial pointer to it.

The scripting host passes the text to the scripting engine

Once the engine is running, the host can acquire a pointer to the engine's IActiveScript interface. The host loads the HTML file's script into the scripting engine using methods in IActiveScriptParse and then invokes the scripting engine's IActiveScript::SetScriptSite method, providing a pointer to its own IActiveScriptSite interface. The basics are now in place for the host and the scripting engine to perform their complementary tasks.

The result of loading the example HTML file.   *Figure 11-10*

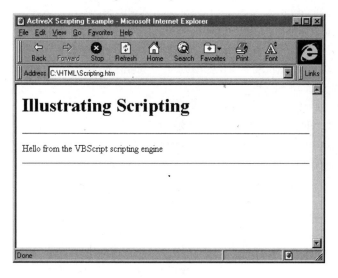

The script that the engine is executing will need to use one or more of the objects supported by the host. Our VBScript example, for instance, sets the bgColor property and invokes the Write method of the HTML viewer's Document object. (Figure 11-10 shows the results.) To set properties and invoke methods of an object in its host, the scripting engine needs a pointer to that object's IDispatch interface. To allow the engine to get this pointer, the host can call IActiveScript::AddNamedItem for one or more of its objects, passing in the object's name as a character string. The HTML viewer, for instance, makes this call for the Window object, the top-level object in its hierarchy. This call isn't necessary for the lower-level objects in the hierarchy, however. Instead, the scripting engine can acquire pointers to these objects through properties on the Window object, as explained earlier.

A host can pass the names of its objects to a scripting engine

Once the host has informed the scripting engine about all the necessary objects, the host invokes IActiveScript::SetScriptState to tell the engine to begin executing its script. When the scripting engine needs a pointer to an object that it learned about through IActiveScript::AddNamedItem, it calls IActiveScriptSite::GetItemInfo with the name of that object. In our example, the scripting

A scripting engine can use an object name to ask a host for a pointer to that object

engine calls this method only once, requesting information about the Window object. This call returns a pointer to the IUnknown interface of the named object. The scripting engine calls QueryInterface on the returned IUnknown pointer, asking for IDispatch. When it acquires the Window object's IDispatch pointer, the scripting engine next uses it to access this object's Document property and acquires a reference to the subordinate Document object. Using this reference, the scripting engine can set the Document object's bgColor property and invoke its Write method, as specified in the script.

Scripting engines receive events using the same mechanisms as control containers

A scripting engine calls its host to invoke methods and access properties. But a host might need to call a scripting engine, too, to inform it of events that have occurred. If an object in the host displays a button, for instance, the object might need to inform the scripting engine that the user has clicked on the button and that some event-handling code in the script should run. This is not a new problem—the process is just like an ActiveX control sending events to its container. Happily, the solution adopted by ActiveX Scripting is identical to that defined for ActiveX Controls. (In fact, the object sending the events to the script might actually be an ActiveX control.) Hosts such as the HTML viewer can provide type libraries for their objects, just as ActiveX controls do. A scripting engine gets pointer to an object's type library and then reads the type library to learn how to build sinks for that object's events. This process is very similar to what control containers do (described in Chapter 9). And, as with controls, connection points are used to pass the necessary pointers from the engine to the objects to allow the events to be sent and received.

ActiveX Scripting allows a host to be transparently scripted from any language

By standardizing the interactions between an executing script and the objects it uses, ActiveX Scripting allows any host to work with any scripting engine. If the simple script shown earlier were written in JavaScript rather than VBScript, for example, nothing would change from the host's point of view, except that it would instantiate a different class of scripting engine. It's even possible to mix VBScript, JavaScript, and (potentially) other scripting languages in the same HTML file and have each script executed by its own scripting engine. And, as mentioned earlier, ActiveX Scripting is useful for more than scripts loaded into a browser— scripting capabilities can be added to any application by implementing the interfaces required of an ActiveX Scripting host.

ActiveX Controls and the Internet

Visual Basic was the first widely used container for ActiveX controls, and its requirements were a driving factor in their original design. However, Internet Explorer 3.0's HTML viewer is a control container, too. An HTML page might contain data, for instance, that requires loading a specialized ActiveX control into the client's browser to view it. The code for this control might already be present on the client machine, or it might be downloaded from a web server when it's needed. Alternatively, IE 3.0 might download a platform-independent *applet* written in the Java language. (An applet is a program, typically a fairly small one, that runs inside a container of some kind, such as a web browser.) In either case, the result is the same: code is loaded as needed (perhaps from a web server) and executed on the browser's machine.

Internet Explorer 3.0 can load controls locally or from web servers

While the most visible effect of the Internet's collision with controls is probably their current name—ActiveX controls rather than OLE controls—the emergence of web browsers as control containers also caused some of the original, desktop-centric design decisions concerning controls to be revisited. As Chapter 9 explained, for example, the requirements a COM object must meet to qualify as an ActiveX control have been greatly reduced, a change made largely to accommodate the process of loading controls over slow Internet links. Loading potentially large amounts of data over those slow links has also led to extensions to the original controls technology. This section examines how ActiveX controls interact with browsers and discusses how a control can better fit into this new environment. Although Internet Explorer 3.0 serves as the example throughout, all the HTML shown here conforms to standards set by the World Wide Web Consortium—it contains nothing specific to Microsoft's browser.

The arrival of the Internet led to changes in the ActiveX Controls technology

Loading Controls into a Web Browser

An HTML
document can
cause ActiveX
controls to be
loaded using
the *OBJECT* tag

Using the *OBJECT* tag in HTML, IE 3.0's HTML viewer can load
and use any ActiveX control. And just as scripts can be written
that use the objects built into the HTML viewer, so too can scripts
make use of dynamically loaded controls. For example, suppose
that the HTML viewer loads the following page:

```
<HTML>
<TITLE>HTML Control Example</TITLE>
<BODY>
<H1>Click An Arrow</H1>
<P>
<OBJECT
  CLASSID="clsid:B16553C0-06DB-101B-85B2-0000C009BE81"
  ID=SpinButton
  HEIGHT=200
  WIDTH=100
  HSPACE=85
>
</OBJECT>
<SCRIPT LANGUAGE=VBScript>
Sub SpinButton_SpinUp()
  MsgBox "(Up arrow clicked)"
End Sub
Sub SpinButton_SpinDown()
  MsgBox "(Down arrow clicked)"
End Sub
</SCRIPT>
</BODY>
</HTML>
```

A control does
not need to do
anything special
to be loadable
into IE 3.0

After the heading *Click An Arrow*, this document uses HTML's
OBJECT tag to load an ActiveX control—in this case, it's the spin
button control you saw in Chapter 9 ("An Application Developer's
View," page 210). When this document is loaded, the HTML viewer
reads the CLASSID attribute and then calls CoCreateInstance with
that CLSID. The ID attribute gives the control a name that can be
referred to in the script, while the remaining attributes determine
the control's size and position on the page. There's nothing special
about the control—this is the same code that was loaded into Visual
Basic in Chapter 9's example. As in that example, the code is loaded locally, not from a web server. If no COM object is available
locally with this CLSID, this example won't work.

Following the *OBJECT* tag is a simple VBScript program that again emulates the example in Chapter 9. Recall that the spin button control generates events when a user clicks on either of its arrows, events that can be caught when the control is loaded into Visual Basic. A VBScript program can also catch those events when the spin button control is loaded into the HTML viewer. (The previous section on ActiveX Scripting explained how the VBScript scripting engine is able to receive those events.) As the example shows, simple subroutines similar to those shown in Chapter 9 can be written in VBScript and executed when the user clicks on an arrow and the control generates an event. Figure 11-11 shows what a user sees after clicking on the up arrow.

An HTML page can contain scripts that use loaded controls

The result of loading the example HTML file and then clicking on the up arrow.

Figure 11-11

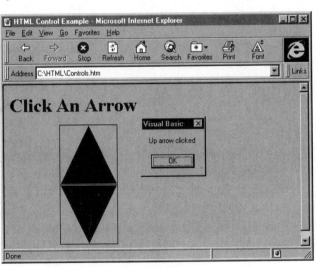

Loading a Control's Persistent Data

An ActiveX control usually has persistent data that it must load when it begins executing. Controls loaded from HTML files have several options for where this persistent data is kept and how it is loaded. This section describes these choices.

A control's
persistent data
can be stored
directly in the
HTML file

Loading small amounts of data How a control loads its persistent data depends on what kind of persistent data it has. Suppose, for instance, that a control has several properties whose values need to be set when the control is loaded. As shown here, those values can be stored in the HTML file itself using the *OBJECT* tag's *PARAM* element:

```
<OBJECT
  CLASSID="clsid:99B42120-6EC7-11CF-A6C7-00AA00A47DD2"
  ID=label1
  WIDTH=150
  HEIGHT=500
>
<PARAM NAME="Angle" VALUE="270">
<PARAM NAME="Alignment" VALUE="2">
<PARAM NAME="Style" VALUE="0">
</OBJECT>
```

When IE 3.0's HTML viewer encounters this *OBJECT* tag, it loads the code for the specified control (which we'll again assume is already present locally) and requests a pointer to that control's IPersistPropertyBag interface. The viewer then reads the *PARAM* elements and hands their values to the control one at a time, as described in Chapter 5. (See "The IPersistPropertyBag Interface," page 125.)

A control's
persistent data
can be stored in
a separate file

This approach works well with controls that can reasonably store their properties as text in an HTML file. But other controls might store their persistent data in a binary form and expect to load this data through IPersistStream. To allow this, the *OBJECT* tag can use the DATA attribute to specify a file that contains the data:

```
<OBJECT
  CLASSID="clsid:99B42120-6EC7-11CF-A6C7-00AA00A47DD2"
  ID=chart1
  WIDTH=200
  HEIGHT=500
  DATA="http://www.acme.com/charts/profits.ods"
  >
</OBJECT>
```

When Internet Explorer's HTML viewer encounters the DATA attribute, it fetches the indicated file and hands it to the control as a stream through IPersistStream::Load. Although it's not shown here, it is also possible to place a limited amount of data for a control directly in the HTML file's DATA attribute.

Loading large amounts of data Both examples shown so far work well with controls that have a relatively small amount of persistent data. But imagine a control whose persistent data includes large graphic or video files or other *binary large objects* (BLOBs). In this case, the control's BLOB data is certainly too big to be stored in the HTML file. It might also be impractical to store this data in the file named with the DATA attribute. Because the file would be loaded using IPersistStream, the file is handed to the control as a complete unit and all data in the file must be present on the local machine before the control can see any of it. Preventing the control from becoming even partially active until all the data has arrived is a less than optimal solution when that data is being loaded over a slow Internet link—users get frustrated when they're forced to spend much time looking at an hourglass icon.

Controls with large amounts of persistent data need to load it asynchronously

A better approach would be to initialize the control with all its "small" persistent data and then load any BLOBs asynchronously. Web browsers do this today with ordinary HTML pages, first loading the page's text and then fetching any embedded images. The benefit is that the user sees an active (although incomplete) page almost immediately and gradually gets the larger data elements which complete the page. Controls with BLOB data can work the same way—first loading any smaller data and becoming at least partially active to the user before gradually loading BLOB data.

This two-part initialization scheme relies on *data path properties*. A data path property is like any other property a control might support except that its value can be a URL. Data path properties are stored in the file identified by the DATA attribute of the *OBJECT* tag and are passed to the control through IPersistStream. When the control receives its properties, it examines them individually

Controls can define data path properties

and uses their values to initialize itself. When the control recognizes a data path property, however, it can extract the property's URL and use it to locate and load the data it refers to.

A control's container typically participates in referencing data path properties

The URL contained in the data path property can be absolute, containing everything needed to locate the machine on which the data resides. For example, the data path property shown in Figure 11-12 contains an absolute URL. More likely, however, a data path property's value is a relative URL, which must be combined with a base URL (such as that of the page in which the control is embedded) to completely specify the data's location. Because only the control's container knows this base URL, the container is typically involved in the process of locating the data identified by a data path property. To allow this involvement, the container implements the IBindHost interface.

Figure 11-12 ***Three properties for a control, one of which is a data path property.***

Height: 200
Width: 100
Data path: http://www.acme.com/image.jpg

Properties

A container might need to give some controls' downloads higher priority than others

When a control needs to load information identified by a data path property, it can invoke its container's IBindHost::CreateMoniker method, passing in the URL contained in the data path property. The host creates a moniker (such as a URL moniker) that identifies the absolute location of the data and returns a pointer to that moniker back to the control. The control is then free to call the moniker's IMoniker::BindToStorage method to retrieve the information refer-red to by the data path property. Normally, however, a well-behaved control won't do this. Instead, it allows its container to participate in the binding process. The container, for instance, might have loaded several controls, each containing data path properties referencing remote BLOBs and all loading those BLOBs at the same time. The container might need to prioritize the order in which BLOBs are loaded, based on information only it knows.

Accordingly, rather than calling IMoniker::BindToStorage directly, a control typically calls its container's IBindHost::MonikerBindToStorage method, as shown in Figure 11-13, passing a pointer to the moniker received from the container. The container then calls this moniker's BindToStorage method. If the moniker in question is a URL moniker, as it usually is, the information referenced by the data path property (the control's BLOB) is now downloaded asynchronously into a stream provided by and accessible to the control. The URL moniker keeps the control informed of the arrival of new chunks of data by periodically invoking OnDataAvailable in the control's implementation of IBindStatusCallback. (The control passes a pointer to this interface as a parameter on MonikerBindToStorage, and the container passes it to the moniker through the bind context object, as described in Chapter 6; see "How Asynchronous Monikers Work," page 148.)

An asynchronous moniker informs a control when a new chunk of the control's data arrives

Moniker binding for a data path property.

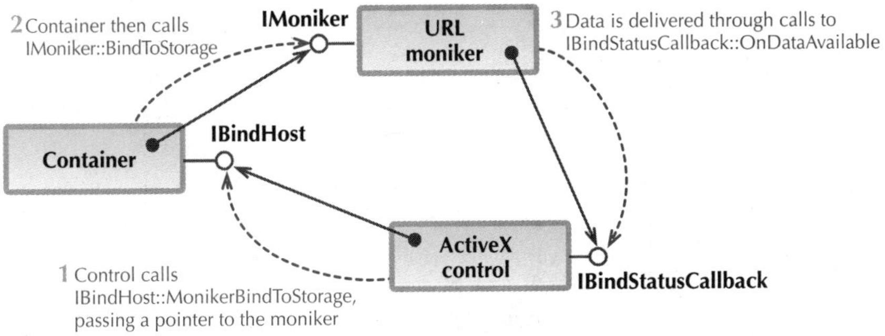

Figure 11-13

2 Container then calls
IMoniker::BindToStorage

IMoniker

URL moniker

3 Data is delivered through calls to
IBindStatusCallback::OnDataAvailable

IBindHost

Container

ActiveX control

1 Control calls
IBindHost::MonikerBindToStorage,
passing a pointer to the moniker

IBindStatusCallback

The benefit of all this complexity is that a control with BLOB data can become at least partially active quickly and then load larger files in the background a bit at a time. This makes for happier users, who aren't required to wait for all the control's data to arrive before beginning to use that control. And should a control find itself loaded into a container that doesn't support IBindHost, it can attempt to fend for itself by converting its data path properties into monikers using MkParseDisplayNameEx and directly calling BindToStorage on those monikers.

Loading large amounts of persistent data asynchronously lets the control become partially active more quickly

A control can inform its container when all data has been loaded

A control with data path properties must take one more action, however. When downloading data using a URL moniker, the control eventually receives an indication from the moniker that all the data has been loaded. The control must then inform its container that initialization has been completed and that it is fully ready for use. To do this, the control can send the OnReadyStateChange event to its container. The control can also set the value of a property called ReadyState, which the container can use to query the control's state. Through this event and/or property, the control can indicate different states: it has loaded all properties except asynchronously loaded BLOBs, it has loaded all properties including BLOBs, and so on.

Controls supporting these features work better in the Internet environment

ActiveX controls such as the spin button control that were created before the advent of these new Internet-related technologies don't take advantage of these new features. Although older controls can be loaded and used by control container web browsers, they don't provide all the benefits of a control written with the Internet in mind. Controls that are Internet-aware are made more efficient with support for data path properties and asynchronous downloading along with the OnReadyStateChange event and/or the ReadyState property. These features are by no means required, but they make a control much better suited for use inside a web browser.

Downloading Controls

A control's code can be downloaded when needed from a web server

In the examples shown so far, a control's data might have been stored on a remote machine, but the code for the control was assumed to be resident on the browser's machine. This need not be the case, however. Why not load a control's code from a web server when it's needed? To tell the browser where the code is, the *OBJECT* tag can include a CODEBASE attribute. Here's a simple example:

```
<OBJECT
  CLASSID="clsid:B16553A0-06DB-101B-85B4-0000C009BE05"
  CODEBASE="http://www.acme.com/welcome/mapshow.ocx"
  DATA="http://www.acme.com/maps/campus.geo"
```

```
  ID=MapDisplay
  HEIGHT=450
  WIDTH=450
>
</OBJECT>
```

HTML's CODEBASE attribute indicates where the code resides

When Internet Explorer 3.0 encounters this tag in an HTML file, it downloads the file named by the CODEBASE attribute (assuming that no code for this CLSID is currently present on the machine) and then instantiates the control. In this example, the referenced object is an ActiveX control, but Internet Explorer 3.0 also supports the downloading of Java applets. An attribute called CODETYPE on the *OBJECT* tag can be used to indicate the MIME (Multipurpose Internet Mail Extensions) type of this object, such as *application/java-vm*, which lets the browser decide whether it's worthwhile to download it.[6] And as the example shows, it's also legal to use the CODEBASE and DATA attributes at the same time, causing the browser to download both a control's code and its persistent data.

How downloading works In some cases, all that's required to download code is to copy a single executable file from a web server to the browser's machine. In other cases, it might be necessary to copy more than one executable file along with one or more supporting files. To deal with this variability, the *Internet Component Download* service used by Internet Explorer defines three packaging schemes for downloaded code:

Three main options are available for packaging downloaded code

- A portable executable (PE), containing a single executable file with an extension such as OCX, DLL, or EXE.
- A cabinet file, identified by the file extension CAB. A cabinet file can contain one or more executables, all compressed into a single package and downloaded as a unit. It also includes an INF file that directs the installation process of the cabinet's files.

---

6 MIME types are used throughout the Web environment to indicate data types. Other commonly seen MIME types are *text/html, image/gif, image/jpeg,* and *video/mpeg.* At the time this book is being written, no permanent MIME type has yet been defined for ActiveX controls.

- A stand-alone INF file, containing only references to other files that should be downloaded. An INF file can contain URLs referring to files on a single machine or on several machines. It can also specify options for which files to download depending on the type of client platform making the request. For example, a request to download an INF file made from a Windows 95 system and the same request made from a Macintosh system might result in copying different binaries.

The filename specified in the CODEBASE attribute can optionally be followed by a version number. If it is, the file is downloaded only if this version number is more recent than any version of this file currently resident on the system.

A call to CoGet-
ClassObject-
FromURL does
everything
required to
download and
install a new
component

When a browser such as Internet Explorer attempts to download the code for an ActiveX control, its real goal is to create one or more COM objects using that code. Ultimately, then, the browser must acquire a pointer to the IClassFactory interface of the control's class factory and call CreateInstance. The Internet Component Download service makes this very easy. When Internet Explorer encounters a CODEBASE attribute inside an *OBJECT* tag and de-cides to download the associated code, it needs to call only the single function CoGetClassObjectFromURL. Like CoGetClassOb-ject (discussed in "Using a class factory," page 61), this function returns a pointer to a class factory. As its name suggests, the caller passes in a URL specifying where to find the code. This URL can name a portable executable, a cabinet file, or an INF file, and the browser takes this value directly from the CODEBASE attribute in the *OBJECT* tag. The caller can also pass in the CLSID from the tag's CLSID attribute or the MIME type of the object indicated by the CODETYPE attribute. (The MIME type is mapped to a CLSID using the system registry.) Making this single call causes the con-trol's code to be copied to the browser's system (if it's not already present), verified as safe using WinVerifyTrust (discussed in the next section), and registered with the system registry. Once every-thing has been installed locally, CoGetClassObjectFromURL calls CoGetClassObject to return a pointer to the class factory of the new object.

Of course, the actual process is a bit more complex. The implementation of CoGetClassObjectFromURL relies on a URL moniker to accomplish the downloading, which means that a client making this call must implement IBindStatusCallback to receive progress notifications. The caller of CoGetClassObjectFromURL must also implement the ICodeInstall interface. This simple interface lets the client learn about any problems that crop up during the download and handle any necessary user interface issues. Also, once a component is downloaded, no automatic mechanism deletes it—it remains on that system's disk indefinitely. For the most part, however, clients such as Internet Explorer are shielded from the messy details of downloading objects.

Ensuring the security of downloaded components Being able to download components as needed is a useful capability. By default, a downloaded Java applet is wrapped in a secure cocoon during execution. Because each applet has its own safe "sandbox" to play in, providing security in this way is sometimes called *sandboxing*. Unlike Java applets, however, ActiveX controls are binaries executing directly on the machine's hardware. Although ActiveX controls have capabilities that sandboxed Java applets do not, they also offer more opportunities for mischief. A malicious developer could easily create controls that, say, reformat the hard drive of any machine that installs them. If users can't have faith that a given control won't damage their system, they can't take the risk of downloading and running that control.

Creating that faith is the goal of the *Windows Trust Verification Services*. Through the single function call WinVerifyTrust, a user of this service can access one or more *trust providers*. In general, a trust provider can answer questions about whether a component can be trusted according to certain criteria. The initial release of this service includes only one choice, the Windows Software Publishing Trust Provider. This trust provider is able to answer the question that most concerns the potential user of a downloaded ActiveX control: was this control produced by someone I trust?

Some mechanism must exist to guarantee the security of downloaded code

A trust provider can provide that guarantee

At first glance, this might appear to be the wrong question. What users really want to know is whether this control will damage their system, not who created it. Unfortunately, there's no general way to determine this. The best users can do is assure themselves that the software was created by a trusted source and that it hasn't been modified since its creation. This is similar to the faith users express when buying packaged software. If the box carries the name of Lotus or Microsoft or another reputable vendor, and if the shrink wrap on the package isn't broken, users can feel confident that the software inside won't intentionally damage their system. Providing this same kind of confidence is the goal of the Windows Software Publishing Trust Provider.

When Internet Explorer 3.0 downloads a component, that component might carry with it a *digital signature*. A digital signature is a byte string that can be used to verify that the associated information was actually provided by a specific entity. More than that, a digital signature also verifies that the information (in this case, the downloaded code) hasn't been modified since the signature was affixed. In essence, the signature plays the role of both the company name on a software package and the package's shrink wrap.

To allow others to verify its digital signature, a component carries with it another byte string called a *certificate*. When Internet Explorer calls WinVerifyTrust, it passes in references to both the newly downloaded control's digital signature and its certificate. The trust provider examines both and returns an indication of success or failure.[7] If the check fails or if the component is from an untrusted source, IE 3.0 informs the user and offers a choice of whether to proceed. Note that because a digital signature verifies that the associated information hasn't been modified from its original form, it's impossible to silently insert viruses into the code. By having the developer add a signature to a component and having the

---

7 The details of how digital signatures work are beyond the scope of this book. For those who are familiar with the technology, the Windows Software Publishing Trust Provider uses PKCS #7 and X.509 version 3 certificates. For those who aren't, well, you can trust me on this.

browser check that signature after downloading, a system is created whereby a user can have a high degree of faith in the component's trustworthiness.

ActiveX and Java

While the length of time required to move from abstract concept to widespread deployment in software hasn't changed radically (writing code still takes time), the interval between development of a new concept and widespread assimilation of that concept certainly has. No technology better demonstrates this change than Java. Created by Sun Microsystems, Java is a programming language, one not too different from C++. But Java is more, too, offering exciting possibilities for the Internet and for COM.

As with most programming languages, it's possible to compile a program written in Java and produce a binary executable. This isn't commonly done today, however. Instead, Java source code is usually translated into a machine-independent *bytecode* rather than a machine-specific binary. This bytecode is then interpreted by the Java Virtual Machine (VM), software running on a real machine. Using this scheme, the same Java code can be executed on any machine that supports the Java VM.

Java programs are executed by the Java VM

One popular use of Java is to create applets, relatively small Java programs that run inside a container such as a web browser. Since Java applets can be distributed as bytecode rather than as machine-specific binaries, the same applet can be downloaded and executed on different systems. All that's necessary is for the target machine to have Java VM software available. It's also possible to create stand-alone applications in Java. Unlike applets, applications don't assume the existence of a container.

A Java applet can be executed on any machine with Java VM software

Java and COM

Microsoft has wholeheartedly endorsed the Java language. Microsoft's Java development tool, Visual J++, allows the creation of both applets and applications. At first glance, it might not be obvious

Java fits very well with COM

why Microsoft would choose to support this new language so strongly. After all, Java was created by Sun, a direct competitor. Furthermore, the machine-independent nature of Java's bytecode has led many to suggest that this new development tool could weaken the dominance of Windows/Intel systems. Despite this, however, Java offers a benefit that's very attractive: it meshes exceptionally well with COM. Although COM is officially language neutral, it's fair to say that COM and its supporting technologies were designed with C++ and Visual Basic in mind. Remarkably, even though it was created in a completely separate environment by a competing company, Java actually fits with COM as well as or even better than these two languages. A key part of this fit is that Java objects, like COM objects but unlike objects in C++, can support multiple interfaces. This, together with a few other features, makes Java an excellent language with which to implement and use COM objects. While this sort of technical serendipity is more the exception than the rule, Java and COM really are a natural pair.

Microsoft's Java VM makes Java objects look like COM objects

Microsoft's implementation of the Java Virtual Machine integrates Java objects and COM objects. Part of this integration is that from the point of view of a COM client, the Java VM makes a Java object appear to be just another COM object. With Java applets, for example, Microsoft's Java VM automatically constructs a dispinterface containing all the applet's public methods. With other Java objects, vtable interfaces are created. These methods are then accessible to clients of this object through a VM-provided implementation of IDispatch, as shown in Figure 11-14. To complete the illusion, the VM provides an implementation of IUnknown for each Java object, allowing clients to acquire pointers to other interfaces the object supports. The VM also implements a class factory, allowing a client to treat Java objects like any other COM objects. The Java programmer creates objects as usual—nothing special is required. All the services necessary to make those objects look like COM objects are supplied transparently by Microsoft's Java VM.

Microsoft's Java VM lets a Java applet look like a COM object.   ***Figure 11-14***

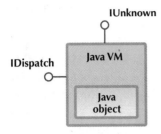

Microsoft's Java VM also provides the reverse translation: from the point of view of a Java object, an external COM object looks exactly like a Java object. Again, this integration is achieved without making any changes to the Java language itself. Instead, the Java VM transparently performs the necessary translations to map between the two kinds of objects.

Microsoft's Java VM also makes COM objects look like Java objects

Java is an excellent tool for creating COM clients, as the Java environment offers services that make life significantly easier for COM programmers. For example, a programmer working with COM objects in C++ must always be aware of reference counting. For a C++ client, this means calling Release whenever an interface pointer will no longer be used. Java programmers need not concern themselves with reference counting, however. Instead, the Java VM notices when an object is no longer referenced and automatically deletes it, a service known as *garbage collection*. When Microsoft's Java VM notices that the "garbage" object being collected is a COM object, it simply calls Release on the object. Unlike C++ COM clients, the creator of a COM client in Java never needs to worry about keeping track of which objects are no longer needed and then releasing them.

For acquiring references to new interfaces on an object, Microsoft's Java VM even hides calls to QueryInterface beneath the Java language's built-in operators. A Java programmer writes the same code to access a new interface regardless of whether that interface is on a Java object or a COM object. (In fact, the Java programmer can't tell them apart.) For a COM object, however, the Java VM intercedes, silently calling QueryInterface on the object and returning

The Java VM hides calls to QueryInterface

the new interface pointer. Unlike C++ developers, COM programmers working in Java never need to make explicit QueryInterface calls.

In order to provide all the translations required to map between Java and COM, Microsoft's implementation relies on the information stored in a COM object's type library. And to further integrate Java into the COM world, Microsoft offers Java class libraries exposing key COM functions such as CoCreateInstance, along with access to monikers, Structured Storage, and more. Although neither Java nor COM was designed with the other in mind, the two fit together very well.

Java Applets and Internet Explorer 3.0

Using Java to create COM objects and to write clients that access COM objects is an appealing idea. By hiding some of the rough edges, Java makes using COM that much easier. But a key purpose of Java, creating downloadable applets that run in web browsers, has no intrinsic connection to COM. How does Internet Explorer 3.0 support this?

Since Microsoft's implementation of the Java Virtual Machine makes a Java object look like a COM object, supporting Java applets is no different than supporting COM objects. The Java VM is implemented as an ActiveX control included with Internet Explorer 3.0. To execute a Java applet, the applet is simply loaded together with this control. To a control container such as Internet Explorer's HTML viewer, the applet looks like any other ActiveX control. And Microsoft's ActiveX control implementation of the Java VM can execute any standard Java applet, not only those created using Microsoft Visual J++.

Implementing the Java VM as an ActiveX control has broader implications, too. Since applets look like ActiveX controls, and since controls can be driven by scripts, Java applets can also be scripted. Using the ActiveX Scripting interfaces, VBScript, Java-Script, or another scripting language can be used to access the methods exposed by an applet. Java applets can also work with other applets and ActiveX controls in the same page. Finally, because the Java VM ActiveX control makes any Java applet look like a control, an applet can be loaded into any ActiveX control container and behave just as if it were a control. Although Java applets have historically relied on web browsers as containers, they can now be used with other control containers as well.

As with ActiveX controls, the *OBJECT* tag can appear in an HTML page to indicate that a Java applet should be downloaded. Internet Explorer 3.0 also supports the *APPLET* tag, an older mechanism for embedding Java applets in HTML pages. When Internet Explorer 3.0 encounters an *APPLET* tag, it internally converts it to an *OBJECT* tag with the CLSID of the Java VM's ActiveX control. Internet Explorer then loads the Java VM ActiveX control and passes it the *APPLET* tag's parameters. The control then does everything required to download and run the applet.

HTML pages can include Java applets using either the OBJECT or APPLET tag

Once downloaded, a Java applet can potentially call other COM objects or native code on the system. Ordinarily, an applet is sandboxed, as described earlier, and so isn't allowed to make these calls. As with ActiveX controls, however, Internet Explorer 3.0 allows a Java applet to be digitally signed and to have this signature checked when it's downloaded. Assuming that the signature identifies a trusted source, the applet is permitted to call other COM objects and local code just as a trusted ActiveX control would. For example, because any COM object looks like a Java object to an applet, it's possible for a digitally signed applet to access the automation services that many applications provide. A Java applet might access Excel's built-in services, for example, as a Visual Basic program might do.

Java applets can be digitally signed

ActiveX Hyperlinks

Part of the reason for the tremendous growth of the World Wide Web is surely the appeal of its fundamental metaphor: browsing. The central notion underlying browsing is the idea of hyperlinks.

Browsing depends on hyperlinks

To a user, a hyperlink appears on the screen as colored or underlined text, or as a graphic element embedded in the page, or perhaps in some other way. Clicking on a hyperlink changes what the user sees. In some cases, clicking on a hyperlink in an HTML document might simply result in displaying another part of that same document. In other situations, clicking on a hyperlink results in loading an entirely new document.

The ActiveX Hyperlinks technology allows hyperlinks to be created among various kinds of documents

Most users like the browsing paradigm—it's easy to learn and powerful to use—and Microsoft intends to integrate it throughout the Windows and Windows NT user interface. Key to this is finding a way to provide hyperlinks between all kinds of elements, not just HTML documents. Why can't we create a hyperlink between, say, a Word document and an Excel spreadsheet? Rather than embedding or linking the two documents using the conventions of OLE, why not tie them together with a hyperlink as if they were HTML documents? This is the goal of *ActiveX Hyperlinks*. By enabling the creation of hyperlinks that reference all kinds of elements, including but not limited to HTML documents, and by wrapping this generality in standard COM interfaces, ActiveX Hyperlinks applies the browsing metaphor to a broad range of documents and applications.

Describing ActiveX Hyperlinks

ActiveX hyperlink objects contain a friendly name, a moniker, and a location string

An ActiveX hyperlink is a COM object that supports the IHlink interface. It also supports IPersistStream, allowing its persistent state to be saved to and loaded from a stream, and IDataObject, allowing its contents to be copied using drag and drop or the clipboard. Every ActiveX hyperlink object contains (at least) three key pieces of information:

- A friendly name that can be displayed to the user when the hyperlink is visible. (Showing the friendly name is not required, however, because how a hyperlink is displayed is ultimately determined by the container that displays it, not by the hyperlink itself.)

- A moniker for the hyperlink's target—that is, for the application and data to which the hyperlink points.
- A string indicating a specific location within the target.

For example, an ActiveX hyperlink to a Word file on a local machine might contain a friendly name such as *Current Status Report*, a file moniker that references the Word file, and a string indicating a location such as a Word bookmark within that file, as shown in Figure 11-15. An ActiveX hyperlink to an HTML document stored on the Internet might contain a friendly name such as *Acme Product Support Info*, a URL moniker that references the link's HTML document, and a string identifying a location within that document. A developer might use this second hyperlink to add an option to an application's help menu that directly connects the user to product support information on the World Wide Web.

An ActiveX hyperlink might reference a location in a file or on a web page

Two example ActiveX hyperlink objects and their contents.

Figure 11-15

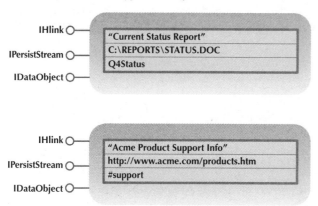

All ActiveX hyperlinks look the same to their clients, who see them primarily through the methods in IHlink. Those methods include the following:

- The **GetFriendlyName** method can be used by a client to learn the friendly name of the ActiveX hyperlink.
- The **GetMonikerReference** method returns the moniker and the location string from the ActiveX hyperlink.

- The **Navigate** method causes the ActiveX hyperlink to navigate to its target, the document to which it points.

Standard library functions are used to create ActiveX hyperlinks

To create an ActiveX hyperlink object, a container need only call one of several standard library functions and pass in the appropriate data. HlinkCreateFromMoniker, for example, lets a container create a hyperlink object by providing the three required components of an ActiveX hyperlink: a moniker, a location string, and a friendly name. HlinkCreateFromString lets a container create an ActiveX hyperlink object by providing a location string, a friendly name, and a character string identifying the hyperlink's target.

ActiveX containers and targets implement IHlinkSite and IHlinkTarget, respectively

However it is created, an ActiveX hyperlink object communicates with its container through the container's implementation of IHlinkSite, as shown in Figure 11-16, and communicates with its target through the methods in IHlinkTarget. Note that a hyperlink can refer either to a location in the currently displayed document or to a location in another document. Supporting this first case requires the hyperlink's container to itself implement IHlinkTarget.

Figure 11-16   *ActiveX hyperlinks, their targets, and a container.*

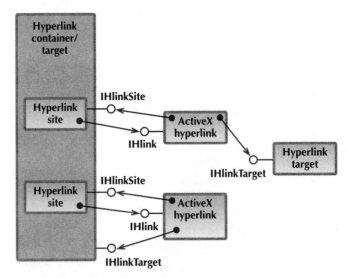

Although they aren't shown in the figure, two other components play a part in ActiveX hyperlinking: the *browse context object* and *hyperlink frames*. The browse context object supports the IHlinkBrowseContext interface, and it is responsible for maintaining the *navigation stack*. This data structure supports an integral part of the browsing metaphor: the ability to move forward and back in the list of visited documents. A traditional web browser maintains this list itself, but it applies only to hyperlinks between HTML documents. Because no single "browser" application might be able to encompass all the documents a user visits through ActiveX hyperlinking, an external object must maintain a list of visited documents. The navigation stack maintained by the browse context object generalizes the traditional web browser history list to include all documents browsed using ActiveX hyperlinks, including HTML documents, Word documents, Excel spreadsheets, or anything else.

The browse context object maintains a navigation stack

Finally, navigating to a hyperlink should ultimately result in displaying something new to the user. To provide some consistency, it's common (though not mandatory) to wrap a single frame around a succession of displayed documents accessed with ActiveX hyperlinks. Internet Explorer 3.0, for example, can be used to browse across many different kinds of data, and it gives the user a common frame for all of them. It can be useful to keep this frame informed about what's happening, allowing it to do whatever is needed to maintain a smooth look for the user. For example, all applications hosted within a hyperlink-aware frame can rely on the frame to locate the browse context object for them. To do this, a frame supports IHlinkFrame, whose methods are called by various components in the hyperlinking process at appropriate times. Internet Explorer 3.0's simple frame, IEXPLORE.EXE, implements this interface, as will Internet Explorer 4.0.

A hyperlink-aware frame provides a consistent environment for displaying a succession of documents

How ActiveX Hyperlink Objects Work
When a user clicks on a hyperlink, the container that receives the click creates an ActiveX hyperlink object containing the correct information and passes it a pointer to its IHlinkSite interface.

An ActiveX hyper-
link object can
refer to a location
in the current
document or in
another document

(With the creation functions mentioned earlier, such as HlinkCreateFromString, all this can be done with a single function call.)
Once the hyperlink object is running, the container calls its IHlink-
::Navigate method. To find out whether this hyperlink refers to
another location in the document the container is currently displaying or to a location in another document, the implementation
of IHlink::Navigate turns around and asks the container for a moniker to the container itself using IHlinkSite::GetMoniker. The ActiveX
hyperlink object then compares this moniker with the moniker it
already contains, the one naming the hyperlink's target. If the two
monikers are the same, the hyperlink knows that it refers to another
location in the current document. If not, it must refer to a location
in a different document.

If a hyperlink
object refers to a
different docu-
ment, it relies on
its moniker to
create that object

If the ActiveX hyperlink object determines that it refers to a location
within the current document, the container for that document must
support IHlinkTarget. (It's the target for this hyperlink, after all.) The
hyperlink gets a pointer to this interface by calling the container's
IHlinkSite::QueryService method. If this hyperlink does not refer
to a location in the container's current document, the hyperlink
object calls IMoniker::BindToObject on the moniker it contains.
For a hyperlink containing a file moniker with a filename such as
REPORT.DOC, for instance, calling BindToObject will typically
start Microsoft Word (because of the DOC extension) and hand it
this file through IPersistFile. If the hyperlink contains a URL moniker such as http://www.acme.com/report.htm, it will fetch the
HTML page identified by this URL and hand it to a web browser
such as Internet Explorer. Whatever kind of moniker is involved,
the initial interface the hyperlink requests on BindToObject is
IHlinkTarget.

The location string
identifies a specific
location within a
document

One way or another, the ActiveX hyperlink object now has a
pointer to the IHlinkTarget interface of the target. The hyperlink
object next invokes IHlinkTarget::Navigate, passing in the location

string that this hyperlink stores. The source finds the correct information and causes it to be displayed.[8] If this hyperlink is to another location in the current document, the current window displays the new information. If necessary, however, a new window is created and correctly positioned to present a smooth transition to the user, much as is done with OLE in-place activation. And although this brief description omits the details, the frame (if there is one) is kept informed about what's going on, and the browse context object is updated with the result of this navigation throughout the process of following the hyperlink.

The Simple Hyperlinking API

Integrating the browsing metaphor throughout their environment is likely to make users happy. Given what's just been described, however, it might leave software developers somewhat less pleased. Developers want a simple, powerful way to implement browsing, and although what we've seen so far is powerful, it's not especially simple. The implementor of a web browser or an application such as those in Microsoft Office might need a detailed understanding of the ActiveX hyperlinking architecture, but most programmers need only a straightforward way to add hyperlinks to their application. A simple hyperlinking API has been created to make this possible.

The simple hyperlinking API makes all this easy to use

The primary purpose of this simple API is to make it easy to navigate to the target of a hyperlink. The API's small group of functions listed on the following page are focused around this goal.

---

8 This is similar to OLE linking using a composite moniker built from a file moniker and an item moniker. In that case, the file moniker identifies both the application and the document, while the item moniker passes the application a string that identifies a location within the document. By identifying a location within a document using a simple character string rather than an item moniker, the ActiveX Hyperlinks technology avoids the overhead of creating a moniker for the common case of hyperlinking to another location in the same document.

- The **HlinkSimpleNavigateToString** function causes a jump to another location, presenting the user with a new set of information. The caller passes in a string, such as a file-name or a URL, along with a location string and a few more parameters. The implementation of this call creates a moniker from the string (using MkParseDisplayNameEx, described in "A Generalized Approach to Naming," page 151) and creates an ActiveX hyperlink object containing that moniker and the location. It then navigates to the object this hyperlink identifies. A simpler version of this call, **HlinkNavigateString**, performs the same task but provides defaults for most of the parameters.

- The **HlinkSimpleNavigateToMoniker** function, like Hlink-SimpleNavigateToString, causes a jump to another location. Its parameters are the same, too, except that the caller passes in a moniker instead of a string. A simpler version, called **HlinkNavigateMoniker**, provides defaults for most parameters.

- The **HlinkGoBack** function causes a jump to the previous location in the navigation stack maintained by the browse context object. This call works only if it is made by an application hosted in a hyperlink-aware frame, such as Internet Explorer. (This limitation exists because the implementation of this call relies on the frame to locate the browse context object—without it, there's no way to find the navigation stack and hence no way to go back.)

- The **HlinkGoForward** function causes a jump to the next location in the navigation stack. Like HlinkGoBack, it works only when made by an application hosted in a hyperlink-aware container.

Using these calls, any application can follow hyperlinks to any other application that supports the basic interfaces required to be a hyperlink target. An ActiveX control, for example, might present the user with a button that represents a link to a predefined Word document. When the user clicks on this button, the control can call HlinkNavigateString with the name of the file, and a hyperlink jump to that document will immediately occur. Rather than understanding and implementing calls to the underlying objects and interfaces, a developer can achieve the most commonly used features of ActiveX hyperlinking with a minimum of effort.

Final Thoughts

We work in a great business. Where else could new technology as transforming as that of the Internet and the World Wide Web so quickly become an important part of our lives? The downside of this enormous rate of change, of course, is that we're constantly forced to learn how to live with and use these new technologies. Sometimes this is easy. For the average software professional, learning to use a web browser takes less than five minutes. Sometimes, though, it's not so easy. Understanding the ActiveX technologies that underlie Microsoft's approach to the Web, for example, requires a firm grasp of COM, persistence, monikers, OLE, ActiveX controls, and more. It also requires understanding basic web technologies such as URLs and HTML. The reward for all this effort should be substantial, however. Whatever can be said about the tremendous amount of Internet hype—and it has frequently exceeded the bounds of rationality—one thing is sure: the Internet and the Web will be part of our lives for quite some time.

New technologies force us to change

So, too, will ActiveX and OLE. COM and the technologies it has spawned have worked their way into the very fabric of Windows and Windows NT, two systems whose popularity is not declining. Understanding the ramifications of COM is essential to understanding software in the Microsoft world. And, one way or another, understanding the Microsoft world is important for nearly everyone in this exciting business we're in.

COM and the changes it has brought are here to stay

Index

H

HandsOffStorage method, 123
History property, Window object, 281
HlinkCreateFromMoniker function, 308
HlinkCreateFromString function, 310
HlinkGoBack function, 312
HlinkGoForward function, 312
HlinkNavigateMoniker function, 312
HlinkNavigateString function, 312
HlinkSimpleNavigateToMoniker function, 312
HlinkSimpleNavigateToString function, 312
HRESULT, 44
HTML viewer (Internet Explorer), 276,
        279–90
    ActiveX Scripting and, 282–89
hyperlink frames, 309
hyperlinking API, 311–13
hyperlinks, ActiveX. *See* ActiveX Hyperlinks

I

IActivation interface, 252–53
IActiveScript interface, 284, 286
IActiveScriptParse interface, 285, 286
IActiveScriptSite interface, 284, 286
IActiveScriptSiteWindow interface, 284
IAdviseSink2 interface, 197 n
IAdviseSink interface, 167, 188, 197 n
    embedding containers and, 181
    notifications and, 161–63
IBindCtx interface, 144
IBindHost interface, 294, 295
IBindStatusCallback interface, 295, 299
ICatInformation interface, 207
ICatRegister interface, 207
IClassFactory2 interface, 61, 232
    license checking methods, 233–34
IClassFactory interface, 60–61, 182 n, 232
IClientSecurity interface, 261, 262
ICodeInstall interface, 299
IConnectionPointContainer interface,
        164–66, 226, 284
IConnectionPoint interface, 164, 166,
        226, 284

IContinueCallback interface, 269, 270
IDataObject interface, 156–63, 167, 306
    data cache objects and, 182, 183
    describing data in, 158
    drag and drop and, 159–60
    FORMATETC data structure and, 158, 159
    linking and, 198, 199
    methods in, 159
    notifications and, 161
    STGMEDIUM data structure and, 158
IDispatch interface, 82–83, 89–106,
        222, 223
    clients and servers and, 91–92
    dual interfaces and, 99–102
    IOleCommandTarget interface and,
        271, 272
    methods in, 97
    multiple dispinterfaces in a single object
        and, 98–99
    multiple instances of, 92
    Visual Basic and, 47, 90–92
IDL (Interface Definition Language), 43
    creating proxies and stubs with, 73
    dispinterfaces described using, 94
    example of use of, 77–79
    type information defined using, 76
IDropSource interface, 160
IDropTarget interface, 160
IErrorLog interface, 126
IExternalConnection interface, 198
IHlinkBrowseContext interface, 309
IHlinkFrame interface, 309
IHlink interface, 306–7
IHlinkSite interface, 308–10
IHlinkTarget interface, 308, 310
IID (interface identifier), 41
IMoniker interface, 130, 146–47
    asynchronous monikers and, 147–51
ImpersonateClient method, 263
implementation inheritance, 13–14, 17, 64
import statement, 44
IMultiQI interface, 255
inheritance
    concept of, 12–13
    implementation, 64
    multiple, 44 n
    types of, 13

O

Object Description Language (ODL), 76 n, 77 n, 94
object exporter identifiers (OXIDs), 247–48
object exporters, 247
object orientation, COM and, 9–14
ObjectPool storage, 178
Object RPC, 245–47
objects. *See also* COM objects
  Connectable, 27, 156, 163–68, 224
    future of, 168
    interfaces for, 165–68
  data, 157–60
  definition and characteristics of, 9–11
  as reuse mechanism, 16–18
OBJREFs (object references), 249–52
OCXs. *See* OLE controls
ODBC (Open Database Connectivity), 32
ODL (Object Description Language), 76 n, 77 n, 94
Office Binder, 267
OID (object identifier), 249
OLE Automation. *See* Automation
OLE compound documents. *See* compound documents
OLE containers. *See* containers (for compound documents)
OLE controls (OCXs), 30. *See also* ActiveX controls
  original vs. current specification, 205
OLE Database, 33
  monikers and, 135
OLE Documents, 22, 28–30
  ActiveX Documents distinguished from, 268
OLE Industry Solutions, 21
OleLoad function, 119 n
OLE (Object Linking and Embedding). *See also* COM, COM-based technologies
  ActiveX and, 4
  Connectable Objects, 27, 156, 163–68, 224
    future of, 168
    interfaces for, 165–68

OLE (Object Linking and Embedding, COM-based technologies), Connectable Objects, *continued*
  defining standard interfaces and, 22–23
  goal of, 1
  service interfaces based on, 32–33
  Structured Storage, 22, 24–26, 108–18
    embedding and, 177–78
    IStorage interface, 115–16
    IStream interface, 117
    library functions, 118
    rationale for creation of, 109–10
    storages and streams and, 110–14
    transactions and, 114–15
  Uniform Data Transfer, 27, 156–63 (*see also* IDataObject interface)
    notifications and, 160–63
  uses of the term, 3–4
OLE Scripting. *See* ActiveX Scripting
OLE servers. *See* servers
OnClose method, 181
OnDataChange method, 162, 163, 181, 188
OnLinkSrcChanged function, 197 n
onLoad event, Window object, 281
OnReadyStateChange event, 296
OnSave method, 181
onUnload event, Window object, 281
OnViewChange method, 181, 188, 194
Open Software Foundation's Distributed Computing Environment (OSF DCE), 43, 246
OpenStorage method, 115
OpenStream method, 115
Open verb, 184, 185, 187
operating systems
  COM's availability on various, 20–21
  services provided by, 5
outgoing interfaces, 164–68, 224–26
[out] parameters, 44
outside-in activation, 221
OXID objects, 253
OXID resolvers, 248
  OBJREFs and, 249–52
  pinging and, 256
OXIDs (object exporter identifiers), 247–48

David Chappell

is principal of Chappell & Associates, an education and consulting firm in Minneapolis, Minnesota. His clients have included most major computer vendors and many large corporations and government agencies. Earlier in his career, David was a senior software engineer at Cray Research, chaired a U.S. national standardization group, and worked as a pianist accompanying ballet and modern dance classes. More recently, David has been a keynote speaker at conferences in the United States and Europe, appeared frequently on the Computer Channel, and pre-sented seminars around the world. He holds a B.S. degree in economics and an M.S. degree in computer science, both from the University of Wisconsin-Madison. He can be contacted at www.chappellassoc.com.

The manuscript for this book was prepared and submitted to Microsoft Press in electronic form. Text files were prepared using Microsoft Word for Windows 95. Pages were composed using Adobe PageMaker 6.01 for Windows, with text in Optima and display type in Optima Bold. Composed pages were delivered to the printer as electronic prepress files.

Cover Graphic Designer
Becker Design

Cover Photo
Peter Poulides

Interior Graphic Designer
Kim Eggleston

Interior Graphic Artist
Travis Beaven

Compositors
Elisabeth Thébaud Pong
Paul Vautier

Principal Proofreader/Copy Editor
Devon Musgrave

Indexer
Maro Riofrancos

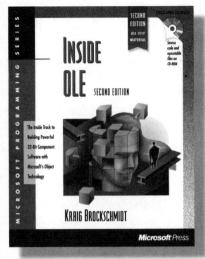

ISBN 1-55615-843-2, 1232 pages with one CD, $49.95
($67.95 Canada)

OLE is a unified and extensible environment of object-based services that enables rich integration among components. As Microsoft's object technology, it represents major innovations in object-based programming, making it possible to create applications and software components with unprecedented capabilities. But with this power come additional complexity and new programming paradigms.

INSIDE OLE provides both a clear tutorial and a strong set of example programs, giving you the tools to incorporate OLE into your own development projects. Written by a member of the Microsoft® OLE team, this book truly gives you the insider's perspective on the power of OLE for creating the next generation of innovative software.

INSIDE OLE provides detailed coverage of and reference material on:

- OLE and object fundamentals: objects and interfaces, connectable objects, custom components and the Component Object Model, and Local/Remote Transparency

- Storage and naming technologies: structured storage and compound files, persistent objects, and naming and binding

- Data transfer, viewing, and caching: Uniform Data Transfer, viewable objects, data caching, OLE Clipboard, and OLE Drag and Drop

- OLE Automation and OLE Properties: automation controllers; property pages, changes, and persistence

- OLE Documents: OLE Documents and embedding containers, OLE Documents and local embedding servers, in-process object handlers and servers, linking containers, and in-place activation (visual editing) for containers and objects

- OLE Controls and the future of OLE: OLE Controls, future enhancements, and component software

If you're interested in fully exploring and understanding OLE and component software, there's no better source than INSIDE OLE.

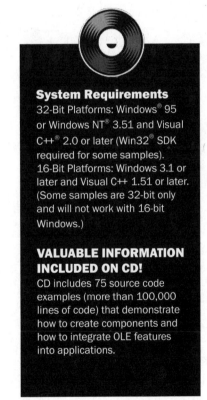

System Requirements

32-Bit Platforms: Windows® 95 or Windows NT® 3.51 and Visual C++® 2.0 or later (Win32® SDK required for some samples). 16-Bit Platforms: Windows 3.1 or later and Visual C++ 1.51 or later. (Some samples are 32-bit only and will not work with 16-bit Windows.)

VALUABLE INFORMATION INCLUDED ON CD!

CD includes 75 source code examples (more than 100,000 lines of code) that demonstrate how to create components and how to integrate OLE features into applications.

Microsoft Press® products are available worldwide wherever quality computer books are sold.
For more information, contact your book retailer, computer reseller, or local Microsoft Sales Office.

To locate your nearest source for Microsoft Press products, reach us at: www.microsoft.com/mspress/, or
1-800-MSPRESS in the U.S. (in Canada: 1-800-667-1115 or 416-293-8464).

To order Microsoft Press products, contact: 1-800-MSPRESS in the U.S. (in Canada: 1-800-667-1115 or 416-293-8464), or CompuServe's Electronic Mall at GO MSP.

Prices and availability dates are subject to change.

Everything you need to know about the best computer books available anywhere.

www.microsoft.com/mspress/

Microsoft Press

Register Today!

Return this
Understanding ActiveX™and OLE
registration card for a Microsoft Press® catalog

1-57231-216-5   *Understanding ActiveX™ and OLE*   *Owner Registration Card*

_____

NAME

_____

INSTITUTION OR COMPANY NAME

_____

ADDRESS

_____

_____

CITY   STATE   ZIP

Microsoft®*Press*
Quality Computer Books

For a free catalog of
Microsoft Press® products, call
1-800-MSPRESS